ANOTHER NORTH

ANOTHER NORTH

essays

JENNIFER BRICE

Book design by Mark E. Cull

Library of Congress Cataloging-in-Publication Data

Names: Brice, Jennifer, author.
Title: Another north: essays / Jennifer Brice.
Description: First edition. | Pasadena: Boreal Books, 2024.
Identifiers: LCCN 2023046971 | ISBN 9781597099363 (trade paperback) | ISBN
    9781597099387 (ebook) | ISBN 9781597099455 (library binding)
Subjects: LCGFT: Essays.
Classification: LCC PS3602.R49455 A56 2024 | DDC 808.84—dc23/eng/20231017
LC record available at https://lccn.loc.gov/2023046971

The National Endowment for the Arts, the Los Angeles County Arts Commission,
the Ahmanson Foundation, the Dwight Stuart Youth Fund, the Max Factor Family
Foundation, the Pasadena Tournament of Roses Foundation, the Pasadena Arts &
Culture Commission and the City of Pasadena Cultural Affairs Division, the City
of Los Angeles Department of Cultural Affairs, the Audrey & Sydney Irmas Chari-
table Foundation, the Meta & George Rosenberg Foundation, the Albert and Elaine
Borchard Foundation, the Adams Family Foundation, Amazon Literary Partner-
ship, the Sam Francis Foundation, and the Mara W. Breech Foundation partially
support Red Hen Press.

First Edition
Published by Boreal Books
An imprint of Red Hen Press
www.borealbooks.org
www.redhen.org

for Carrie

Contents

AUTHOR'S NOTE

These essays were written over twenty-five years, when I was living in some far-flung places. They are arranged not by chronology or geography but in a way that makes intuitive sense to me.

ANOTHER NORTH

I truly cannot understand the language of my former heart.
Who was *that person?*
    —Zadie Smith, "Some Notes on Attunement"

To make sense of this place, the idea of true north must be banished.
—Maggie Shipstead, *Great Circle*

Another North

Winter solstice, 2014. Alaska Airlines 145 carves through ice fog on final descent into Fairbanks, then *thunks* onto frozen tarmac. The woman in 10E checks her iPhone: 2:20 a.m., forty-four below zero. She looks out the window at a world simplified to grayscale, like a grainy sixties home movie. A stranger seeing this landscape for the first time might find it austere and otherworldly, even lunar-esque. She finds it beautiful—attuned, in the words of a writer whose work she loves, to her "most profound sense of how things ought to be."

As the jet bleeds off speed, this woman—middle-aged, a middling writer, no longer beautiful (if she ever was)—presses her forehead to the window, scanning the runway shoulder. She's looking for a sign. It's not a metaphor, this sign, but a solid object of aluminum and steel. She's seen it hundreds, maybe thousands, of times. She knows what to expect: no words, just numbers, three to be exact, the first one offset from the last two by a dash. To interpret these numbers requires a working knowledge of aeronautical charts. The woman in 10E—a gray-haired professor of English at an East Coast college (is she coming into focus yet?)—has a working knowledge of aeronautical charts, a fact about which she is ridiculously vain. Soon, soon, the sign she's looking for will flash by. When it does, then she knows she will be really, truly home.

Her story could begin anywhere. Let's say the summer of 1961, when the woman who will become our protagonist's mother says goodbye to New York City, goodbye to Columbia-Presbyterian Hospital, goodbye to the medical student who recently flew her to Texas to meet his socialite mother and, afterward, regretfully asked her to return his diamond ring. Fresh out of nurse's training, Carol Ann Heeks had applied for exactly two jobs, the first on the Good Ship Hope, the second in Fairbanks, Alaska. She vowed she'd take the first offer. After two weeks of driving all day, then camping at night alongside her dusty Plymouth Valiant, Carol Ann pulls into a gas station along the Richardson Highway, about a hundred miles north of Delta Junction, in the geographic center of the state. What does the attendant see? A young woman in her early twenties with Irish coloring—cap of brown hair, bright blue eyes—and a confused expression.

"How do I get to Fairbanks from here?" she asks.

"Lady," the guy says, "you just drove through it."

The sign I'm looking for is meant to say "1-19." Pronounced out loud, it's "one-dash-one-nine." These numbers—"one" and "one-nine"— have been the identifiers (yes, plural) of the main runway of the Fairbanks airport ever since it was built in the early fifties. What the runway is called, at any given moment, depends on the direction one is traveling. Northbound traffic uses runway one; southbound, one-nine. The one and the one-nine correspond to the azimuth of the runway's two possible headings, expressed in deca-degrees (meaning, nineteen rather than 190; one rather than ten). Based on wind speed and direction, and sometimes, in the wee hours, the desire to be considerate of slumbering city-dwellers, the air traffic controllers decide which runway should be in use. They broadcast this information over something called the Automated Terminal Information Service (ATIS) to pilots preparing for takeoff or landing. On first contact with the tower, the pilots are duty-bound to declare they've "got" the ATIS.

If you think assigning two different names to one single runway seems needlessly complicated, picture a two-hundred-ton object hurtling 250 miles an hour down a one-way street in rush-hour traffic.

Now picture it going in the wrong direction.

Head pressed up against the germy window, I see the sign right where I expect it to be, close to where the runway intersects with the taxiway. Everything about it is right—size, shape, color—except for the numbers. These are completely wrong: 2-20. Startled, I bang my head on the glass. How can this be? In my sleep-deprived state, did I board the wrong plane in Seattle?

When the terminal trundles into view, it's the one I recognize from my childhood. I gather my things—purse, computer bag, Patagonia puffer coat—and prepare to disembark, that familiar drill. But everything feels strange. How am I supposed to interpret a sign that tells me my hometown is literally not in the same place I left it the last time I visited? I feel like weeping from the mixture of disorientation, weariness, and loss. This new sign has set me to wobbling like a compass needle, like my mother's murky memory, my father's fibrillating heart. This particular case of wobbliness is just one more sign of how unsettled I feel most of the time these days in the new state of in-betweenness that is late middle age.

Why didn't anyone warn me?

A July day in 1962—high cirrus clouds, winds aloft out of the north, five to ten knots—a young man, Carol Ann's husband of just a few months, takes off southbound from the Fairbanks airport in his Aeronca Champ. It's a two-passenger taildragger equipped with a 65-horsepower engine, a compass, and an altimeter. For his first solo flight, he turns toward the east, then tools out over the Tanana Flats. He carves a few S-turns to get used to the new center of gravity—first time with no instructor in the backseat—then, half an hour later, heads back to the airport. With no radio onboard, he waggles his wings at the tower. A controller flashes a green light: permission to land granted. On the first try of his first solo fight, Alba Brice sets the Champ down as gently as the baby—me, who will be born eight months hence—on runway one-nine.

When we talk about our love for certain places, we tend to talk as if the love flows in only one direction. It's easy to forget that places are capable of loving us back. "They give us continuity," writes Rebecca Solnit, "something to return to."

Early summer now, 1964, the northern air peppery with fresh paint and wild roses. Wearing plaid pedal pushers and a sleeveless blouse, Carol Ann propels my pram down Fairbanks's Second Avenue. Chitina, our Husky, trots off leash at her side. Outside the Co-op, Carol Ann sets the stroller's brake and tells Chitina to stay. "Mind the baby," she says, then shoulders her pocketbook and heads inside. To pass the time while she's shopping, Chitina and I swap stories out on the sidewalk.

Fast-forward to August 1967, the end of the rainiest summer on record. We're living in a low-ceilinged apartment on the westernmost edge of town. It sits at roughly the same elevation as the airport, 434 feet above sea level. Carol Ann is now taking care of three toddlers and Chitina. She's been on her own with us for the past several months while my father's company builds a runway near the village of Wainwright on the coast of the Arctic Ocean. Even if he wanted to fly himself home in his new Bellanca, he couldn't: the Fairbanks airport is under a flood watch. Only big jets from the Lower 48 ("heavies," they're called) are permitted to land.

On the day I'm thinking of, my mother seems not quite herself. There's a small playground in the center of our C-shaped apartment complex. Instead of standing at the bottom of the slide to catch me, she huddles in conversation with the other mothers. At one point, to emphasize something she's been saying, she sweeps her right arm in a wide arc, as if taking in the whole complex, the unpaved road that runs past it, and our whole town beyond that.

Headed home for lunch, I let go of my favorite bouncy ball. When I try to shake free of Mom's vise grip, she won't let me go. "Forget it," she says. "It's dangerous."

Why is my ball dangerous? I wonder but don't ask. I am a tractable child, so I do as I am told. I eat my peanut-butter-and-honey sandwich, then go down for my nap.

An hour or so later, I wake in the arms of our upstairs neighbor, Mr. M. He's wearing hip waders, which is a good thing, because café au-lait water is now lapping at our stoop. He passes me, still wrapped in my green blanket and clinging to Baby Dear, to a man I don't recognize, a stranger struggling to stand in a canoe. My mother is already in the bow, cradling my two-year-old sister in one arm and clutching my three-year-old brother with the other. The stranger settles me on the bench in the middle, then picks up his paddle. "Hold on," Mr. M shouts. Chitina is flailing in his arms. He dumps her in the canoe, nearly tipping it over. I grab the gunnels, the stranger swears, then the dog curls up in a ball at my feet, as if she knows she's there on sufferance.

The canoe ride is short, just a few hundred yards to the base of a nearby hill. There, National Guardsmen lift us into the back of a troop carrier that transports us to the KUAC radio station, a couple of miles north of town. Next, my mother finagles a ride to my grandparents' eighty-acre farm in the hills a few miles farther north. The word "lark" isn't in my vocabulary yet, but that's what this feels like: a frolic, a spree, or (in the earliest meaning of the word) "rough play in the rigging of a ship."

For the next two weeks, the farm and its outbuildings overflow with refugees: aunts and cousins and friends, but also the friends of friends who are strangers to me. Because my father, his brothers, and their father are all working in Wainwright, nearly all the grownups are women. Looking back, I wonder how on earth my grandmother found the resources to feed and shelter so many of us. But my four-year-old self was unconcerned with such prosaic things. Instead, I reveled in the romance of being uprooted, playing outside all day, keeping watch for the man on the motorcycle—yet another stranger—who roared down the half-mile-long driveway every evening with panniers full of milk bottles for the babies.

After the flood, we return to an apartment made moldy by floodwaters. Two more years pass. I attend first grade at a school roughly a third of a mile away. I walk there and back every day, along a route that traverses the shoulder of a secondary road. I'm a dreamy child, a reader of fairy tales who likes to fantasize she's really a princess fallen into the hands of coarse commoners who force her to eat liver and Brussels sprouts, and who sometimes swat her for forgetting to pick up her toys or look after her siblings. I pretend that someday my true parents, who are kind and beautiful and omnipresent, and who fix me my favorite combination of pork chops and lima beans for dinner every night, will claim me. Together, we'll ascend the stairs to the first-class section of a Pan Am 747, which will fly us home, to a castle just like the one in the opening credits of *Wonderful World of Disney*.

I'm halfway home one day when the sky starts pelting me with rain. Probably I'm wearing my pink slicker and rubber boots. I might even have an umbrella. I don't remember. One thing I *do* remember is how a dun-colored Ford Granada just like my grandfather's swims up alongside me and stops. Two middle-aged white men sit in the front seat. Strangers. The passenger rolls down his window, asks how old I am and where I live. I tell him. Then the driver leans over and opens the back door for me. I get in.

Dear Fairbanks: you know I had to leave you, right? Had to leave the same way every girl has to leave her mother to see the possibilities for her own self. It took me nearly forty years—half the total number in my account, if I'm lucky—to achieve exit velocity.

When the next big thing comes along, I'm still in elementary school. Unlike the earthquake of '64—9.2 on the Richter scale, still the strongest tremor ever registered in North America—and the flood of '67, the trans-Alaska pipeline seems like something we might all survive.

Fairbanks smartens itself up for the men in cowboy boots who stagger out of the Hideaway Bar in the wee hours, windmilling on ice or howling at the midnight sun. For men who leave fifty-dollar tips on three-dollar meals at the Co-op lunch counter. The Fairbanks airport gives itself a middle name: "International." A popular bumper sticker reads, "Happiness is 10,000 Texans headed south with an Okie under each arm." In truth, the happiest people are the ones headed north, to Prudhoe Bay. Everywhere you look, the mood is giddy. Some of my friends have older brothers, and these boys drop out of high school on their sixteenth birthday to sign on with Bechtel or Alyeska. Why break your brain with algebra when you can work in the oil field for union scale?

It's 1980 now, the summer before our senior year of high school. Dana and I cruise Airport Way in her orange VW Bug, hair blowing in the wind, blasting the Bee Gees' "Stayin' Alive." I have a wild crush on Dana's long-haired, much older brother who plays the drums in a rock band. My actual boyfriend is on the cross-country ski team. He's a year younger than us and doesn't have a driver's license yet. For a while, Dana was dating an older boy with a job and a car. Then one afternoon, he tried to change the cassette in his car stereo while navigating rush-hour traffic. Now Dana doesn't have a date for the senior prom.

The prom (theme: Stairway to Heaven) is held on a sixty-below night in January. Ice fog so thick you can practically cup it in your hands. Tires square up at these temperatures, thwacking like helicopter blades for the first few minutes until they heat up. Fan belts freeze and fly into the roadway, a plague of black snakes.

The entrance to the Elks Lodge or Masonic Temple or Moose Lodge, where the prom is held, lies at the base of some stairs. Dana and I waft in on a cloud of ice fog. She wears a white off-the-shoulder Grecian gown, sewn by her mother. The zipper on my floral chiffon sundress broke when I was changing, so my mother stitched me into it. We're both wearing spike-heeled sandals.

In Alaska, we dress for the occasion, not the weather

After graduation, I spend four homesick years at an East Coast women's college (nothing to see here, reader), then take a job answering phones and writing obituaries for the *Fairbanks Daily News-Miner*. The first place I move after leaving my parents' house is a one-room cabin in the woods. It has no electricity or indoor plumbing. I work long hours, then come home in the dark, chop wood, build a fire, cook pasta on the propane stove. For a while, I'm happy. At least, I think I'm happy. At the very least, I'm home.

The late eighties bring a fresh bumper sticker: "Dear God, please give us another oil boom. We promise not to piss this one away." The Woolworth's on Second Avenue closes, then the Co-op. Nordstrom decamps for more moneyed pastures, followed by JC Penney.

What happened to Lori King, who was my best friend back in sixth grade, is front-page news. Like me, she accepted a ride from a stranger.

The men in the Ford Granada just like my grandfather's who offered me that rainy-day lift took me straight home. When I walked in the door, my mother turned from the sink, startled.

"How did you get here so quickly?" she asked.

"I got a ride in a car," I said.

"Whose car?"

"I don't know."

The color drained from her face, and she gripped the counter behind her as if it might keep her from sinking to the floor. In a low, dangerous voice, she said, "I am going to spank you into next week, and then I am going to call your father so you can tell him exactly what you did."

A quarter-century after my father's first solo flight, I take off southbound from the small-plane ramp of the Fairbanks airport in an Arctic Tern equipped with a 165-horsepower engine, compass, altimeter, and voice-activated two-way radio, along with more instruments than I will ever have the knowledge or occasion to use. I am learning to fly in order to prove something to myself, though it's not yet clear just what that might be—maybe that I'm smart in the ways a person needs to be to survive and thrive in this place.

On this particular day, I'm flying light, with no instructor in the back seat. I putter around the Tanana Flats for half an hour or so, sketching a few wobbly S's, then head for home. Two miles from the airport, I radio the tower on 118.3, tell them I've got the ATIS, and request permission to land on runway one-nine. The permission is granted.

I try three times to land but keep bouncing (*Not a lark!*) back into the sky. On my fourth go-round, the controller warns me he's about to switch runways. An electrical storm is muscling in, and the wind has swung around to the north. If I stay up any longer, I'm going to have to execute the aerial equivalent of a U-turn.

I grit my teeth and stick my next landing.

A June evening on the deck at Pike's Landing, a restaurant so close to the airport it's practically in the slipstream of arriving jets. My husband and I are having burgers and beer with his aunt and uncle. They've just flown in from Nebraska or Kansas or Oklahoma. They strike me as Midwestern staid. Tonight, I'm up for anything, though, what with the solstice sun warming the back of my neck, a Corona sweating in my hand. Instead of looking at each other, the four of us watch the Chena River, tamed by a flood-control project upstream, flow sedately by, silt rustling like silk underskirts. In just a few years, my marriage will founder, and I'll head south down the Richardson Highway at the helm of a U-Haul, bound for a new life in Virginia with three toddlers in tow. But, on this evening, I am in love with my life, in love with this place.

"So what do you think of Fairbanks so far?" I ask my husband's uncle.

"Trashy little burg, isn't it?" he replies.

Dear Fairbanks, when I was young, I never saw you as beautiful. Like my mother, you just *were*. Sometimes on winter nights, she'd wake me from sound slumber, wrap me in a scratchy blanket, and tug me out the back door. By then, we were living in a three-bedroom house five miles from town. It was so big it had a back porch into which we dug a network of snow tunnels every winter. On the nights I'm thinking of, Carol Ann would place me in front of her, then tilt my sleep-tousled head toward the sky. "Look up," she'd say, in her gentlest, most rapt voice, the one she usually reserved for church. Streamers of green and pink unfurled soundlessly across the star-studded sky. "It's the northern lights. They're dancing. Isn't it wonderful?"

To see something as wonderful—literally, as a miracle, a mystery, a prodigy of nature—you must also see it as strange. Because I was born here, I've never been able to see Alaska through a stranger's eyes. When I was a child, and everything seemed new, nothing ever surprised me either—nothing, I should say, but the sight of my no-nonsense, loafers-wearing, public health nurse mother undone by the beauty of her chosen home. To please her, I looked up.

And fell into the sky.

"I assure you that this region is so far north that the Pole Star is left behind toward the south," writes Marco Polo in *The Travels of Marco*

Polo. His *I assure you* gives him away, of course. As his editor, R. E. Latham, notes drily, "A more learned writer might have avoided Polo's gaffe about travelling farther north than the Pole Star." I don't blame him for exaggerating: Marco Polo was an explorer, not a cartographer, and he was pursuing a truth more abstract than longitude or latitude. True north has always been a figment of mapmakers' imaginations, a fixed point on the globe that doesn't correspond to any real place on earth. It's like the pot of gold at the end of a rainbow: the closer you get, the farther it recedes. The romantic in me will always be seduced by that phrase, *true north* (also: *magnetic azimuth, pole star*), especially as a metaphor for the companion of one's heart. The practical side of me knows where the compass needle points instead: toward plain-old magnetic north. The magnet is earth's fiery core. Fluctuations in its temperature mean that magnetic variation—meaning, the compass gap between true north and magnetic north—is most extreme at literally the most extreme places on earth: the North and South Poles.

This has been a long peregrination. I'm returning to the place where I started, with the sign that gave me such a turn on that December night nearly a decade ago. By the time I got around to asking my father for an explanation, I'd already begun to work it out for myself. In 2014, the Fairbanks runway was nearly seventy years old. Over the decades, magnetic variation had done what an earthquake, a flood, and time alone could not: shifted its compass heading ten degrees.

Bewildered is the word for what I felt, on realizing this—literally stumbling around in a wilderness of not-knowing. Dislocated and estranged from myself. I was like a drunk who'd tumbled out of the bar a few martinis in, only to discover her house two blocks west of where she'd left it. The external world no longer aligned with my inner compass.

Here, in a place simultaneously home/not home, is where I found myself at fifty-one, the same as Clarissa Dalloway in her narrowing bed. The same age as my grandmother when she rescued my family from the flood. Now, for the second time in my memory, the fabric of the natural world had ruptured. What was I meant to do with this new information?

Who was I meant to be?

Ten days from now, a little bit after midnight, my Seattle-bound flight will lift off from Fairbanks runway two-dash-two-zero. I will be on board. I will be unmoored.

Playing Bridge with Robots

1.

Memory is a cheat and a sieve. I forget whether the queen of hearts has already played—she hasn't—and go down three tricks. The distant past irrupts, sending me back to August 1993. Sitka, Alaska. My friend Sherry and I walk along the sea. Clamorous gulls, briny smell of rotting salmon, wind whipping her long hair into our mouths. We've flown here from Fairbanks for a weeklong writers' symposium, though we don't regard ourselves as writers yet—just "recovering journalists." That's Sherry's joke. All the jokes are Sherry's. She's the funny one. (Once, at a writers' dinner, she discovered the woman we were talking to had been married five times and blurted, "You poets have the best sex!")

What are the two of us talking about? It would be nice to say, from the vantage of years, that it's something serious and deep—the nonfiction writer's obligation to tell the truth balanced against her desire not to betray any confidences, say. More likely, it's a glittery bit of gossip we got hold of and are picking apart like magpies—a semi-famous writer caught showering in the dorm bathroom with a much younger symposium attendee. (You know *that* happened.) Regardless, we're so giddy with whatever it is that we don't hear a stranger shout, don't see him until he jogs up alongside us.

"Did one of you drop this?" he asks, holding up a peach-colored pacifier.

"Oh gosh," I say (or something like it, because all memory is reconstruction, not retrieval, another favorite topic of mine and Sherry's). "Thank you *so* much. It's the only one I've got, and I'd be a goner without it."

"Living on the edge, huh?" the young man deadpans, then with a quick wave, goes on his way.

The nine-month-old baby girl in my backpack shifts, sighs, then settles back into sleep.

2.

If you don't know anything about bridge, don't worry: you're not going to learn it here.

3.

It never occurred to me the world held something as wonderful as online bridge until I read a story about it the *New York Times*. The name, *Funbridge*, sounded vaguely bullying: you will enjoy this . . . *or else*. Since downloading it, I've played 4,163 hands.

That's an average of fifty per day, which, to be honest, is probably on the low side. The *very* low side. After every hand, the app rates your performance vis-à-vis other live players, which makes it a diabolical little dopamine generator. The goal becomes not simply to win but to win bigger, more interestingly, than anyone else. My average is 42.5 percent. Through a serendipitous and irreproducible combination of novel (reckless) bidding and elegant (lucky) card play, I've scored 100 percent exactly twice.

4.

After the great travel writer Bruce Chatwin died in 1989, another great travel writer, Paul Theroux, published in *Granta* a eulogy that was really just thinly disguised character assassination. Theroux didn't so much as stab Chatwin in the back as fillet him. He described him as a fabulist, a braggart, a boor, and (horrors) a closeted homosexual who'd probably died of AIDS, not a mysterious wasting disease contracted in some far-off jungle, as Chatwin had led people to think. Theroux begins his piece unsubtly: "When I think of Bruce Chatwin, who was my friend, I am always reminded of a particular night, a dinner at the Royal Geographical Society, hearing him speak animatedly about various high mountains he had climbed. And that struck me as very odd, because I knew he had never been much of a mountaineer."

No *de mortuis nil nisi bonum dicendum est* for Theroux, who, years later, wrote a vicious book about (the still living) V. S. Naipaul after stumbling on one of his (Theroux's) books in a secondhand bin, bearing an inscription to his mentor. When I think of Paul Theroux (who is not, thank goodness, my friend), I am always reminded of how a prodigious but unreflected gift for observation can sometimes be pressed into the service of cruelty.

5.

Bridge is a game for four players divided into teams of two. In this respect, it ranks near the top of activities—doubles tennis, tandem cycling, whitewater canoeing—with a high potential to blow up relationships. Each player in a bridge game corresponds to a point on the compass; North partners with South, East with West. In Funbridge, the human nearly always plays North, except when North is dummy, in which case, North and South switch hands. This way, the human always gets to play instead of going along for the ride, in the dummy position.

The robots—all of them—are named Argine.

6.

I met Sherry in 1985, when we worked together on the Fairbanks newspaper. I did the weather and obituaries and also answered the phones. She was the features editor, the coolest person in the newsroom, the sun around which the rest of us orbited. With some people, it's easy to pinpoint the source of their charisma. Not so with Sherry. She was taller than average, five foot eight or so, with shoulder-length blonde hair and bangs. In all the years I knew her, she never changed that hairstyle. She wore baggy khakis, button-down shirts, and wool blazers. The overall effect suggested she thought she was fat, which she was not. What drew people to her were maybe three qualities: intelligence, a sense of humor (nearly always at her own expense), and the groundedness one sees in people whose sense of right and wrong is in their DNA.

Alaska's oil-driven economy was humming along in the eighties, and the newspaper was fat with features: food, youth, education, arts, and religion. Also a Sunday magazine. The staff wasn't big enough to fill all those pages, so we hired stringers. One poor guy was so desperate to come on board that he turned up every week with one or more stories so labored it was hard to get anything out of them besides the image of a writer laboring. "Someone ought to tell him to stop writing so hard—he might hurt himself," Sherry said after the fourth or fifth time he left her office with his head hanging.

Eventually I got promoted from receptionist to reporter, and then to arts editor, but I spent those years in tongue-tied awe of Sherry, simultaneously hopeful and terrified that her gaze would someday fall on me—that she'd say something as pithy and precise about me or my writing as what she'd said about that wannabe stringer.

Then, in the early nineties, we both enrolled in the same MFA program in creative writing, and, just like that, we were best friends. Those were heady years for me. I'd never had a best friend before. We were each other's first and smartest readers, real and—in the days before email and texting, when you had to hold onto your thoughts until you saw someone in person—imagined interlocutors. We traveled to conferences together, sharing meals and hotel rooms and confidences for three, four, or five days at a stretch. Several times a summer we'd gather up my daughters and a bunch of groceries, then fly or boat into my family's cabin on the Salcha River. Once there, beyond the reach of a telephone, we'd spend a few blissful days entertaining the girls, going for long walks, reading, writing, and talking. We talked about other people's poems and essays and films and books, and we talked about our own—the ones in progress and the ones we hoped to write someday. We were intensely interested in the demands the northern landscape placed on our writing. We told each other everything—our secret fears, our childhood traumas, our ambivalence about the men we'd married and the things we wished we'd done differently. We were capable of walking along the riverbank in companionable silence or even working quietly alongside each other without speaking, of course, but the most vivid image I have of those river trips is of me and Sherry in folding chairs beside the campfire, she poking the embers with a stick, while we talked about the wilderness all around and also inside us.

In those years, ours became that "single dominant friendship," in Montaigne's terms, that "dissolves all other obligations." He goes on to say (in Donald Frame's translation): "The secret I have sworn to reveal to no other man, I can impart without perjury to the one who is not another man: he is myself."

I imagine that lots of people—maybe even most people—live their whole lives without the gift of such friendship, but also without the fear of losing it. The young man who raced after us to return my baby's binky got it right: I *was* living on the edge. But then, aren't we all?

7.

When you lose at bridge, you are said to "go down." (Don't linger over that: bridge is the least sexy game I know.) Sometimes, going down is a strategic maneuver: it's better to lose 200 points than allow your opponents to gain 500. More commonly, you go down because you screwed up by waxing overly optimistic about your own hand or your partner's; you misread or failed to heed a warning telegraphed during the bidding phase; you got so caught up in the thrill of taking five club tricks in a row that you accidentally cut off the path between the good cards in your hand and the useless ones on the board. When the dust settles, you must ask yourself where you went wrong—in the bidding or the playing? In the wanting or the getting?

8.

I learned to play bridge at sea, on a freighter bound for South America. I was twenty-five and not keen to take up a game that smacked of rubber-soled shoes and shuffleboard. But it wasn't as if I had anything else to do besides reread a tattered copy of *In Patagonia* or polish my fingernails while running down my Walkman batteries listening to Kate Bush on repeat. There were ten passengers on the trip, and only three of them were bridge players. By the time they circled back to me for the third or fourth time, they were getting pretty frantic, so I relented. They consisted of an older couple—he: retired military and gruff; she: whippet thin and ironic—and a man in his fifties. They weren't traveling companions and had nothing in common but bridge. The bachelor was heavyset and unhandsome, slow moving, with round glasses. He reminded me of a very large and very learned tortoise. Back in the sixties, he'd been forced to withdraw from Berkeley, and his philosophy studies there, on account of a bridge addiction. After that, he'd stayed clean for years but was willing to join our little group, as long as there was no betting involved. With the stakes reduced to nothing but pleasure, he, along with the elderly couple, turned out to be an excellent—patient, unpedantic—teacher. At sea, in between ports, time was measured in weeks, not days. The four of us would gather after lunch and before cocktails at a table in the dining room, where crewmembers sometimes brought us sodas and snacks, then stayed to kibitz. My grandmother, whose traveling companion I was meant to be—a role I fulfilled erratically, and not always kindly—was usually napping. This was years before marriage and babies, and I was on leave from my job as a journalist, so there were no competing claims on my time. To this day, the pleasures, for me, of bridge are inseparable from the rolling of the sea, the sense that someone has given me a gift I don't deserve, and the taste of Danish butter cookies.

9.

Every hand of bridge begins with a coded conversation. While bidding, partners try to convey to one another as plainly as possible what cards they possess. The first bid (or pass) is the easy part. It's like the opening gambit in online dating. The bidder swipes left, saying, "Here's what I've got. Any chance it might be just what you're looking for?" After that, the conversation either fizzles or complicates. Opportunities for misunderstanding abound. Both partners are hamstrung partly because they don't know what cards the other holds; partly because of the need to find out what's in the other person's hand using the same code employed by their opponents. One way around this is the use of shortcuts or conventions that constitute a kind of secret language within the code: Blackwood, Jacoby, and Landy; short club, scrambling, and cue. If your partner bids One No Trump, and you want him to know you have a whole slew of hearts, you bid Two Diamonds. Weird, I know. My favorite convention is the cue bid, in which you hitch a ride to the next level by bidding your opponent's suit.

Is this what I'm doing here, I wonder? Using bridge as a kind of Trojan horse to carry me a little closer to my real destination? If so, why not dispense with both of them—bridge and Trojan horse? Why not simply say what I mean?

10.

Let me try. For many years, when we were both in our twenties and thirties, Sherry's friendship was a fire at which I warmed myself. I think I'm being honest, with myself and with you, when I say the only fire she lit was in my brain.

At the Sitka conference one time, she spent hours on her belly in the mud, using milk to lure the stray kittens living under our dorm. She finally caught one with minutes to spare before we had to be at the airport for our flight home. To please her, I cached it in the cavernous pocket of my barn coat and slipped it past security. Because she already had two cats at home, I adopted this one and named it Max.

Sherry's moods were as changeable as the weather. She hated to go more than two days without washing her hair. She used to make me laugh so hard I'd pee myself. Both of us knew to the ounce what the other weighed and what we thought our best features were (me: legs;

Sherry: breasts). We had crushes on all the same writers. She was brave enough to fly with me at the controls of a small plane. We went into business together, briefly, teaching bureaucrats to write in plain English. A few days before Christmas every year, we set aside an afternoon to bake and wrap biscotti to give to friends. She loved chocolate and wine and held (as I do) that in a pinch any brand will do.

She was a thrilling observer of the natural world, gifted with what Rilke called "inseeing," the uncanny ability to move from the surface of things to the heart of them. She did not anthropomorphize so much as empathize with the non-human. Here she is in an essay from her first book, *The Way Winter Comes*:

> Lying in my tent, I could hear the whales parting the air with wet gasps, slapping monstrous tales against the water. Sometimes long, yearning tones hummed through the night, as if an organist had picked one note and then bore down hard on the pedal. The sound hung in the trees, the way I imagined it echoing through the vaulted ocean. It was the sound of wanting what you don't have.

Her writing swung between the twin poles of science and poetry, precision and mysticism. Every word in a sentence had to earn its keep. Another excerpt:

> The wind blows from the northeast across the Arctic Ocean, exhaling the ache of winter into my nose and throat. Waves heave along the stony beach that fronts Barrow as I scan the horizon for signs of pack ice. A milky nimbus brightens the margin between ocean and sky, and I say to myself, "Ice blink."

Both of us were mortally afraid of bears, though only she was willing to risk a week alone on an island along with them. To keep bears away when we were bushwhacking, I'd sing Sunday school hymns and she'd sing Carpenters tunes. Once, when the two of us were perched on a large boulder in Glacier Bay eating lunch, I announced that I didn't think there was any point in having bear spray if we were never going to test it. *Waiiii*—, she said, as I stood to spritz it. The wind blew it back in our faces, and we spent the afternoon in glum silence, wiping our eyes and noses with bandannas. Nothing—not even a seal paddling alongside our kayak or a whale breaching nearby—would induce her to speak to me.

11.

Sherry wove me into a couple of her essays, including "A Nuisance to Myself and Others," which is about that trip to Glacier Bay:

> We chipped at beached icebergs to melt drinking water. Our shoulders ached, and our fingertips grew tender from exposure to brine, rain, and wind. The colder and wearier we became, the more we chafed against each other's personalities. Jennifer's perky "Good morning!" made me want to throw myself in the bay. She called me sullen. I thought her natural bossiness lent her the charisma of a supply sergeant. She suggested that I was too picky about the food. But we were deeply grateful for the companionship of a steady friend, because the most terrible thing of all was to imagine being in this dreadful place alone.

That's a compare-and-contrast construction imbued with generosity: *we chafed against each other's personalities, but, in the end, we were grateful for each other's friendship.* In my memory—and, doubtless, in hers—we ended the week barely on speaking terms. It didn't help that I'd forgotten to pack the rudder for our collapsible sea kayak, which meant we had to work ten times harder, in relentless rain and wind, to paddle a straight line.

12.

I wrote Sherry into my essays too. In "The Metaphysics of Being Stuck," I wrote:

> One of my close friends is a woman who has always wanted to have children but, for reasons too complicated to go into here, cannot. She tells me that I want it both ways, as if the occasional public rant against motherhood ... sometimes nullifies a deeply felt private emotion. The truth is, I love my daughters—love them as a sow bear loves her cubs, protectively, unambig-

uously, and with a force and breadth beyond the reach of language. Is it OK to confess that sometimes I love them best when they are sleeping?

In this passage, I summon what Sherry once told me in a moment of extreme vulnerability—revealing the thing that was most painful to her in her life—and hold it up to the light where everyone else can see it too. Then I knock it down with the force of my own eloquence, the essential rightness of my thoughts and feelings. In rhetorical terms, this is a straw man argument. In bridge terms, I spoke for Sherry; I made her my dummy.

It's no surprise, really, that eventually she stopped speaking honestly to me. The wonder is that she ever spoke to me again at all.

13.

Reader, you know this moment is coming. I, of course, had no warning. Like a long sea voyage, the pandemic had scrambled my internal clock. By the fall of 2020, I no longer thought in hours and days but in weeks and months. I could not possibly tell you when I downloaded Funbridge except to say it was a couple of weeks after I received a Facebook message from a man I'd never met. I'll call him D. I recognized his name as belonging to a colleague and close friend of Sherry's, a man about whom she'd spoken often, and warmly. In his message, he mentioned this connection—Sherry's status as the bridge between us—and asked me to call him at my earliest convenience.

14.

The Englishman I live with informs me that *dummy* is British slang for "pacifier." Someone who loses their temper over a trifle is said to have *spat the dummy*. There was no big fight or falling out, and neither of us lost her temper. The friendship simply foundered. It wasn't about competition; at least, I think it wasn't. Neither of us ever earned the kind of acclaim or advances that might lead a person to envy. Is it possible to feel ambitious for oneself without feeling a flare of competitiveness toward someone else? Maybe not. Still, I like to think ours was the kind of competition that spurred us to work harder and better, not to hold the other back. And we cheered each other's successes sincerely, full-throatedly.

One of our mentors in graduate school was the poet Peggy Shumaker, who memorably said—in response to another poet, a small man with a big ego who'd unjustly accused her of trying to hurt his career—"I am not diminished by the success of others."

15.

A few bendable rules of bridge: When playing no trump, always lead the fourth card from the top in your longest and strongest suit, and never lead away from a king. Lose your losers. Always cover an honor with an honor. Try to make your bid (of course); failing that, go down one or two tricks to avoid letting your opponents make their bid: in bridge, you *are* diminished by the success of others.

16.

I've lived since 2003 in a three-stoplight college town in upstate New York. A year or two before moving here, I lucked into intimate friendship with another woman, a relationship that has, over the years, nurtured, sustained, and civilized me. It has carried me through a divorce and the aftermath, through the suicide of another close friend, the plane-crash death of my uncle, the falling into dementia of both our beloved mothers. This friend, with whom I walk and talk on the phone nearly every day, is a novelist who has taught me a million things about the workings of the human heart. One of these things, in particular, I seem to need to learn over and over: when people behave badly, it's usually because they're in pain.

I like the life I've made in this snowy town. During the pandemic, the friends in my circle text the whole group whenever they're headed to the nearest big city, asking if anyone needs anything. And we leave little gifts—meringues, Nutella brownies, chocolate cake, kosher salt, Bag Balm—on each other's doorsteps. If there's anything I pine for besides my daughters—now grown and gone—it's a bridge partner. *Pine* is probably too strong a word. If I really wanted to find one, I could post a notice on the town's message board. My expectations would not be high. (I'm thinking of a grad school classmate's dating profile: "ISO lesbian with good teeth.") Every week or two, I meet up with a new colleague—decades younger—for a walk on the towpath near our homes. A while back, she confessed she'd met someone. She wasn't looking for romance (she has a partner), just ordinary female friendship. (It goes almost without saying that I am an OK dog-walking companion but too old for true friend material.) She and this new woman bonded at first over their anti-social dogs, then they fell into the habit of letting each other know when they were headed out for a walk. A couple of weeks ago, I asked Lucy how things were going with her new friend. "That got a little weird," Lucy said. Her new friend had started texting her obsessively, several times a day, and also pressing little gifts on her: a manual for training difficult dogs, potted succulents, homemade toothpaste. *Homemade toothpaste!*

The truth is, my hunger for bridge isn't about anything other than a hunger for bridge. The possibility of loneliness doesn't frighten me nearly as much as the reality of other people's neediness.

17.

Argine the Funbridge robot plays with a steady cadence that can best be described as (sorry) "robotic." Like Anton Chigurh in *No Country for Old Men* or the eponymous Terminator, Argine is a machine with only one purpose, which is to annihilate her enemies. She (definitely a "she") goes about her mission without vindictiveness or mercy. She does not bluff. She has no sense of humor.

And yet—she can be solicitous. If I get carried away and try to bid Seven No Trump—meaning, I intend to take *all* the tricks—she asks, "Are you sure you want to do this?"

Thanks to Wikipedia, I know that Argine really is a she, her name an anagram of Regina. She was the queen of clubs on eighteenth-century French playing cards. In the economy of bridge, spades are the most valuable and clubs the least, meaning that Argine is barely even royal.

She suffers, I decide, from professional jealousy toward the other queens: Judith, Rachel, and Pallas.

Every once in a while, I play a card so unexpected (read: so dumb), it causes Argine to pause briefly, almost as if she's not an algorithm but a human being who's been knocked off guard.

18.

"The last time I saw my father was in Grand Central Station." A colleague of mine once taught a whole class on that sentence—the opening of John Cheever's "Reunion"—the shimmering indeterminacy of it. Was the man referring to the most recent time he saw his father—as in, "The last time I went to Wegman's, I stocked up on coffee, paper towels, and toilet paper"? Or was he talking about the last time he ever laid eyes on his father? The first interpretation would have been true the day after that encounter in New York City; the second, only years later.

The last time I saw Sherry was at a nonfiction conference in Melbourne, Australia. We hadn't seen each other in maybe five years, but we fell quickly into our old groove of skipping out on the plenaries and panels and cocktail parties in order to explore the city together.

At the time, both of us were living in places where it was already winter, so we soaked up the tropical plants and sun along with the Victorian architecture, the restaurants, the night market, and outdoor book stalls. We walked so much I wore a hole in one of my shoes. We talked too. In my experience, it's nearly always easier to talk to someone when you're walking alongside them than when you're sitting across the table from each other. Someone had broken my heart recently, and I'd whittled my body down to near invisibility. I thought she might remark on this—the old Sherry would have—but she did not. She did say she'd begun seeing a therapist who'd helped her a lot. *With what?* I wanted to ask but did not.

"Do you ever do yoga?" I asked instead. We'd just stepped inside a boutique. I picked up a pair of strappy cornflower-blue sandals. They were on sale, and I liked the color, but they wouldn't last two hours at our pace.

"Yes," she said. "Sometimes. My favorite is the pose you do at the very end, you know—savasana." She closed her eyes and lolled her tongue, pretending to be dead. That cracked us both up.

19.

In a 1936 letter rebuffing a prospective biographer, Freud writes, "Anyone who writes a biography is committed to lies, concealments, hypocrisy, flattery, and even to hiding his own lack of understanding, for biographical truth does not exist, and if it did we could not use it."

20.

Lately, I've been dreaming in bridge.

21.

When the university where Sherry was teaching scaled back its graduate writing program to a low-residency one, she and her husband moved to New Mexico. They cultivated hummingbirds and joined the local fire brigade, an experience that led them (I learned much later) to draft living wills. Sherry wrote her third book there, a deeply researched and gorgeously written study of the animals who'd been haunting her dreams forever. *Dominion of Bears* won this country's most prestigious prize for writing about the natural world, the John Burroughs medal. You'd think that when I heard this news about my friend, I would have picked up the phone to call and congratulate her.

You would think.

22.

Here is a partial list of things I've learned from playing bridge with robots: Being profligate with riches is likely to lead you to overbid an already strong hand. Projecting your own strengths or weaknesses onto your partner can prevent you from listening with your deepest ear to the story she's trying to tell you. The tiniest missed cue can set you on the path to certain destruction.

Also this: Sustaining a grudge requires more than mere stinginess of spirit. It feeds off memory. Argine's memory ends with every bridge hand. This feels a lot like forgiveness. If someone, even a game engine, forgives you often enough, you begin to be able to forgive yourself.

Finally, this: Once in a blue moon, a blunder gets rewarded. Luck matters, in bridge as in life. So does courage.

23.

Etymological notes: A trump card is one that is temporarily invested with superpowers. If diamonds are trump, then the two of diamonds beats every other card in every other suit. The word *trump* comes from *triumph*. A rare but not unheard-of complication arises when two partners turn out to hold nearly all the trump cards between them. Instead of complementing one another, their hands are too similar. The phrase for this is *trump rich*.

This condition is nearly always fatal.

24.

A partial list of things that Sherry and I never talked about: The impulsive behavior that led me to wreck two marriages, only one of them my own. Her suspicion that I might have been behind some anonymous emails sent to her editor, urging him to cancel a book contract on account of her bad character. (I was not.) The irrational anger I feel whenever I am thwarted. The men we loved who drank too much. The toxic stew of ambition, anxiety, compulsion, and existential desire that led her to gambling, me to bridge, and both of us, sometimes, to drink too much. The fact that no doctor could diagnose the cause of her fainting spells, and how she made peace with that. Whether her life was, in the end, enough for her—revolving as it did around her husband, her writing, her teaching, her hummingbirds, and her beloved blue heelers, the children of friends (including one of mine, her goddaughter) but never any of her own.

25.

In "Strawberries Under Ice," David Quammen writes, "Pure friendship, uncomplicated by romance or blood, is one of the most nurturing human relationships and one of the most easily taken for granted."

26.

What was fatal to my friendship with Sherry? It's hard to say. There was no big fight, no falling out, even—just a slow falling off over time. Probably there's no single explanation for what happened in the same way there's no single story of anything. Despite my fear of having done so, I actually don't think I wounded her with what I wrote in that essay about her decision not to have children. And I know she didn't hurt me by saying I was perky in the morning and as bossy as a drill sergeant. (I will cop to both charges.) For one thing, what we each wrote about the other was factually and emotionally accurate. For another, we both harnessed the other person's words in pursuit of some unrelated fugitive truth. We weren't doing what I am doing right this minute, which is trying to capture some fugitive truth about her. Or about me and her. Or maybe just about me.

Did I take our friendship for granted? (Or, as a student of mine once wrote, Did I take it for "granite"?) Did I fail to feed and water it sufficiently? Even scarier, did I somehow reveal my deepest, truest, meanest self—the Paul Theroux at the heart of me—causing her to recoil in horror?

Or was it none of these things? At the risk of sounding solipsistic (another crime I'll confess to), maybe it wasn't me, but her. I'm thinking now of something that another friend, an up-and-coming poet, once said about her lover, who was a very famous poet: "All of his emotional and erotic energy goes into the poetry." And I'm summoning Montaigne again, this time on the necessity of solitude if one is to live a happy and productive life. We should dine and sleep well, he said, and cultivate friends and family. But we must also reserve a kind of "back shop" for ourselves, a space in which "our ordinary conversation must be between us and ourselves, and so private that no outside association or communication can find a place." Maybe Sherry didn't leave me for a new best friend, or because I inadvertently revealed my real self to her. Maybe she left me for her own back shop.

27.

What does it look like when intimate friendship slides into ordinary friendship?

Maybe like this: Two women are riding together in a car. It's going somewhere interesting, somewhere they both want to go. Suddenly, one woman taps the driver, says, "I've changed my mind. Please let me out here." The car stops, she gathers her things, and shuts the door firmly behind her. As the car drives on toward its destination, she does not linger but turns and walks briskly in the opposite direction.

Or like this: North and South are sitting at a table with thirteen cards each fanned out in front of them. South opens one no trump—a sign of strength. North passes. "Two hearts?" South pleads. North passes. Desperate now, South bids three clubs. North passes. East and West both pass. South ends up playing alone. She goes down three tricks.

28.

In *How We Die*, Sherwin Nuland writes that the myth of an easy death is just that—a myth. Sherry's death was merciful by most standards. If there was suffering, it didn't last long. And she spent her last waking moments with the man she loved and whom she married at eighteen.

When I reached D on the phone, he told me that she'd woken up a few days earlier, unable to form words properly. It was a holiday weekend, so she had to wait a few days to see a doctor. When she finally got in, a scan of her brain revealed an ominous mass. Within hours, an aneurysm ruptured, and she fell into a coma. I knew none of this while it was happening. She'd already been airlifted to a hospital over the Texas border by the time I telephoned D and heard him say, in a voice clotted with grief, "Our friend will never wake up."

So what am I doing here? Not writing a eulogy, certainly. Sherry was sixty when she died, and the silence between us fell twenty years ago.

Even if I could fill that gap with words, others have already done it, and done it better than I possibly could. D wrote about her for the *Anchorage Daily News*, and another friend, a colleague from our newspaper days, published a piece in the Fairbanks paper. The graduate programs where she taught have hosted readings in her memory. Words have been spoken—eloquent words—and tears shed by people who knew her better and longer, who loved her better, than I did. One of the ironies of her dying first is that she's one of the few people who would have appreciated the impossibility of writing honestly about someone else when there's a great big obstacle in the way, and the obstacle, of course, is the eulogist's own self.

29.

Who was my friend. The phrase hangs over Theroux's Chatwin essay like a sostenuto note. Are we meant to read it as a claim? A clue? A rationale? Or is it, perhaps, the sound of wanting what you don't have?

30.

One thing Sherry and I agreed on: essay-writing flushes out those fugitive truths, things you maybe didn't even want to know when you sat down to write. This is from "Lucky You," an essay Sherry wrote about her jones for gambling. It was published originally in the *Harvard Review*, then Hilton Als selected it for the 2018 *Best American Essays*:

> When you were standing in line at the cashier's window borrowing money (again), you suddenly recognized the terrible emotional transaction under way: you felt awful about what you were doing, but the only way to stop feeling so bad was to continue doing the one thing that could help you forget how bad you feel.

31.

D and I spent less than five minutes on the phone together. When Sherry's heart stopped beating, three days later, he let me know by email, apologizing for the impersonality of it but saying he was too broken up to talk just then. A few things about our earlier phone conversation have stayed with me. The first is that D thought to get in touch with me in the first place; the second is that he called her "our friend." Together, these things made me wonder how she described me to other people. The third thing is the most poignant, and it's what D told me just before hanging up. His son had died tragically a few years earlier—I had a vague memory of this—and when she heard the news, Sherry caught an overnight flight to Anchorage. She was there for him and his wife when they woke up the next morning. She stayed for as long as they needed her. Then, gradually, over the months and years that followed, she began to distance herself from them. I couldn't tell, then or now, whether he was simply trying to put something into words for his own sake, or whether he was trying to tell me something he felt I needed to know. I could have told him yes, I know what it's like, that partial eclipse of the sun. Such a surprise. So chilling.

32.

In linguistics, a word that exists solely to make a construction grammatical is known as a dummy, like the *it* in these sentences: "It's not clear to me why our friendship cooled," or "It's a mystery how, having been dealt a once-in-a-lifetime twenty-six-point hand, I managed to down five tricks."

33.

Dear fearless, unlucky friend: I said my desire for you wasn't erotic, and I meant it. And yet. The formula for the erotic (Anne Carson writes in *Eros: The Bittersweet*) is desire plus an obstacle. Now that you're gone forever—*fallen asleep, flown off, in bright repose*—I see that somewhere deep inside I'd been holding onto the irrational belief that one day we'd find our way back to each other. We'd strap on our walking shoes and talk our way back into a kind of intimacy that blocked out the rest of the world.

The other day, I happened on your recipe for fudge truffle cheesecake, set down in your ornate, old-fashioned handwriting. I realized that, in recent years and without being aware of it, I've begun elongating the tails of my *y*'s and *g*'s, just like you. Our friend Martha has the same recipe in your handwriting, with an extra note at the bottom: "After eating, install butt on Stairmaster to prevent immediate enlargement."

This afternoon I baked a chocolate cake with rosemary-honey syrup, strapped on my winter boots, and walked the snowy streets of my little town, placing tins of cake on friends' porches. Each tin was accompanied by a note, the tone of which varied, depending on the nature of the friendship. The gist of each one was the same, though: "You don't think you need this, but, really, you do." What I meant in every case was, "Here is my one heart. Please don't leave me stranded."

All of the notes were scrawled on two-by-four-inch cards with a *J* at the top. It's been a quarter of a century since you gave me five hundred of these cards as a gift. Against all logic, it seems sometimes as if the box of them will never run out.

34.

According to the American Contract Bridge League, the average age of a competitive bridge player is seventy-one, which makes me old for my age.

35.

It's 5:00 p.m., the end of one more yoga-pants workday day in the Pandemic States of America. I could complain, but I won't: I'm one of the lucky ones who hasn't lost anyone I love to the virus. How to pass the hours stretching from now until bedtime? I could walk the dogs or call my daughters, ride my stationary bike or leaf through a cookbook, hoping for inspiration.

I grab my phone and click on the Funbridge app. *Just one hand*, I tell myself. Half an hour later, I'm still at it. *Just one more hand*, I tell myself. *Shtick, shtick.* Eleven points, no suit. South bids one club. *Hello, Argine!*

All of a sudden, I'm sick of robots. Talking to them bores me. Bridge bores me. I bore myself.

I click *pass*.

"This bid," says Argine, "is strictly forbidden."

Whatever the mind is wrapped up in, it is all wrapped up in it, and domestic occupations are no less importunate for being less important.
—Michel de Montaigne, "Of Solitude" (trans. Donald Frame)

On Keeping House

The Graduate's Guide

Nearly half a century has passed since the spring day I'm thinking of when the president of Smith College bestowed her blessing on the graduating seniors assembled on the lawn outside the neo-Gothic quadrangle. Like thousands of women before and since, the seniors were black-capped, bobby-pinned, and shellacked with hair spray; they wore white dresses (cotton, silk, or voile) and white shoes under black gowns. If they were inclined to fidget, they would have settled when Jill Ker Conway took the podium. I know this not because I was present on that particular spring day but because I was present a few years later, and I remember the effect that President Conway had on my own graduating class. Tall and slender (she'd worked as a model, briefly, before taking her PhD in history), she had limpid eyes and a halo of brown curls. Her lilting accent conveyed an upper-class upbringing in a remote outpost of the Empire: Aussie without so much as a hint of twang. Her erect carriage bespoke intelligence, good breeding, grace, shyness, and wit. On that May day in 1981, President Conway said a few things that were exactly what everyone expected her to say to several hundred women on the cusp of Real Life. Then she said something that no one expected her to say, and that caused a kerfuffle in the coming days: "Hire someone to clean your house."

Lavish intelligence, joie de vivre, and beautiful bone structure are gifts that befell my friend Alison, one of the 1981 graduates, and the person who first told me about President Conway's admonition. Together, Alison and I have parsed that single sentence for hidden meanings, turning it over in our minds with a thoroughness that would probably surprise or even shock its author. Was she a closet Nietzschean, believing in a world made up of people who are either gold or dross, never both? I doubted it then as now. Maybe she was playing to her audience, going for a laugh at the image of a Smithie spurning four years of top-drawer liberal arts education for the pursuit of dust bunnies. That seems more likely: I like to think I knew her well enough to say that, as a rule, her humor tended more toward the dry than the vernacular.

I graduated from Smith in 1985, the year President Conway stepped down. This was several decades after the dreaded (apocryphal?) nude "posture pictures"; the "open-door, three-feet-on-the-floor" rule for entertaining male visitors; lessons in how to descend a flight of stairs without letting your date, standing at the bottom, see up your slip. (Think *traverse*, as in downhill or telemark skiing.) However, a few customs persisted into the mid-eighties, among them high tea in the parlor on Friday afternoons and, for seniors, sherry at the president's house.

Like many of my classmates, I, too, fell under the spell of Jill Conway's aristocratic bearing, shy smile, and penetrating mind. My friends and I never wearied of the story of how she'd fallen for, then married, her history professor at Harvard. (To prepare for their first date, I learned from reading *True North*, she spent a *whole day* at Boston's Elizabeth Arden salon.) Heck, I was probably a little bit in love with her myself. I tell you these things because I want you to believe, as I do, that my motives are pure. Language is, literally, the currency of my life: I make a living by writing and teaching writing to college students. What I do with words—sifting, arranging, coding, decoding—is more compulsion than talent. Over and over, I've repeated President Conway's words until they've become a kind of mantra: "Hire someone to clean your house. Hire someone to clean your house. Hire someone. To clean. Your. House."

In her mid-forties now, my friend Alison has a husband, two daughters, and a PhD in neuroanatomy (meaning she knows one or two things about rat brains that you and I never will). She is articulate and forceful when it comes to expressing her views on a range of topics, from social Darwinism to Henry James to the politics of academia. She has few, if any, hang-ups: For Independence Day one year, she dressed up as the Fourth of July Fairy. She painted her dining room walls Chinese lacquer red before anyone of our other friends thought to do it. In her red dining room, Alison has thrown dozens of parties over the years: progressive dinner parties, birthday parties, book group parties, Christmas parties, pre- and post-concert parties. At these occasions, the food and wine and conversation are so fabulous, so effortless, so scintillating, that few guests, if any, could possibly notice Alison's bookshelves. There, chaos reigns: novels and children's books crammed together with hairbrushes, ponytail holders, barrettes, Happy Meal toys, homework papers, stray recipes, newspaper clippings, party invitations. Her bookshelves speak to me in my language. They say important things about my own life and house, about the unholy alliance of cowardice and fear and repression that drives me to tidy up every visible surface or, failing that, to keep the world at arm's length.

The Feminist Guide

I'm old enough to remember the day my parents replaced our black-and-white RCA with a color TV. Reception was dicey—we got only two channels—and I soaked up the storylines in commercials as avidly as those in a Disney fairy tale. In one, a woman was brought to the brink of despair by her husband's collars—"those dirty rings, you try scrubbing them out." In another, a woman with a rag tied around her head, just like Hattie McDaniel in *Gone with the Wind*, joyously mopped the kitchen floor with a revolutionary no-wax formula that didn't require her to strip and reapply the wax inch by painstaking inch, on her hands and knees.

Then, in the early seventies came the commercial that shook me to my core. I was lying on my parents' bed in my flannel nightgown, fluffy slippers, with Dippity-Do and pink foam rollers in my hair. The television played a sultry melody, and I watched a high-heeled, briefcase-toting, business-suited woman step into her apartment at the end of the workday. Suddenly, she whipped off her horn-rimmed glasses, shook out her chignon, unbuttoned the top few buttons of her blouse, and, *Voila!* She magicked herself into being the woman as well as the man: she could bring home the bacon *and* fry it up in a pan. She was no longer a high-powered lawyer or accountant but a domestic goddess!

I thought, *Wow, that's* exactly *who I want to be when I grow up.* That perfume ad was my first lesson in feminism: women could (and should) do it all—hold down a job, cook, clean, and, at the end of the day, put on a frilly apron and hand their husband a martini as he walked through the door.

By the time I graduated from high school, feminism was evolving into its woman-as-CEO phase. If there was anyone in the apartment wearing a frilly apron or fixing a martini, she was probably the hired help. For the women I went to college with, the only field worth excelling in was the corporate one. I wouldn't be surprised if, among my graduating class, future investment bankers outnumbered aspiring doctors *and* lawyers two-to-one. And all of them outnumbered the "Mrs." degree-seekers by twenty to one, at the very least. We were going to bust through the glass ceiling, goddammit, just try to stop us. As soon as we busted through the glass ceiling, we'd hire someone to shop for us and fix our meals, drop our Armani suits at the dry cleaners, drive us to work in the Range Rover, and clean our Upper East Side apartment as well as our home in the Hamptons or on Nantucket. Kids weren't part of the picture yet, but, heck, if push came to shove, we could hire someone to have our babies and rear them too.

The twenty-first century has brought more firsts: the first woman CEO (Mattel) to be fired for incompetence, the first woman director (Christie's) to be convicted of price-fixing, the first woman gazillionaire (Martha Stewart) to be tried, then convicted, then serve jail time, in an insider trading scandal.

I don't mean to make cartoon characters of my own generation. If I do, then I'm just as implicated as everyone else. (Well, maybe not as implicated as Martha Stewart, but definitely not as rich either.) I've identified myself as a feminist virtually from the moment I was capable of political thought. The forerunners—Bella Abzug, Gloria Steinem, Adrienne Rich—fill me with admiration, even awe. For the sake of all of us who came after them, they had to be simultaneously fierce and inspirational. Their courage, outspokenness, and activism made everything possible for me and my daughters.

If ante-lib women felt themselves to be enslaved to ring-around-the-collar and no-wax floors, we post-lib women find ourselves contracting with other less fortunate, less educated—let's face it, less *American*—women to do our dirty work. Herein lies the conundrum: Women's lib freed us *for* something, which was to be whoever or whatever we wanted to be. It also freed us *from* something, and that thing was our houses. We weren't going to live in squalor, *nuh-uh*, not us. We stood ready to write a check or pay cash under the table for someone else to do the work that was no longer worth our while. No matter how courteously or even generously we treated these hired helpers, the fact remained that they were doing our dirty work. "Dirt," observes Barbara Ehrenreich in her essay "Maid to Order," "tends to attach to the people who remove it."

In a speech to the graduates of Barnard College, the Nobel laureate Toni Morrison once admonished them not to become like Cinderella's stepsisters. Bear in mind, she told them, that a career as an investment banker, CEO, plastic surgeon, social worker, circuit court judge, college English professor, novelist, airline pilot, lobbyist, marathon runner, or deep-sea diver is not an entitlement but a privilege. Success doesn't grant women carte blanche to trample on other women, to metaphorically enslave those who, for one reason or another, find themselves excluded from the pell-mell pursuit of happiness in the form of two-hour commutes, Lincoln Navigators, McMansions with backyard swimming pools, investment portfolios, and summer places on the Cape or Martha's Vineyard. Just because the dirt we produce doesn't stick to *us* doesn't mean it ought to stick to someone else.

The Marxist Guide

So the world is divided into two classes: people who clean, and people who can afford to treat them as commodities. What are we supposed to make of that fact? The people who clean are almost always women, almost always non-white, almost always less educated than their employers. Many are newly arrived immigrants not yet fluent in English.

The typical cleaning lady rides the bus or the train from the part of town where she lives to the part of town where her employer lives. On the way, she looks out the window and watches the houses grow bigger, the streets become cleaner, the lawns more expansive, the shops more exclusive. In her part of town, men walk the sidewalks on weekday mornings, ambling along singly or in pairs, greeting friends and neighbors, gazing in shop windows as if they have all the time in the world. In her employer's part of town, the sidewalks are patrolled by women with ramrod posture and straight-ahead gazes, pushing single or double (even, occasionally, triple) strollers, or holding a clutch of dogs on leashes. Even if they're just walking in a big circle, they stride along for all the world as if they have someplace else to be.

The cleaning lady gets off at her stop, walks five or six blocks to her employer's house, and lets herself in the back door. If she's not already wearing a uniform, she may change into one in the room that used to be (so quaint!) the maid's quarters. Her employer has already left for the day, having roared off in her Volvo Cross-Country or Mercedes SUV to work at her part-time job in real estate, or to play doubles tennis at the club, or to make pancakes at her children's private school. On the dining room table, she's left a list of instructions (clean the refrigerator, wash the screens, use a toothbrush on the bathroom fixtures) and an envelope full of cash (social security and unemployment insurance are so *messy*).

It's an arrangement that (mostly) suits both parties. From the cleaning lady's perspective, she doesn't have a boss twittering around, offering criticism, or—worse—pretending to help. Perhaps she daydreams a bit, whiling away an hour or two pretending *she* is mistress of the enormous house with more bathrooms than bedrooms, with walk-in closets the size of her own bedroom at home.

From the employer's perspective, the cleaning transaction feels as impersonal as buying veal at the grocery store. Step 1: Leave money on the table then go away for a few hours in the morning. Step 2: Return in the early afternoon to a sparkling house. By now, the cleaning lady has changed out of her uniform, let herself out the back door, walked five or six blocks, and is waiting at the bus stop in the rain. Except for the shiny floors and the missing envelope with her name on it, you could almost imagine she'd never been there at all.

When we tell ourselves that housekeeping is a job like any other job, we're lying to ourselves. If we really believed it, we wouldn't have any trouble looking our house cleaner in the eye, the same as we do with waiters or flight attendants or yoga instructors. For better or worse, our home reflects who we are. It smells of us. Its floors collect mud dragged in after a rainstorm, fallen leaves trapped in the treads of our shoes. The washing machine traps gunk from our soiled clothes. The underside of the toilet seat is smeared with blood and shit. Sloughed-off cells glom onto sheets and towels. We tweeze, shave, shampoo, brush and blow dry: all those stray hairs have to go *somewhere*. Likewise the clippings from our nails, the end-products of our depilations. None of it simply melts into thin air.

Still, we kid ourselves. Who's got time to clean up after themselves these days? Not us. The very suggestion has an antiquated, even reactionary feel, like urging us to get milk and butter straight from the cow.

The Mother's Guide

Like children everywhere, mine are self-absorbed, absent-minded, slavish adherents to the pleasure principle. Just about any afternoon, you can find them wrapped up in one of the two kinds of projects at which they excel: (1) constructing complicated works of art that require oil-based paints, cornstarch, cotton balls, uncooked macaroni, food coloring, glitter, and/or pipe cleaners; (2) building forts out of every sheet, blanket, coverlet, and piece of furniture in the house. They never clean up after themselves without being asked at least 582 times, and then only grudgingly. I feel lucky if they change the kitty litter once or twice a week, or help me carry in groceries from the car. At least once a day, I'm forced to appeal to the only emotion that really motivates them: fear. They hate it when I scream and curse at them. They hate it even more when I threaten to revoke their phone, computer, guest, or allowance privileges. In the end, I find the begging, wheedling, cajoling, and threatening more exhausting than simply shooing the girls outside and tidying up all by myself.

Housecleaning, for me, is never a linear narrative with a clear beginning, middle, and end. It's more like a postmodern riff that begins nowhere in particular and ends in roughly the same place. It's like a heap of junk in the center of the room: unmatched bedroom slippers, Barbie doll shoes, fabric swatches, Beanie Babies, marbles, bits of Play-Doh, book jackets separated from their books, doll dresses, silk butterfly wings, Magic Markers. You can put each item in a specially marked container, but it won't stay put. Order is at best temporary; at worst, utterly illusory. This is what it feels like to live inside the messy story of one's own life.

As a woman and mother, I often think in terms of connects and disconnects. Invisible strings run from my body to my daughters', to their classrooms, to the mothers of other children in their class. The strings form intricate patterns when I carpool, chaperone a field trip, buy a birthday present for a child I've never met, say yes to a play date on a Saturday afternoon, drive a hundred miles each way for an Odyssey of the Mind competition. I know the voices of the parents on my telephone tree better than their faces at soccer games. Even so, my daughters ground me in a kind of community, one made up almost exclusively of other women. The women in the particular community in which I find myself hire women from outside our community to clean.

As a college professor, I tend to feel far less connected to a community, especially a community of women. At my old job, a wiry Black woman named Isabel used to clean my office early in the morning, before I got there. Whenever we passed each other in the hall, we'd say hello and wonder whether it would rain, but I knew nothing of Isabel's life. Actually, I take that back; I knew something I wished I didn't. One day, I got to the office without my keys, so I went in search of Isabel and her master key. I found her in the downstairs housekeeping closet hurriedly burying a bottle in the trash. There was no mistaking the smell of alcohol on her breath. It was eight o'clock in the morning.

A talkative and efficient woman named Linda cleans my house every two weeks, and sometimes, when I'm feeling flush or out of my mind with stress, or both, she comes every week. She's only a few years older than me, but she's already a grandmother. Linda is married to one of the groundskeepers on campus, one among the invisible army of men and women who cut the grass, trim the hedges, plant and replant the flower beds that make our campus one of the most picturesque in the South. Groundskeepers and housekeepers are a time-honored tradition here: up until the Civil War, the estate that is now a women's college was a working southern plantation. No need to spell out what that meant in terms of unpaid labor, right?

Linda prefers to clean when no one is home, although she's sweet and accommodating toward sick children and snow days. Every other Wednesday morning, before I leave for work, I put two twenty-dollar bills in the center of the dining room table. In the late afternoon, I return to a house that is gleaming, and the money, of course, is gone. Linda seems to think this is a good deal for her. I *know* it's a better deal for me.

When I was growing up, my mother expected me to make my own bed every morning, pick up my room once a week, and, on Saturday mornings, to help with the household chores. With few exceptions, the chores rotated among us five children. I remember hating to fold laundry, loving to dust my mother's knickknack shelves. Ever so carefully, I would remove the pieces one by one, spray the shelves with Lemon

Pledge, wipe them clean, then replace everything, piece by precious china piece. My mother was often emotionally unavailable in those years—a consequence of too many children born too few years apart, a husband who was often away, her own part-time work as a nurse, and the family's financial struggles. I was constantly being reminded that I was the oldest and, therefore, the one from whom the most was expected. When my mother was around, I was at her side, her special helper. When she was away, I served as her surrogate. Those Saturday mornings of handling her demitasse collection—twenty-some tiny patterned teacups and saucers—made me feel closer to her somehow. When I finished the job, she would inspect it and, more often than not, pass it. I could bask for a whole day in the glow of her gratitude for a job well done.

Years later, when I was grown and living on my own, my mother and I were drinking coffee at my kitchen table. She said something that shriveled my heart: "I wish I'd done a better job of teaching you how to clean."

The Girlfriend's Guide

Every week if you can afford it; every two weeks if you can't. That's the consensus in my community, among my friends, professional women between the ages of twenty-five and sixty. It may sound gross to go fourteen days without vacuuming the living room, mopping the kitchen floor, washing the sheets, or even cleaning the toilets, especially with a houseful of kids, but it can be done.

A poet friend of mine was born in America to immigrant parents. In India, her mother ran a household with several servants. In America, as the wife of a dentist and university professor in the sixties, she was expected to clean the house by herself. My friend says, *You know that trick with the old toothbrush? How you're supposed to use it for the fixtures and base of the toilet? My mother never learned that.* A kind neighbor took my poet friend under her wing when she was young and taught her, among other things, the trick with the toothbrush. As soon as my friend sold her first collection of poems, she hired a cleaning woman.

Another friend is a former investment banker and current full-time mother to three active boys. She actually likes to vacuum. When I asked her why, via email, I could almost see her grin: "When the vacuum is turned on, I can't hear anyone calling *MOM*!"

My friends and I have excellent educations: Smith, Wellesley, Harvard, Brown. We have jobs we love, even if our job is staying home with our children. (One overachieving friend stays home with her children *and* writes novels, good ones, at the rate of roughly one per year.) Almost without exception, our household income is higher than that of our parents. As the years go by, we have fewer wishes for ourselves, more for our children. We love them *so* much. We show our love by fixing them healthy meals and washing up afterward, while they concentrate on their homework. We pick up their dirty clothes and damp towels, and we put them in the laundry hamper, from whence we eventually retrieve them, wash them, dry them, fold them, and put them away. We get down on our hands and knees to clean the toilet that they, in their early-morning grogginess, sometimes miss. On Saturdays, in lieu of housework, we drive them to soccer games or birthday parties or ski resorts or the beach. We are constantly deferring our own needs and gratification in order to meet theirs. If the housework becomes too much for us to handle during daylight hours, we put it off until evening, when the children are asleep. Toward midnight, we fall into our beds, bone weary and brain numb, perhaps—if we could even articulate it right then, which is unlikely—a teensy bit resentful.

The Man's Guide

Here's the comedian Dave Barry on cleaning: "Women, for some hormonal reason, can see individual dirt molecules, whereas men tend not to notice them until they join together into clumps large enough to support commercial agriculture."

Silly women.

Here's a riddle for Dave Barry: In what way is a woman's body just like a woman's house?

Answer: Men like to make big messes inside them both.

My favorite babysitter of all time was a bright and motivated college senior named Laura. One evening, when I returned from a dinner party, she asked me where she could find a corner sink strainer just like mine. She'd never seen anything like it before, and she thought it was a wonderful invention—a truly useful tool that might make her life easier. *Oh, how so?* I asked. It turned out Laura had a fiancé in law school thirty-five miles away. Being a nice southern boy, he saved his dirty dishes all week long, just for her. (*And* his laundry, I found out later, but that just goes to show, doesn't it?) With a sink strainer, at least he could dispose of uneaten food instead of leaving it to rot until Laura arrived on Friday evening.

In a wonderful essay called "Compression Wood," Franklin Burroughs writes of his bachelor friend McIver whose house is "bad to look at"—possessions thrown everywhere like so much flotsam and jetsam. He continues:

> You let appearances slide, and it is harmless; then you let them slide further, let them go altogether, and discover that there was more reality in them than you thought. They take away whatever energy and self-respect you had invested in them, and they keep it.

That's the question at the heart of housekeeping, whether you're a man or a woman. At what point does the appearance of something like slovenliness slide into the reality?

For the eight years in which I lived inside a marriage, the burdens of cooking, cleaning, and laundry fell largely on me. I'm not complaining. For most of those eight years, the arrangement made sense. My husband worked full-time and traveled a lot on business. I was in graduate school for many of those years, which meant it was easy for me to be home during the day. After the girls were born, I taught part-time, but I was still home for all but a couple of hours a day. I convinced myself that my doing the housework was best for everyone. For one thing, I clung to the adage, "If something is worth doing, it's worth doing right." My husband's motto, à la Dave Barry, was, "One pass is good enough."

My husband meant well. It's not as if he was the kind of guy who walked in the door at 6:00 p.m., gave me a peck on the cheek, grabbed a Bud from the fridge, then plopped down on the couch to watch TV. We never watched TV. In a pinch—if we were having company, say— my husband could run the vacuum and clean the toilets. But he was more comfortable doing manly chores—emptying the garbage, mowing the lawn, putzing in the tool shed, even placing dishes in the dishwasher after I cooked. I accepted his help grudgingly; not surprisingly, over time, he came to offer it the same way. At the time when we're being batted around by our emotions, we can't possibly name them. Now I can say that asking for help with the housework made me feel as if I were surrendering a mantle of power that defined as well as oppressed me. If I couldn't go to grad school, work full-time, *and* take care of the house by myself, then what *was* I doing? *Who* was I?

The twins came along after six years of marriage. Those first few months after they were born are still a blur. I remember breast-feeding for eight to ten hours a day. I remember a panic attack that sent me to the hospital emergency room. I remember seeing the doctor for the fifth urinary tract infection in as many months, and her telling me to stop holding just because the urge came at inconvenient moments. I remember crawling into bed, spent but angry, at 1:00 or 2:00 a.m. beside my snoring husband. I hated him for sleeping when I couldn't, hated him for being able to read the newspaper when he was at work. I hated him because I couldn't hate the babies and the preschooler who were draining me with their endless claims on my mind and body. I'd lost all sense of myself as anything but a machine for dispensing milk, changing diapers, picking up toys, pushing swings, heating up food, processing yet another load of laundry. At night, if my husband tried to touch me, I rolled over and pressed myself against the wall. "Resentment about household tasks is the strongest anaphrodisiac in the world," observes Monica Szabo, the main character in Mary Gordon's *Spending*.

The Martha Stewart Guide

Sally Quinn once criticized Martha Stewart for being all about things ("how to make the perfect tablecloth, the perfect apple pie"), the less-than-subtle implication being that she, Sally, set more store by people than pies.

A summer issue of an old *Martha Stewart Living* featured a spread on the domestic diva's birthday party for herself and a few dozen friends who share her astrological sign. In one of the photographs, an assistant is shown using a tape measure to make sure that the tables are an equal amount of space apart. (I would just like to observe that it is behavior like this on the part of certain autocratic perfectionists that brings out the mean streak in their critics.)

Being something of a perfectionist myself, I've felt the urge to whip out the tape measure once in a while. Being an occasional memoirist, I also know one or two tricks about the construction of a self. The idea is to make the final product—whether it's a wedding cake, birthday party, checkerboard paint job on a child's dresser, an essay, or even *you*—look effortless, breezy, seamless, and inevitable, as if perfection was the destination stamped on the ticket from the outset. *Use the tape measure if you must, but for God's sake, don't let the whole world know about it.*

I understand what's at stake when throwing a party; I can even guess at what's at stake when throwing a big party that will eventually be the subject of a magazine spread. What's at stake every day, though, in my keeping a clean house? What would happen if I left the beds unmade for a couple of days in a row? If I cleaned the kitchen floor with a mop instead of on my hands and knees? ("Never, ever use a mop on the kitchen floor," my mother told me. "It just pushes the dirt into the corners.") What if a friend were to drop by at 3:00 p.m. and find me at the computer in my pajamas, the breakfast things gathering flies on the dining room table?

The answer is, I'd feel ashamed. And shame—an existential conflict between who we think we ought to be and who we really are—eats away at a healthy sense of self. I swear there are days when nothing stands between me and wholeness but a basket of ironing.

Remember the parable of Martha and Mary? It appears only in the Book of John, not in any of the other canonic gospels. You might not remember it because it's only four verses long. It concerns ordinary women whose roles are defined not by their relationship to men (mother, sister, prostitute) but to each other. Martha and Mary are, in fact, sisters of Lazarus, a fact that is largely irrelevant to this story, except that it helps to explain why they feel so grateful to Jesus. Something else, something less easy to name, draws me to their story time and again. It's not just a paradox, as many of the parables are. As a story, the parable of Martha and Mary feels to me incomplete in some essential way. Here it is, in toto, as it appears in the King James Bible:

> Now it came to pass, as they went, that he entered into a certain village: and a certain woman named Martha received him into her house.
> And she had a sister called Mary, which also sat at Jesus' feet, and heard his word.
> But Martha was cumbered about much serving, and she came to him, and said, Lord, dost thou not care that my sister hath left me to serve alone? Bid her therefore that she help me.
> And Jesus answered and said unto her, "Martha, Martha, thou art careful and troubled about many things.
> "But one thing is needful: and Mary hath chosen that good part, which shall not be taken away from her."

That's it. Just as it's really getting going, the story ends. What happens next do you think? Does Martha say, "Oh, of course, I've been such a ninny!" then scurry to join Mary at Jesus' feet? If so, who finishes fixing the meal? The servants?

I've talked this over with friends, and they tell me I expect too much. They say biblical truths are meant to be universal and archetypal, not personal or psychological. But I can't stop myself from wanting it all, psychological verity on the same table as spiritual nourishment.

Maybe Martha did join Mary at Jesus' feet. Maybe Jesus performed his famous sleight of hand, turning a single fish into bouillabaisse for two dozen. If he were capable of doing that, why not also resolve the "many things" about which Martha is "careful and troubled"?

Dinner parties are never easy. Imagine throwing one on the spur of the moment for a multitude of guests, among them the savior of the known world. The details that might cause a hostess to feel troubled or full of care are legion. Herein lies the rub: Women get the message in myriad ways that we're supposed to make whipping up a healthy five-course meal, or stitching up fallen hems, or keeping an immaculate house seem absolutely effortless. Why? Because these pursuits, in inverse proportion to their needfulness, are unworthy of a valued person's time or energy.

One of the cattiest things one woman can say to another is: "Wow, your house is always immaculate. And to think you've got three kids and a full-time job: I don't know how you do it. I sure couldn't." What that woman really means is, *Here you are, a woman with full-time work and three kids, and you spend all your free time on something as superficial and meaningless as housecleaning. If it turns out you have so much as a trace of an inner life, I'll be shocked.*

The hostess makes a little moue of denial and says, "Oh no, the house isn't nearly as clean as it looks. See the red wine stains on the rug? Let me pull out my junk drawer and show you. Watch out! Don't open that closet too quickly—a person could get hurt that way."

Back off, bitch.

The Contemplative Life

"Which does a man prefer? Bacon and eggs, or worship? Sometimes one, sometimes the other, depending on how hungry he is," writes Margaret Atwood in *The Blind Assassin.*

Imagine the parable of Martha and Mary from Martha's point of view. Instead of helping with dinner, Mary sits at Jesus' feet, listening to the Word. She is still, rapt, attentive—the very image of a nun or disciple. Mary is an empty vessel being filled with the Holy Spirit. Martha, on the other hand, is emptying herself out. She bustles to and fro, carrying dishes of food, directing servants, refilling glasses of wine. Tendrils of hair stick to her sweaty forehead. There's a pebble in her sandal, but she's too busy to stop and shake it out. Exhaustion rings in her ears. Can't stop now. The fire needs building up. Flasks need replenishing. Blistered feet—*men's* blistered feet—need salving and bandaging.

Martha is hostess, housekeeper, nurse, cook, and bottle washer: Woman as Study in Perpetual Motion. Every time she steps over Mary, sprawled at the feet of Jesus, she feels a prickle of annoyance. As the afternoon wears on, the irritation turns to anger. Being the type of person she is, she'd rather slit her own wrists than ask for help, though. To do so would be to reveal a flaw or weakness in her character, to admit not just that she has failed at something but that *she* is a failure. By the time her bitterness overflows, it is so strong, so full of self-loathing, so polluting of herself and everyone within earshot, that her voice sounds whiny, even to her own ears. *Doesn't anyone care about me?*

"*Martha, Martha,*" Jesus implores. "*Calm thyself.*"

In a striking rhetorical inversion, Jesus tells Martha she is "careful," meaning full of care—perhaps for the well-being of others; Mary, on the other hand, is "needful," meaning full of need (read "desire") for the Holy Spirit. One sister gives; the other receives. To "take care" of something or someone is to be active; to "be needy" is passive. Everything I've seen of women in the world tells me that caring is good, needing bad. Yet here is a woman who gives out of her own generous emptiness, a sister who receives out of her selfish need.

The Writing Life

Hiring someone to clean my house makes me queasy, but I do it anyway. On Wednesday mornings, when I put forty dollars on the table, I feel my deepest convictions (clean up after yourself, don't pay another woman to do your scutwork) clash with my deepest desires (a cleaner house, more time to write and play with the girls). I feel lucky beyond belief to have a job that pays me a decent salary to do what I love best, which is writing and teaching.

Because I love to write, and because I was reared in accordance with the precepts of the Church of Delayed Gratification, I tend to feel as if I have to *earn* my writing time. At this moment, I've got an itch to get up and clean out the linen closet and the cupboard under the bathroom sink. After that, I need to wash the windows and screens. And then there's mending and ironing to be done. *Dearest Cinderella, if you can pick two bowlfuls of lentils out of the ashes in an hour, you may go to the ball.*

Hemingway and his expat pals in Paris in the twenties and thirties wrote hard during the day, then tore up the town at night, carousing in bars and cafés. The *writing* was the work; the drinking and storytelling, the all-around frat boy behavior, was the reward.

If I let myself get up from the computer and start on the chores, I'll get through them, but I'll be too worn out to write. Is that what I want? Some days, the answer is yes. A deadly voice whispers in my ear: "You can clean the linen closet to your satisfaction in thirty minutes or less, but everything you write in the next thirty minutes is likely to be crap. Which activity—cleaning or writing—constitutes the best use of your time?"

I dislike the image of myself as a drudge, cleaning out closets, scrubbing toilets, and washing windows. I embrace the image of myself as a writer, clicking away at the computer. They cannot be reconciled, these two images. What if I let go of them both? To live in this world, I must clean up after myself and my children sometimes. The trick is to feel satisfaction in a job well done but not to be carried away by compulsion. To be a writer, I must write, which means being stingier with time that could be spent on projects with quicker, more tangible results. It means that writing badly must be its own reward.

Zen and the Art of Household Maintenance
Here's Thich Nhat Hanh on the Zen of housework: "Let us light the torch of our awareness and learn again how to drink tea, eat, wash dishes, walk, sit, drive, and work in awareness. . . . We find that life is a miracle, the universe is a miracle, and we too are a miracle."

Yeah, right.

A Few Definitions

Cleaning House: An idiomatic expression meaning to rid an institution or organization of inefficient, lazy, or corrupt workers.

D & C: Dilation and curettage. A common medical procedure for clearing unwanted detritus from a woman's uterus. *See also* Dusting & Cleaning.

Dusting & Cleaning: See D & C.

Keeping House: Keeping *the* house, that is, making the mortgage payment within a week or so of when it's due each month so the bank doesn't foreclose; fighting the highway expansion project that would raze the house for a high-speed exit ramp; declining the job offer that would require selling the house and moving across the country.

Messy vs. Dirty: The summer before my first year of college, I received a questionnaire in the mail from Smith. I'd be sharing a room with a stranger that year, and the person in charge of matching us up wanted to know if (A) I liked my surroundings neat as a pin, (B) I liked my surroundings clean but not necessarily neat, or (C) I was a total slob. Like 90 percent of my classmates, I checked B. Even then, I was conscious of dissembling: if you can't keep the surfaces reasonably clear, then you can't very well get under them to clean, now can you?

(Update: my freshman year roommate and I are nearing sixty, and we're still friends. I seriously doubt whether either of us remembers the other's cleaning habits.)

Pre-cleaning: What one does the night before the cleaning person is scheduled to arrive. Because cleaning is a seller's market in the part of the country where I live, failure to pre-clean is apt to result in one's being fired by said cleaning person.

Random Thoughts Related to Definitions (Above)

A well-kept house creates the illusion of a well-kept, intact self. In straightening my room, do I straighten myself? Do I need straightening? Do I want it?

By nature, cleaning is a rule-bound activity, subject to certain universal standards. Like assembly-line work, it requires one to subjugate oneself to the work. It discourages self-expression or eccentricity, encourages self-effacement, even self-erasure. Ideally, one ought to become a robot, an inanimate extension of the vacuum cleaner, feather duster, toilet bowl brush.

A radical thought: is it possible that our passion for cleanliness is really a passion for something else—a passion, perhaps, for hiding our true selves? I shower every day to cover up the smell of the real me. I clean my house for pretty much the same reason. Can it be that existential terror we feel in the face of a really big mess is the terror of being stripped naked, exposed for the flawed, decrepit, and smelly beings we naturally are?

Housekeeping and the Simple Life
A recent issue of the lifestyle magazine *Real Simple* features a recipe for "beer-can chicken." Instructions: Drink half of a 12-oz. can of beer, then pour the rest on the chicken.

I like it. Truth is, I like Martha Stewart too. She strikes me as refreshingly honest. (Also, I'm crazy about the CBD gummies she developed with her pal Snoop Dogg.) Publishing a picture of a woman measuring the space between tables is a tacit acknowledgment of the man (or woman) behind the curtain. The subtext of Martha's magazine, Martha's TV spots, Martha's merchandising empire, Martha's *life* seems to be, *Yes, housekeeping is hard work*—but it's *good* hard work, as someone once told me about homesteading in Alaska. Our strength lies in caring for, in keeping up, the things we've chosen to surround ourselves with. In that sense, housekeeping is a meaningful undertaking, a gauge for measuring our larger failures and successes as human beings.

Postscript #1: Desire
I'm writing this in one of the four applewood chairs that my grandmother left me in her will. Before sitting down to write, I had to drag the chair from its place beside my bed, where it doubles as a nightstand. Before that, I had to clear the seat of detritus from last night. If last night had been a good night, the detritus would have been an

empty wine glass and a hardcover novel or volume of poetry. Instead, there were crumpled Kleenex, two or three Dixie cups half full of water (careful, lest they disintegrate when you try to pick them up), and a fever thermometer. The water was for the child who was coughing, the one curled up in a nest of pillows on the bedroom floor with a snoring beagle on her feet. The thermometer was for a second child, the one who had seemed to be on the mend from the coughing virus and a nasty case of pink eye but who developed, in the middle of the night, a startling, blotchy rash over her entire body. Her temperature turned out to be normal, thank God. This second child ended up in bed with me, entangled in my acres of flannel nightgown, curled up next to the third daughter, the one who'd begun the night in bed with me because, early in the evening, she'd suffered a round of burning diarrhea.

Entropy in action. But now I'm writing, tidying up, setting the room to rights (such a wonderful, virtuous phrase!), stitching up the tatters, making worlds out of words. Is it vanity to think I can hold things together this way? I don't think so. I *can't* think so. Real life is bound to reassert itself shortly in the form of laundry to be folded, friends to be bolstered, daughters to be driven to school, to ballet, to soccer, to the doctor. This business of running in circles bothers me less, somehow, if I shore myself up with something that lasts. Build breakwaters out of paragraphs. If only I can shake the illusion that beautiful, orderly surroundings cause me to have beautiful, orderly thoughts.

When my house is in a shambles like this, a voice in my head says, *Don't despair, it will get picked up eventually. And even if it doesn't, the world won't end.* I usually ignore that voice. Instead, I listen to the irrational and therefore stronger voice that says to throw a temper tantrum, throw china at the walls, smack a child on her bottom, dissolve in a puddle of tears on the floor. Not today, though.

Today is Linda's day to clean.

Postscript #2: Entropy
Outside the plate-glass windows of my high school classroom, birch branches filigreed a sky awash in the tropical colors of an Arctic sun-

set. Inside the room, my economics teacher—a stoop-shouldered man whose thick, horn-rimmed glasses kept sliding down his nose—droned on about the relationship between supply and demand. I tuned in every few minutes, then went back to meditating on the flickering patterns of branches against sky. It deepened from the palest peach-blue, like veins under the skin, to the violent red of bloodshed. *There* was drama for you.

I tended toward dreaminess in every subject but literature. Words on the page made worlds, and they reflected my own weird adolescent reality back at me. One sentence of *Tess of the D'Urbervilles* made more sense than a semester's worth of lectures on the vagaries of the stock market. Even then, I was interested in order and beauty—what they were, and whether I would know them when I saw them. Were they related and, if so, did beauty beget order, or the other way around? I wondered about ugliness and disarray too. Were they the opposite of beauty and order, or only the obverse?

I had no answers then. Still don't, truth be told. With age (my fortieth high school reunion just passed) has come not wisdom but the occasional glimmer of insight. Most of the time, knowledge comes to me as apprehension of the inverse. I know how it is to feel good because I've felt crummy a time or two. I know beauty exists because I've glimpsed it elsewhere—in other people's homes, other people's gardens, other people's faces. As for order, I know it purely in the breach: it's the lovely thing already gathering dust. It is, at best, partial. If order prevails in the living room, then the kitchen must, ipso facto, be a train wreck. If the spice jars are alphabetized, then heaven help the silverware drawer. And these are only the little things. What about orderly work habits, an orderly mind, an orderly *life*? What's so bad about wanting what I cannot have?

Molly Peacock poses the question in her poem, "Why I Am Not a Buddhist." Her answer: "Because want leaves a world in tatters? / How else but in tatters should a world be?"

How else indeed.

We've been locked in the world's box,
Love sets us free, time kills us.
                    —Adam Zagajewski, "Little Waltz"

In Praise of the Perfect White T-Shirt

It's 2002, and I have a temporary teaching position at a horsey women's college in the South. A few of my students are fragile, and they sometimes linger after class for a bit of coddling: *Sorry I was late again. The doctor gave me some new meds.* On the day I'm thinking of, the conversation ran long. I glance at my watch: 2:35 p.m. It's imperative that my ten-year-old daughter be fetched by 3:00 p.m. from her private school. The school is thirty miles away, in a suburb of Lynchburg, Virginia. On this day, like so many others, I hit the road fuming—at myself for losing track of time; at the indicator light in my car that warns I'm about to run out of gas; at my daughter whose first words will be, "You're late, Mom—*again.*" What seems to be most at fault in this situation, however, is not me or my job or my daughter but time itself for being as relentless, inexorable, and powerful as a fifty-foot wave propelling me, a helpless shred of flotsam toward a distant shore that was never on my itinerary.

My fury finds an outlet in the other southbound drivers on Route 29: construction workers jammed four abreast on the bench seat of a pickup, their beefy arms dangling out of open windows; stop-and-start driver's ed students with that ridiculous yellow hat bungeed to the top of the car; Realtors (you can tell from the license plate) closing a deal on the cell phone while creeping along at forty-five miles per hour in the left lane; quivering ancients propped up on pillows in order to see out the windshield. *Hey, Buddy! Guess what? The road is for driving!* No one has pulled a gun or a baseball bat on me yet. I haven't yet been stopped for speeding, though (knock wood) I richly deserve it.

Speeding is just a symptom, of course. The larger problem is not that I'm running late on a particular Tuesday in March, but that I'm *always* running late—always rushing to catch up to the woman off in the distance, just a few miles or minutes away, the one vanishing around a distant bend just as I'm entering the straightaway. I sense that the woman in the distance is another, better, possibly even truer, version of me. Who, then, is this caricature slaloming down Route 29, lobbing obscenities at other drivers, willing time to tick backward or even just to stop for just a moment? Dear reader, I, too, would like to know.

Even for physicists, time is abstract, an inchoate concept that can be grasped, explained, quantified only in terms of the relative concrete. If you try in casual conversation to talk intelligently about time, you will lapse almost immediately into metaphor. *Racing time. Killing time. The test of time. Time on your hands. Time to burn. Running late. Running behind.* Even *running early.* As metaphors, these are pretty much DOA; over time (!), the words have untethered themselves from the image. When we say we're killing time, we're anthropomorphizing it. When we say that someone (meaning, someone *else*) has time on her hands, we imply that time has mass. "Running early" strikes me as particularly insipid; if you're likely to be early, why bother running at all?

A week or so ago, I found myself in the unusual position of being early—*ahead of time*—to pick up my daughter. The handful of extra minutes made me feel lazy, decadent, unencumbered, foreign inside my own skin. I stopped at a bakery to buy a loaf of crusty bread for dinner, a couple of molasses cookies for me and my daughter to share on the drive home. Next door was a whimsically named boutique, Pheasant's Eye. For a few seconds, I stood outside the plate-glass windows, soaking up the still life of jewel-tone blouses, scarves, stemware, beaded bracelets, and crystal drop earrings. I asked myself what, if anything, I needed. Nothing. I still had grading to do, but classes would soon be over for the summer. If I wanted to, I could spend the next couple of months wearing nothing but shorts, tank tops, and sandals. No make-up or jewelry, just sunscreen and a watch. I checked it again. There was time to burn.

Ten minutes later, I left the boutique with a creased paper bag under my arm. The clerk had curled her lip slightly as she wrapped my purchase in a sheet of petal pink tissue, then, wordlessly, handed me change for my twenty-dollar bill. The Lynchburg matrons who comprise the shop lady and country club set—blonde, bobbed, wallpapered in Lilly Pulitzer—might have looked down their overbred noses at my purchase. I couldn't have cared less. I was flying high on shopping endorphins: the tension of desire giving way to the rush of fulfillment.

At home later, I'd slide my purchase out of the crackling bag, reverently unwrap the tissue paper, snip the tags, and place my neatly folded purchase in the middle drawer of my dresser. To the untrained eye, the contents of that particular drawer might appear to be a dozen or more identical white T-shirts. To me, the T-shirts are as easy to tell apart as my three daughters. Made by Fresh Produce, the one from Pheasant's Eye is constructed of thinly ribbed white cotton with a wide crew neckband. Among the rest are cotton crewnecks from Old Navy and Target; a cropped running shirt in a breathable cotton-polyester blend; a jersey shirt that tends to pill; a pair of boxy ribbed crewnecks from Chico's; a boatneck version with three-quarter sleeves; a long-sleeved, form-fitting jewel-neck; a plain V-neck; and an oversized crewneck emblazoned with my college's logo. As white T-shirts go, I guess that's a lot. As collections go, however, it's negligible. Alice Harris, author of a pictorial history called *The White T*, confessed to an interviewer that she owns literally hundreds.

One of my students, a young woman of modest means, collects amber necklaces. Another student, a woman of significantly greater means, collects matchbooks. A decade or so ago, a friend from work borrowed my kayaking gear. She kept it for two years. Shortly after she'd moved into a new apartment, she returned it in a battered cardboard box labeled "Little Black Dresses."

Why do people collect one thing and not another? Silver spoons instead of stamps? Jazz CDs instead of Baccarat vases? Swatches of fabric instead of pincushions? Porcelain dogs, not salt-and-pepper shakers? Post-Impressionist paintings, not abstract sculptures? White T-shirts, not little black dresses? I know a woman who collects friends. Her address book is thicker than the *Oxford English Dictionary*. Normally, I wouldn't count people as objects unless I were actually to treat them as collectibles: the thrill of pursuit, then the fleeting pleasure of possession, followed by the inevitable letdown, disappointment, heartbreak. Come to think of it, what is collecting but a compressed version of a love affair, endlessly repeated? Once the shine is off, friends gather dust as readily as antique cranberry glass.

Like other compulsions, collecting must strike the uninitiated as profoundly strange. A behaviorist might say collectors are the unwitting victims of imprinting at an early age, the urge to collect no more than a fetish writ large. A Freudian might say the impulse arises from childhood loss or trauma; the sooner we realize we can never obtain that which we desire most—our father's exclusive love, say—the better. A capitalist might say we seek to corner the market on a particular good, to define ourselves not by who we are but by what we own: whoever dies with the most wins. What seems inarguable is that collecting is highly subjective, depending on the upbringing, income, passions, and pains of the individual collector. In his eyes, the desired object accrues value that transcends cost, usefulness, or beauty. In fact, these things are beside the point. Collecting is about love. "Ownership is the most intimate relationship one can have to objects," says the philosopher Walter Benjamin in his essay, "Unpacking My Library": "Not that they come alive in him; it is he who lives in them."

Why do I care so much about white T-shirts? Perhaps because I grew up in Fairbanks, Alaska, the farthest north city in North America, where function nearly always trumps aesthetics. Patagonia, Filson, Royal Robbins, Carhartt, and Xtra Tuff are the designers of choice for the cabin-dwelling crowd. My grandmother might have had something to do with it too. She was a passionate—some would say pathological—collector of antiques: china, silver, crystal, applewood furniture, oil paintings. I sometimes think my own aesthetic—rustic, minimalist—was shaped in opposition to hers.

A simpler possibility is that I settled on white T-shirts because I'm now a single mother trying to survive on an assistant professor's salary. I couldn't collect Stickley furniture or Kate Spade handbags even if I wanted to. That sounds more flippant than I intend. In truth, the decorative arts strike a chord in me: a framed lithograph by an artist friend, a vase of fresh-cut lilacs, a cunning arrangement of dried starfish on the mantel. What I love best, though, are things I can use: a patchwork bedspread from Guatemala, a sleek cast-iron teapot from China, a hand-painted olive bowl from France. A new white T-shirt from Gap.

One of my younger sisters is an incontinent shopper. She can't walk into Walmart without dropping a couple of hundred dollars. Target and Old Navy induce a kind of frenzy in her that I find frightening. She is nearly pure id, this sister. Before shopping, she was addicted to food. She ate fast and furtively, hunched over the plate. Watching her, I once thought she would eat the world. Then she ballooned to over 300 pounds and nearly died from a rare medical condition that was complicated by obesity. To save her life, the surgeon stapled her stomach. Now my sister is svelte; now she satisfies her cravings by shopping.

"Why do I let her drive me so crazy?" I'm on the phone with my other sister, girding myself for a family weekend.

"Because," says my baby sister, "she wears on the outside all the insecurities we carry around on the inside."

In the mid-eighties, the *Boston Globe* ran a profile of Sissela Bok. The reporter marveled at the way she juggled roles as scholar, teacher, mother, and wife of Derek Bok, then president of Harvard University. The reporter asked, *What's your secret?*

"I don't shop," replied Sissela Bok.

I ping between the psychology of my sister, who would buy everything, and Sissela Bok, who would buy nothing (or so she says: in what universe is it really possible to *not shop*?). Do I belong to the realm of ideas? Or to the world of January white sales? Where lies moderation, "the silken string running through the pearl chain of all virtues" (Joseph Hall, d. 1656)? The truth is, I love to shop and I always have. When I was little and when my grandmother gave her some money, my mother would take my sisters and me to The Carousel, which was as exclusive as any shop in the Frozen North could aspire to be. The dresses were hung beneath clear plastic shields. New clothes—especially *these* new clothes—were a near-unfathomable luxury. Most of the dresses I owned then were either handmade by my mother on her Singer sewing machine or handed down from my older cousin Andrea. I associate The Carousel with other things that were out of place in that frontier childhood: my mother's diamond solitaire engagement ring from Tiffany's, for example. And I still remember the smell of the place: sweet and dry, like talcum powder, with overtones of starch and old lady. We were on our best behavior there, speaking in hushed voices, as in church. The owner died when I was in high school, and the store was liquidated. At that final sale, mother bought me a sleeveless white pique dress with grass-green piping at the neck and waist. It was the most elegant thing I'd ever owned up to that point. Wearing it made me feel like Audrey Hepburn. I loved it so much I once tried to sneak out the door in the middle of winter with it on under my winter coat, but my mother caught me and forced me to change into jeans and a sweater.

As a grown woman, I've become a bit of a snob about where and when I shop. I hardly ever go to the mall, and never in December. I like tiny, dimly lit, quirky boutiques like the Pheasant's Eye, places where it's possible to imagine finding the one and only perfect thing—and simultaneously discovering that it is now marked down 50 percent. It seems to me that as a form of work, shopping resembles nothing so much as writing. Like writing, it demands vast, uninterrupted stretches time in which to imagine a self (*Is that me in a Cubist-print shirtwaist?*), reimagine it (*What would happen if I wore a cashmere swing coat with a faux fur collar to the next faculty reception?*), and to wreak the tiniest of transformations (*I now must reckon myself a woman who* *possesses a pair of $164 sandals*). Swiping my American Express Gold Card makes me feel rich, even when I can't possibly pay it off at the end of the month. "Some important part of consumption is really about and for oneself," writes Richard Todd, in *The Thing Itself.* "It represents our desire to enlarge, to complete, to reify ourselves. With our purchases, we try to become more acceptable not fundamentally to others but to ourselves." I've come to think there are worse things than buying a new pair of Donald Pliner square-heeled pumps I can't afford—to match a lifestyle I will never have—and one of them is slinking out of the shoe store empty-handed.

(It's 2022, and I've just returned to this essay, which I drafted twenty years ago. My current, fifty-nine-year-old self would like to inform the thirty-nine-year-old I used to be that those super-stylish Donald Pliner pumps, now best described as *vintage* pumps, are still in my regular rotation of Things to Wear While Introducing Booker Prize–Winning Novelists in Front of Large Audiences.)

The truth is, I'm less neurotic about clothes than a lot of women I know. I might spend one morning in fifty rifling through my wardrobe, in a tizzy over nothing to wear, or—to be honest—nothing that doesn't make me look fat. I own three-season basics in taupe and black. Blouses in sage, sky and teal, garnet and amethyst. Shoes, boots, and sandals in the requisite colors of bone, black, brown, navy, and even red. I love running my hands over the fabrics: silk, linen, flax, cotton, wool, cashmere, and a slinky washable polyester. For the most part, I love my clothes, and they love me back.

On chilly mornings, a white T-shirt is the perfect thing to layer beneath a sweater or button-down shirt. In the summer, I like to wear a white T under white linen. For a trip to the farmers market, a white T (long- or short-sleeved) worn with a wide brown belt, faded blue jeans, and cowboy boots (memo to self: buy cowboy boots!) seems to me to strike a note of carefree chic.

I sometimes think of myself as having been raised more by my friends than my mother, especially when it comes to clothing. One evening, a quarter of a century ago, I was having drinks with friends in the pub of the university where most of us worked then. We were none of us prudes, but we *were* mystified, we all agreed, by the growing trend of turning underwear into outerwear: bra straps under a camisole, overalls over nothing but a bra—that sort of thing.

"I want to say to these girls, 'Didn't your mother tell you always, always to wear a flesh-colored bra under a white shirt?'" asked Helen, in her lilting South African accent.

"Yes!" chimed my friends.

Researching this essay, I asked my friends to tell me what they thought of white T-shirts. Lisa is a college librarian, tall and slender with green eyes and a shock of hennaed hair. Like me, she went to college in the eighties. Nearly every day, she wore Levi's 501s, a Hanes white T-shirt, size extra small—"so it was just a little bit tight"—and a string of pearls. She fully intended to be sending mixed signals: man/woman, innocence/experience, passion/restraint.

Dean is a red-blooded cowboy-cum-newspaper reporter in his mid-thirties. As soon as I asked, his mind leapt straight to wet T-shirt contests. Women reveal a lot about themselves through the fit of their T-shirts, he says. "The tighter they are, the more likely you'll be feeding your illegitimate brood with food stamps."

My friend Carrie has a sense of style so fresh and imaginative that another friend once called her sui generis. She owns sundresses so complex they could be described as architectural: billowy translucent overskirts and silk underskirts in a mix of colors and patterns that would constitute a crime on anyone else. Checked gingham blouses over bias-cut polyester skirts, striped, worn with suede clogs or Birkenstocks. One Saturday in summer, when the temperature climbed to a hundred degrees, she wore a straw hat, a white tank top, and gauzy white pants to go blueberry picking.

Blueberry picking!

On a man, few things are sexier than a white T-shirt. On a woman, nothing is sexier than a man's white T-shirt. It's clean, forceful, uncompromising in its plainness—not coy or prevaricating, like cream or ecru. It is underclothing that (unlike a fire-engine red bra) can properly be worn on the outside. A worn-out white T can do a useful turn as a child's paint smock or nightgown before hitting the ragbag. A writer friend wraps a strip of a worn-out white T-shirt around his head, pirate-style, when he works. "It helps to hold my brains in," he told me.

I wear white T-shirts instead of perfume. The air freshener in my car is a Yankee Candle creation called Clean Cotton. It has a picture of (what else?) white T-shirts on a clothesline. In the house I share with my daughters, mine is the bedroom closest to the bathroom. Rather than schlep all the way to their own room for a pair of pajamas after their nightly bath, my daughters often help themselves to the contents of my middle drawer. With flushed skin and tousled hair, wearing one of my white T-shirts, a twin snuggles up to me on the couch while I read "Little Red Riding Hood."

"Grandmother, what big teeth you have."

"Mommy," says Eme, burying her nose in the fabric. "It smells like you."

America's obsession with white T-shirts started in World War I, when soldiers abroad observed the Europeans wearing a cotton undergarment to protect their skin from itchy wool uniforms. By World War II, the white T-shirt was standard issue as underwear for American soldiers. To wear a white T-shirt by itself—think Marlon Brando, Elvis Presley, and John Wayne—in the fifties was regarded as edgy and risqué. Picture James Dean in a white T-shirt and black motorcycle jacket, lounging against a brick wall in the publicity poster for *Rebel Without a Cause*. Two things happened in the sixties and seventies: T-shirts became more acceptable as outwear, but only if they were silk-screened, tie-dyed, or stamped with a logo. Then, in the eighties and nineties, white T-shirts were reinvented for women's bodies and began to come into their own.

That phrase gives me pause. What does it mean to say that something has come into its own? That it's popular, certainly. But why? The shape of the white T-shirt is rigorously plain: a vertical line topped by a quick horizontal dash, the capital T, vague allusion to the cross and Christ crucified. Its color conjures clouds, snowflakes, wedding gowns, a nun's wimple, the blank page. Whiteness welds surface to depth. It is what it is: no pretense.

I sometimes think I'm made of nothing but pretense. My friend Carrie would catch me up short for saying this—for selling myself short again, she'd say—but I'm the sort of person who's nearly always read the review instead of the book, seen the trailer instead of the film, and who's not above faking having read or seen it all either. I'm up to date on back issues of *Harper's* and the *New Yorker*, but Bachelard's *Poetics of Space* sits on my bookshelf, barely cracked.

Emerson admonishes us to live as simply as possible, to build ourselves plain houses and to furnish them plainly, thereby discouraging any would-be visitors with lavish tastes. Like a house stripped of all but necessities, a white T-shirt implies that its wearer's beauty is in the bones, the clear skin (testament to clean living), not in the chiffonier stuffed with stuff. A well-fitting (not *too* tight!) white T-shirt doesn't snag a stranger's gaze. It allows a woman to travel under the radar, to become invisible. It becomes a vessel into which the body—fat thin buxom budding muscle-bound suntanned tattooed pierced scarred— pours itself. It is form; the body, poetry.

This whole subject makes me vaguely anxious, as if it's some kind of moral failing on my part to love material things, especially clothes. Thoreau warns against "all enterprises that require new clothes, and not rather a new wearer of clothes." He's right, of course, but I can't help feeling like a high school sophomore who fervently believes the right clothes will buy her not merely happiness but belonging. Object lesson 1, from high school: One of the most popular and beautiful girls in my class wore a white blouse to a disco dance. The strobe light had the effect of making everything disappear—skin, jeans, blouse— everything, that is to say, except her brilliant white bra, which glowed blue and appeared to be dancing by itself. Of the dozens of people in the room, the only person who didn't see this was her. Next day, her popularity plummeted. She ended up marrying the class geek whose family owns a run-down convenience store on the outskirts of town.

Object lesson 2: At a meeting for alumnae recruiters to my alma mater, we learned about a recent financial aid application that would, in the Twitter era, have gone viral. Under the heading of "family budget," the applicant's mother had penciled in $2,000 per month for "recreational shopping." This woman needed $2,000 a month to *re*-create herself. My own grandmother spent that and more; she was a restless spirit, given to parking herself for months at a time in hotel suites in Seattle or Rochester, Minnesota. Wherever she traveled, she bought things and sent them home by the literal truckload. She had the surest sense of style of anyone I've known (except, perhaps, my friend Carrie), yet she'd drop $500 for a clutch of silk scarves she didn't need if the saleswoman at Tiffany's acted—as salesladies often did—as if my grandmother had taken a wrong turn on the way to Filene's Basement. The only thing separating my grandmother from your run-of-the-mill obsessive-compulsive shopper was good taste.

I know of a woman of roughly my grandmother's age whose children had to move her into a new house just a few years before she died. She'd filled the old one from floor to ceiling with newspapers, receipts, canned goods, dime-store jewelry, even coils of hair salvaged from the bathtub drain. When the woman died, her heirs had to rent two industrial sized Dumpsters just to clean out the *new* house.

Unbridled desire (itchy palms, pounding heart, stealthy looks to ensure that no one else has seen it too) attaches itself to whatever is near at hand or just out of reach: that's the dark side of collecting. What of the light? What if, as Walter Benjamin would have it, we find a way to live—and love—through our things? Can buying something beautiful be a placeholder for love? I guess I think it can.

Desire is tension; fulfillment, release. Western culture—art, exploration, and science—has shaped itself around the trope of "I want": as often as not, knowledge is the object of desire, but so are things. Perhaps we humans are programmed at the molecular level to want, to get, then to want all over again: three steps that, after all, perfectly describe our relationship to food, sleep, and sex. I've spent so much of my life being kneecapped by desire. To go through life not knowing who or what that desire will attach itself to, or when, terrifies me. It's like living at the edge of an abyss. If I can't contain the wanting, then I might not be able to control the getting either.

Maybe a collector is that rarity among human beings, a person who has figured out how to proscribe the possibilities for desire. (Meanwhile, in his single-minded pursuit of, say, one copy of every book in the world, he might ruin himself financially and force his wife and children to live in squalor, as did Sir Thomas Phillipps, back in the nineteenth century).

The bloom is off the rose the instant it is picked. The value of a car plummets as soon as it is driven off the lot. The same is true of painted tiles and porcelain knobs, T-shirts and toile lampshades. Don Juan was a serial seducer of young virgins; as a woman, Liz Taylor felt obliged to marry her conquests. With collectors, the latest find ceases to enchant as soon as it hangs on the wall, ornaments the body, or says, "I do." Even so, I think getting and spending don't lay waste to the collector's powers; they *are* the collector's powers. What's the harm of believing that somewhere in the world exists the one elusive thing that, if found, would complete the collection, complete *the collector*, if it's enough to get a body out of bed in the morning?

The difference between the pathological collector (Sir Thomas Phillipps) and the casual one (me) is time. I don't mean to suggest he had more time than I do, but rather that his relationship to time—his need to control it—was stronger than mine. True, I would have liked to stop the clock a time or two. That rare and unforeseen stretch of fifteen unscheduled minutes feels like such a gift that, caught unawares, I might fritter it away in the unwrapping, in trying to figure out how best to use it. How many errands can I run in fifteen minutes or less? The post office and the dry cleaners? The post office, the dry cleaners, *and* the bank? Would that be pushing my luck? What if I were to just dash into the bookshop to buy a card for the friend whose mother just died?

No, no, no: it's futile. It's too much. The question is not how much I can do today but what absolutely must be done in the time available to me today. See the big white rabbit with its enormous pocket watch?

Tick tock tick tock. I'm late, I'm late, I'm late for a very important date. There is so much to see and accomplish, so many people to meet and places to go, chores to do, meetings to prepare for, groceries to buy, books to read, data to sift through in the endless pursuit of gold among the dross. Sometimes it feels to me as if the search for the perfect white T-shirt is the best and perhaps only way to short-circuit despair.

Once, foolishly, I made an appointment for 2:30 on one side of Fairbanks and another for 3:00 p.m. on the other. When I confessed to a friend what I'd done, he laughingly told me I'd made a "hole in time." What is a hole in time but that fleeting moment when internal emotion and external representation—id and ego—slip into equilibrium? Likewise, when we buy something we really want, we make a hole in time. It becomes the objective correlative of our desire somehow to transcend what cannot be transcended, to arrest our headlong, helpless skid toward death.

To love something well nearly always means exposing it to the elements most likely to destroy it. In the case of a white T-shirt, these would have to include ketchup, soy sauce, makeup, guacamole, paint, blueberry pie, and red wine. Oh, and fried chicken too. I seem to be congenitally incapable of getting through a single meal without spilling, a trait I come by honestly. In her later years, my grandmother—the collector—was a chronic dribbler. She wore blouses made of the finest linen or silk, Hermes scarves, intricate lace collars—all of them stained, by day's end, with remnants of her lunch or dinner, with ink from her pen, with the paw prints of her adoring dog, Ripper. She loved beautiful things, especially clothes, and she loved to eat. She embraced the latter with little heed for the former. She knew the clock was ticking. She knew that a woman can save time, save money, save furniture, save clothes, save *herself* until the day she dies. Or she can be a happy wastrel, spending every bit of it, every minute of the day.

If, by some miracle, one of my white T-shirts cheats an early death by spillage, it will, with time, grow limp and dingy, its neckline stretched and armholes yellowed. The clothes dryer wreaks its own kind of havoc with shrinkage. For a while, Clorox is my friend, but eventually the fabric weakens and falls apart like wet tissue paper.

Have I mentioned that once upon a time, I did actually own the perfect white T-shirt? My grandmother and I were on a freighter bound for South America when I pulled it out of one of her trunks. Generous as always, she let me keep it. That was decades ago now, but still I recall the substantial heft of the fabric, the cunning flattery of the cut, the way the T-shirt seemed to work with everything else in my wardrobe. If I'd known then that I'd probably never see its like again, I'd have savored it more—and worn it less. "The essence of being human," writes George Orwell, in "Reflections on Gandhi," "is that one does not seek perfection." Perfection is static. One may arguably seek it, but one will never find it because of the human necessity of engaging, moment by moment, with time. Not to seek perfection leads to one kind of death; finding it, to another.

Once or twice, sifting through stacks of neatly folded white T-shirts at Gap or Banana Republic or Chico's, I've run across what I thought, fleetingly, might be the long-lost twin of the perfect white T-shirt. At such times, I've bought compulsively, not bothering with the dressing room, only to discover later that my find was not, in fact, perfect—that it possessed one or more of the flaws endemic to the type. The neck was too high or (rarely) too low. The fabric tugged or, worse, sagged across the bust. The hem was too long to tuck into a pair of jeans without creating bulk at the waist. Occasionally, the shininess of the fabric drew attention to itself, asserting that it ought, by rights, to be the star of the show that is me. I've known women who were worn by their clothes and not the other way around. I don't intend to be one of them.

A few weeks ago, my daughters and I met up with friends for a weekend at Virginia Beach. After a day of paddling in the surf, we drove back to our hotel and showered. Then we rendezvoused in the hall to figure out our dinner plans. Suzanne appeared in khaki shorts and a gorgeous white T-shirt fashioned of cotton so thin as to be nearly translucent, like linen, with a jewel neckline and beautifully finished hem (a cut I've come to know as European).

"I love that T-shirt! Where'd you get it?" I asked, not hiding my envy.

"Silly girl," Suzanne replied. "You gave me this T-shirt last year. You said it looked terrible on you."

To buy a new white T-shirt constitutes a leap of faith. I'm not Catholic, but everything in me embraces the idea of transubstantiation, of host becoming Host through a mystical process involving a cassock-wearing priest muttering magical phrases. At the moment of the transaction, time hangs in suspension; then the moment passes, leaving the recipient fundamentally altered by contact with the Divine. The vehicle (bread or wine) is commonplace; through faith and language, it becomes timeless, transcendent.

When I get it home, the Fresh Produce T from the Pheasant's Eye in Lynchburg disappoints: the fabric turns out to be too thin for work wear. The neckline is of a type that tempts a particular kind of man to talk to my breasts instead of my face. Even so, I can wear it around the house on weekends. And it will do as a stopgap until the next time I'm able to go shopping. One day soon, I'll drive into Charlottesville. On my last trip, I spotted a promising white T in a Patagonia store. It was made of thick cotton, pre-washed to baby-blanket softness. The cut alluded to the traditional man's T but made some concessions to a woman's curves. I checked the price: $49.95—a small price to pay, really, for the promise of re-creation, for a still point in the spinning world, for a blank slate on which to write the story of me.

If only it had been available in my size.

And now with some pleasure I find that it's seven; and must cook dinner.
Haddock and sausage meat. I think it is true that one gains a certain
hold on sausage and haddock by writing them down.
—The final entry in Virginia Woolf's diary

Occasional Lapses into Indulgence

The first phone number I memorized after my own was my grand-mother's: 907-479-7449.

"Did you call Grandma again without asking first?" my mother would ask, cupping her hand over the receiver.

"Uh-uh," I'd reply, shaking my head.

"Sure," she'd say, speaking back into the phone. "That would be fine. What time do you want to pick her up?"

There were five children in my family, and my father spent long stretches working in what we referred to, unselfconsciously, as "the Bush." Left on her own in Fairbanks, Mom was often frazzled by the demands of her nursing job and all of us kids, especially my youngest brother, Ben, who seemed bent, most days, on burning down the house. Money was tight. We couldn't afford to eat out, so Mom cooked nearly every night. She leaned on a handful of staples: Hamburger Helper, spaghetti, tuna casserole, something she called "goulash," which was leftovers warmed up with canned tomatoes and peas. I was agnostic about food in those days, so long as I wasn't forced to stay at the table until I finished every bite of liver and onions, or lamb and mint sauce, weeping bitter tears. The thing I *did* care about was escaping the chaos of our household for the tranquility of my grandparents' farm.

The farm wasn't really a farm—that's just what we called it because it came with a barn, a worker's cottage, and eighty acres. It had been an orphanage before my grandparents bought it, and it still retained something of the smell of group living. It was located about twelve miles north of our house on the outskirts of town, a drive that could take anywhere from twenty minutes to two hours, depending on hitchhikers. Grandma *always* picked up hitchhikers—male or female, respectable or scruffy—and she *always* drove them wherever they wanted to go. One time, when my sister and I were staying at the farm, Grandma left us alone for so long we thought she'd forgotten us, so we struck out for home on foot. I was wearing tights and a turtleneck; Hannah might have been barefoot. When Grandma passed us on the highway in her Mercedes sedan, coming back from whatever errand she'd just run, she hit the brakes, swung a U-turn and pulled up alongside us. I'd never seen her so angry. *"Do you have any idea what kind of people pick up little girls from the side of the road?"* she hollered.

Evenings at the farm, when it was just the two of us, or maybe the two of us plus my easygoing grandfather, Grandma would busy herself in the kitchen and I'd busy myself in her bathroom. I'd run myself a bath, then soak in it until my fingers turned pruney, reveling in the triple luxuries of unlimited hot water, green Vitabath, and total privacy. Afterward, I'd rummage in the wicker trunks stored in an unused bedroom, emerging with a nightgown, negligee, and fur-trimmed mules. Wearing this get-up along with some of Grandma's lipstick and Enjoli perfume, I'd park myself at the kitchen table just in time for her to conjure a bubbling casserole from the oven. She seemed to think it was the most normal thing in the world to eat lima beans in cream sauce alongside an eight-year-old child dressed as Eva Gabor in *Green Acres*. I can't possibly overstate what that meant to me then, means to me now.

She was a wizard in the kitchen, my grandmother. By this, I don't just mean she was a wonderful cook—she was—but rather that I almost never saw her in the act of cooking. Come to think of it, I don't believe I ever saw her shop for ingredients or set the table or do the dishes, though somehow these things must have gotten done. (When I asked him about this, my father observed that the dishes usually got done by someone other than my grandmother.) Did she even *own* a cookbook? This question stumps my father, as does the next one: How did she learn to cook? From her mother? Not likely, Dad says. His grandma Jessie was uninspired in the kitchen. "I guess she must have taught herself," he says.

In the forever-time of memory, Grandma wears an apron to protect her work clothes—crisp white blouse or fawn cashmere sweater—and oven mitts that come to her elbows. The casserole she's pulling from the oven is always the same: lima beans in cream sauce. Maybe with a slice of ham or crisp green salad as well, but those would have been beside the point. The casserole by itself was heaven, the apotheosis of beans, love in a 9½-by-11-inch baking dish. The limas had browned and split in the oven, sponging up the fresh cream, a luxury that was never on offer at my house. (Dad put Carnation canned milk in his coffee, and Mom drank hers black.) If I'd known then what I know now—that I'll probably never taste its like again—I'd have gorged myself on that lima bean casserole every time, letting (as M. F. K. Fisher writes) an overdose "teach restraint by the very results of its abuse."

My grandmother was such a fabulist that not even my father, her first-born, knows the particulars of her early life. Dad believes she was born in 1909 in Augusta, Michigan, and grew up in Augusta, Georgia. She definitely attended Wesleyan College for Women in Macon, Georgia (I checked), but did not graduate, as my father had always believed. For two years, from 1928 to 1930, she was at the center of nearly every-thing at the college—president of the dramatic society, vice president of the literary society, a member of the debate society, often mentioned in the local and college newspapers as being in company with other students at various academic and social events. After the spring of 1930, the end of her sophomore year, the trail grows faint. She took a teaching job in Otter Creek, in northern Florida, near Gainesville. She married my grandfather, who belonged to a family of loggers and sawmill owners in Bronson, Florida. They embarked on my grand-mother's lifelong habit of taking in strays, fostering three orphans (or runaways—the record is not clear). According to the 1940 census, Luther and Hellen [sic] Brice, both thirty years old, had a household with seven dependents. They ranged in age from one to fifteen, and only three (my father and his two younger brothers, Sam and Thom) were their natural-born offspring. The question of why Grandma left Georgia and Wesleyan and moved to the Gulf Coast of Florida in 1930 nags at me. It was the start of the Great Depression. Did tuition money dry up? Or did she get into trouble of one kind or another? Did she meet a boy—my grandfather? someone else?—and decide to follow him to Florida? Or was she simply restless after two years in the classroom, eager to get on with her real life?

Luther Liston Brice was movie-star handsome, mischievous, and mild-mannered. Helen McNutt was a firecracker whose flair for amateur theatrics is still talked about in Otter Creek (or so my father's cousins tell me). Theirs was a long but tumultuous marriage. During the war, my grandfather served with the SeaBees in the South Pacific, and Grandma moved around with the boys—my father and what ended up being three younger brothers, as well as the two older adopted ones—working for a while as a radio journalist in California. She ended each evening broadcast with a coded message to the boys about whether she'd be home in time for dinner. After the war, my grandparents resumed their on-again, off-again marriage. In the late fifties, they both moved to Alaska to reinvent themselves in the northern woods. They thought they'd start a logging business, maybe another sawmill, but they quickly turned to road-clearing, then road building, then even bigger projects that required bulldozers, log skidders, graders, dump trucks, tractor-trailers, airplanes, and a small fleet of barges and tugboats.

I'm glossing over the lean years that preceded the construction of the trans-Alaska pipeline. They were the years of hand-me-downs and hand-sewn clothes, of powdered milk and Tang. The rooms at the farm where Grandma stored her wicker trunks of flimsy negligees smelled of dust and dog poo. Then, suddenly (or so it seems, in my memory), everything changed. Grandma hired a crew to do a gut renovation on the farm, which suddenly gained a library, greenhouse, and in-ground swimming pool. Grandma took me to London, where the company was wooing (or being wooed by—it was never clear) British Petroleum. We had a chauffeur-driven Rolls Royce at our disposal and tickets to the theater: *La Traviata* one night, *Bubblin' Brown Sugar* the next. To escape the worst of Alaska winters, she began hunkering down for a few months every year in the same suite at the Mayflower Hotel in Seattle. Granddad hightailed it back to Florida, buying a cattle ranch near Gainesville and taking up with a redhead named (I kid you not) Mildred. His brother Harvey, who'd been living in Florida with his own difficult wife, moved to Alaska and eventually onto the farm with Grandma. My father, not prone to hyperbole, has more than once referred to his uncle Harvey as the love of his mother's life.

In the perpetual present tense of memory, Grandma is always moving toward me, and I am always backing away. Compared to my mother with her New England self-restraint, Grandma seemed embarrassing: volatile and vain, self-pitying, self-dramatizing, and prone to histrionics that often played out noisily, humiliatingly in public. Her appetites—for food, drink, clothes, attention, affirmation, and even (yes) sex—were Brobdingnagian. She could be charming but when that failed, she fell back on her usual bag of tricks: bullying, accusations, temper tantrums, tears. When foiled or frustrated, she didn't merely weep. She wailed like a giant pink-and-white baby. My entire extended family lived in thrall to her moods.

Workdays she spent prowling the halls of the family firm, a general construction company, pretending to be in charge and forcing everyone else to pretend too. My father and his brothers—the ones who *really* ran the company—employed a full-time secretary to do her bidding. Also to keep her out of their way. Evenings when she was not otherwise occupied, she worked the telephone, dialing one son and haranguing him for ten minutes, hanging up, dialing a second son, complaining to him about the first, then circling back to the first, picking up where she'd left off, often in mid-sentence. My father mostly just listened: "Yes, Mother . . . I know, Mother . . . Uh-huh, Mother."

She wore sneakers to work, high-heeled pumps to play. The heels showed off her perfect posture and shapely legs. She had excellent taste—what Patricia Hampl calls "the beauty disease"—and, it seemed, an inexhaustible budget to buy whatever caught her fancy: silk scarves, embroidered tablecloths, rare books, and antique furniture. Once or twice a year, she'd take me shopping, which meant parking me in a dressing room at Nordstrom or Lord & Taylor while she brought me armloads of things to try on. More than once, I heard her say, in reference to a fashion victim, "She *feels* pretty."

She was often joyful, but she lacked a sense of humor; if she laughed at anything, it wasn't other people, and certainly never herself. She loved horses and sat them well. She was an avid traveler, not least because of the opportunities that travel afforded to stage oneself in a new city, among strangers. As soon as she checked into a hotel, she'd ask the concierge to make a dinner reservation at the best restaurant in town, then she'd whisk herself off in a taxi to get her hair, nails, and makeup done. On her way back to the hotel, she'd make the driver stop at a flower shop where she scooped up armloads of blossoms. Wherever she went in the world, she took her own vases, linens, and silver.

What else? She grew hothouse roses outdoors, in the interior of Alaska where temperatures regularly dipped below minus fifty in the winter. She was a Democratic kingmaker. One of my earliest memories is of a helicopter landing on the lawn in front of her house and disgorging US Congressman Nick Begich. For her, though, all politics were personal, which meant she could be pressed into fundraising for the occasional Republican who was also a close friend. She always said she was the one who introduced Sen. Ted Stevens to his second wife, Cathy. She didn't lie outright so much as evade and embellish, claiming, for instance, to be godmother to Ted and Cathy's daughter, Lily. (A thank-you note in the child's handwriting, found among her correspondence after she died, was addressed to "grandmother-at-large.") Like many insecure people, she loved to give gifts but not to receive them. She was ardently pro-life, referring to anything that offended her sense of politics, propriety, or proportion as an "abortion." She taught me the ins and outs of tipping, and also that it was déclassé to steal toiletries from hotels.

She had a vision of herself that did not always comport with reality. (One of her favorite lies was about being the CEO of a company with a fleet of ships: *My captain tells me . . .*). I regret to say that in the nearly three decades when I knew her, I felt duty-bound to roll my eyes every time she lied, thereby drawing strangers' attention to the space between my grandmother's projection of herself and the far more prosaic reality. "We find truth—human truth—by pretending to be people we're not," writes Hilton Als in *White Girls*, a lesson I didn't learn for myself until long after she'd gone.

Grandma consumed books. By this I mean to say she read them, of course (at least, I think she did), but also that she bludgeoned people with them. She was a reading bully. It occurred to me more than once that she might have modeled herself on characters she found in Hemingway, Fitzgerald, Faulkner, and Tennessee Williams. Or Larry McMurtry's Aurora in *Terms of Endearment*: "Only a saint could live with me, and I can't live with a saint." When she was alive, people used to say, "I know your grandmother. She's a real character." Now that she's been dead thirty years, people still say, "I knew your grandmother. What a character." The older I got, the more I resented my status as her pet. I resented being roped into a supporting role in the ongoing saga of her life. I wanted to buy my own clothes, in colors more subdued than the saturated pinks and purples that she thought suited me. After graduating from college, I turned my nose up at the internship she arranged for me in Sen. Stevens's Washington, DC, office, instead taking a job on the Fairbanks newspaper. I became interested in facts, training the cold lens of a documentarian on her. She became the supplicant in our relationship, calling every couple of weeks to invite me to dine with her. "Pick up a bottle of Möet on the way," she'd say, but I couldn't afford it on my fourteen-dollar-an-hour paycheck, so had to pretend I'd forgotten.

She was a writer who found her medium in letters. She kept all that she received, and she had her secretary, Bev, make copies of the ones she sent. In one of these, she urges a friend to purchase a fax machine, arguing that the speed and convenience outweigh the $2,500 price tag. To close friends and acquaintances, she wrote by hand in her angular, sprawling script that sometimes curled up the sides of the page. For family and friends, she used cream-colored, with "from the desk of . . . helenka Brice" printed across the top. She also had notecards and matchboxes emblazoned with her first name, which she always spelled with a lower-case *h*. Whether handwritten or typed, written on personal or company letterhead, her letters did all the things she herself did in the range of a single day: scold, exhort, harangue, preen, brag, bully, and flirt.

Here she is writing to James Michener in February 1983. Apparently, she d just met him while on her way to Rochester, Minnesota, and a sojourn at the Mayo Clinic:

> Since seeing you on the plane and your request to borrow *Toward Freedom and Dignity: The Humanities and the Idea of Humanity*, my secretary has been trying to obtain a new one from Johns Hopkins Paperbacks. I mark my books as my mood pleases, knowing full well that if I read it the next day, I would mark it as I understand it then.

In this paragraph, three things seem clear. She wishes to (1) remind him that she is the woman he met on the airplane, (2) inform him that she is an important-enough personage to have a secretary, and (3) express some anxiety about how he might interpret the marginalia in the book she loaned him. Later that same day, she wrote to him again. The second letter is more bold and unbuttoned, possibly composed after a scotch or two. In it, she quotes Archibald MacLeish, Carson McCullers, Felix Frankfurter, and Jim Hagarty ("Ike's ex-press secretary who was a friend of mine"). Then she gets down to what one senses is the real purpose of this burgeoning correspondence, which is to present herself as a potential model for a major character, if not the *main* character, in his as-yet-unwritten novel about Alaska:

I am leaving the winter dullness of the Clinic on Thursday to go down to a New Orleans shipyard to finish up for our tug and a couple of barges. I am going to join the skipper and my crew sailing through the Panama Canal Zone to Alaska which is much more troublesome now with the Panamanians in charge than when the Americans were in charge. I am not saying this as a regret or a social statement, but rather a fact. I am taking Mr. Brice with me—he says he wants to sleep in the sun.

In the next paragraph, she brags about the company, which has, she writes, "been in" more villages in Alaska than any other and which is now constructing a sea wall on St. George Island in the Pribilofs. The company has five planes and employs a company pilot, even though her oldest son, a bush pilot, prefers to fly his own planes (she writes). "Feel free to call and ask to thumb a ride at any time." And then a languid coup de grâce: "Sitka is a favorite place to me but, alas, all of Alaska is a favorite place to me. When I get home, perhaps in two months, I will call." (She called, he answered, and that summer I met him at the farm, at a party she threw in his honor. "This is my granddaughter, the one who is at Smith," she said. "It's a pleasure to meet you," he said. "Some of my best secretaries went to Smith.")

Years later, long after Grandma's death, her secretary began sending me her correspondence, one Priority Mail packet at a time. Each one came with a note saying something along the lines of, "I think Mrs. Brice would have wanted you to have these." (In life as well as death, Beverly—who is so much a part of the family as to be named godmother to one of my twins—never called my grandmother anything but "Mrs. Brice.") Every time one of these packets turned up, I felt a surge of resentment, as if Grandma was reaching out from beyond the grave, grabbing my arm, and intruding into my life. What could she possibly want from me now? To become her biographer? No way. For years, especially when my daughters were young and needy, I stuffed the packets, unopened, into plastic file boxes. To be the person I was going to be, to write the books that were inside me, I needed to get my grandmother off my back, out of my head.

Then came COVID-19. By then, the girls were fledged and their father long gone, living in Costa Rica with his second wife. My grandmother had been dead for nearly three decades. With no social life to speak of, I finally had time to clean out the basement and the garage, then all of my closets, drawers, and filing cabinets. Helenka's letters, while still importuning, seemed less reproachful than before. Even (dare I say it?) mildly intriguing.

The first packet contained a thank-you note I wrote in 1974, when I was eleven. The envelope was addressed to Mrs. Luther Liston Brice. I still remember her reply, which was blistering: "I am not Mrs. Luther Liston Brice. I am *helenka Brice!*" (Actually, she was Helen Brice, but she added the pseudo-Slavic ending and the lower-case *h* around the time she moved to Alaska. She pronounced it "el-LEN-ka," and pretended not to hear when someone inquired as to the origins of it.) My mother, the daughter of East Coast socialites and herself a graduate of the Emma Willard School in Troy, New York, taught me the proper way to address a thank-you note. The score of that particular skirmish between her and my grandmother: Mrs. L. A. Brice 0, helenka 1.

For someone who craved contact with other people, she was surprisingly adept at self-sabotage. In the summer of 1987, when Steve McAlpine was running for reelection as lieutenant governor of Alaska, Grandma sent him this handwritten note:

Dear Steve,

You look so healthy—you have beautiful hair—. . . except you look all of the time in public like a banker or an attorney. I feel that you feel you cannot look handsome and with it if you are too avant-garde—but my message I guess is that you need to look at the same time as one who works as a professional—yet has the common touch and availability of the majority of men who punch your X in the ballot box.

You need to dress some of the time unbecomingly.

helenka Brice

If Steve McAlpine ever replied, it is not reflected in the record.

Grandma's favorite subjects were (in no particular order) clothing, books, politics, and food. In the house where I grew up, the one ruled over by Mrs. L. A. Brice, food and love sometimes got tangled up in each other, and there wasn't always as much of either of one as I might have liked. Partly this had to do with my mother's upbringing. Her parents were well-to-do high-functioning alcoholics who outsourced child-rearing to summer camp and boarding school. My mother was not exactly obese as a child, but she was what she describes as a "hefty girl." She punished and rewarded with food. Misbehave, and you got sent to your room without supper. Get straight As, and the whole family splurged on dinner at the fanciest restaurant in town, The Switzerland. With Grandma, food was far less complicated. She didn't punish herself for eating too much (though she often did), and she never punished any of us kids for turning down something we didn't like. For her, food was separate from power; instead, it was all about sensory pleasure. She enjoyed fixing food and she enjoyed eating it. Most of all, she enjoyed being at the table with good company. In the letter I'm about to quote from, she seems to be following up on what must have been a plaintive conversation with her friend EC, a painter who suffered from bipolar disorder:

> You do not need to be sensible. Sometimes we just need to do what we want to do to feel the least stress and the most stimulation. If you listen to your video that I listened to with you, you will see that the doctor considers food a blessing. He certainly would not consider it a sin when you ate something that was delicious to you.

In another note from around the same time, she seems to be nudging EC back into her studio:

> What is it that you know that apparently you have known for a long long time that makes it possible for you to paint canvas after canvas?

Grandma died during the Clinton administration, long before George W. Bush came to power, but she was no fan of his father. To another friend, Alaska state senator Bettye Fahrenkamp, a fellow Democrat, she dictated this letter during early days of the first Gulf War:

> I yearned . . . that Bush would simply look squarely at the mistakes that he had made, that members of his family have made; mistakes committed by inner circle advisors, and during his presidential campaign, then look hard at the critical mistakes and say, "We've made mistakes." And not brought the whole world into starvation, ruined crops, refugees, despoiled sea waters and no waters and no food—babies suffering and families sundered for a no win war. His contra sins, his son's financial ambitions, the whole S and L debacle apparently overwhelmed him. Whatever—it's all too terrible.

Just above her signature, she scrawled a few sentences by hand: "Have much to say. But my house is in disarray. More soon." Much to say, house in disarray. *Story of my life, Grandma. Story. Of. My. Life.*

In his poem "Thursday," James Longenbach calls cooking an "act of radical imagination." I love everything about that, especially the word *radical*—as if cooking a risotto for Thursday night's dinner requires the same level of commitment as marching in a protest. I'm not a gifted cook, but I can follow a recipe, and I enjoy doing it. As activities go, cooking is blissfully more bounded than writing, and it nearly always yields concrete results. I'm roughly the same age now as my grandmother during the years when I used to sneak-call to ask if I could spend the night with her. In search of comfort food one night, I decide to reproduce her lima beans in cream sauce. I turn first to the cookbooks I lean on most: *Good Housekeeping, Silver Palate, Moosewood, 500 Three-Ingredient Recipes.* Nothing. The Internet offers up a recipe that says to cook the lima beans according to package instructions, then add heavy cream and a little bit of salt, heating gently until everything coheres. The beans turn out chewy as nuts, sprinkled in a white sauce that is both too thin and strangely sweet. "An abortion," Grandma would have called it. I eat one or two spoonfuls, then pay for it the rest of the night in stomach pains.

The next day, I leafed through the least radical cookbook on my shelf. If cookbooks, like lawns and hairstyles and the insides of people's refrigerators, declare their political allegiances, then *The Joy of Cooking* by Irma Rombauer strikes me at first blush as Republican to the core. Or so I think. Mine is a well-thumbed copy from 1953, its binding held together by tape, its pages yellow with age and, in places ("Pies Baked with Fillings"), stained with food. It's a hand-me-down from my other grandmother, who gave it to my mother when she moved to New York City to start nursing school. Mom gave it to me, along with an assortment of odds and ends from her kitchen, when I moved into my own place after graduating college. Over the years, I've pulled it out for staples such as French toast and beef stroganoff, but mostly I regard it as so seriously uncool as to be almost embarrassing. For one thing, the title (like *The Joy of Sex*, which my parents kept under their bed) has a whiff of coercion to it. If cooking (like sex) is such divine pleasure, then why should it require a manual?

The index lists two lima bean casseroles, one with onions and the other titled, unpromisingly for my purposes, "Mexican." Other possibilities include a soufflé with lima beans, bacon, and tomatoes; lima beans with mushrooms; lima beans with cheese; lima beans (boiled); and lima beans with piquant sauce. My interest piqued, I turn to page 270. The first sentence I read throws me for a loop, knocks me off my pins, bowls me over—all the clichés. Pleasure catches at my throat. I read it again and find myself transfixed. Transported. Literally dislocated in time and space, because this woman—long-dead, slyly self-aware, author of my dowdiest cookbook—is writing for an audience, yes, but mostly for her own amusement. Here is what she says: "In order to provide a canned Lima bean with glamour, you must do a fan dance with it."

That's all the incentive I need to spend the next couple of hours skimming the cookbook from start to finish, reading it in a way that no cookbook is really meant to be read. Every page is a revelation, beginning with the introduction, which contains this snippet of dialogue between Irma Rombauer and her daughter:

> "Mother," said Marion, "the book needs an introduction." "Why?" said I. "Will cooks ever read it?" She replied: "Perhaps they will read it if you tell them a story, for if they do not, how will they know that an ingredient in parenthesis means 'optional' and 'chocolate' means the bitter kind unless otherwise stated?"

Just who *was* this Irma Rombauer, I wondered. It turns out she was born in St. Louis in 1877, a generation earlier than my grandmother. Her father served as a US diplomat in Europe, a period when Irma went to finishing schools in Germany and Switzerland. On returning to the States, she was briefly wooed by Booth Tarkington. (The passive construction "was wooed" seems right and inevitable here.) Her family opposed the match, so she married a lawyer, Edgar Rombauer, instead. For the next three decades, she threw herself into motherhood and civic life and playing hostess (such an interesting turn of phrase, no?—as if a hostess is not someone who hosts but someone who plays at hosting). A competent though not, by most accounts, dazzling cook, she was intelligent, self-possessed, charming, dignified, and playful. "It is an open secret," Marion said, "that Mother, to the very end of her life, regarded social intercourse as more important than food."

I now rank *The Joy of Cooking* among the two or three most irresistibly, addictively readable books that I own. The cover of the first edition (which I had to buy, in facsimile) is a gem all on its own, depicting St. Martha slaying the Tarrasque, a mythical creature with a lion's head, a bear's claws, and a turtle's carapace. It was said to have poisonous breath and to swallow its victims headfirst. In images from the sixteenth and seventeenth centuries, it is usually depicted with a pair of flailing legs sticking out of its mouth. On the cover of *The Joy*, Martha, patron saint of housewives and servants, is beating the monster with a broom she holds in her left hand. A black pocketbook dangles from her right.

Mrs. Rombauer seems to have been compelled, or moved, to write a new foreword for virtually every edition. The first one reads less like an invitation than a warning—or maybe an apology. "Whenever I leave home and begin to move about, I am appalled to find how many people with a desire to write feel impelled to share their emotions with the general public." Translation: Nothing to see here!

I kept going. Farther down, I found this gem: "In spite of the fact that the book is compiled with one eye on the family purse and the other on the bathroom scale, there are, of course, occasional lapses into indulgence." *Wowie.*

In 1931, *The Joy* ran to 395 pages. My edition from the fifties is 1,013 pages, and the latest edited edition, from 2019, tips the scales at 1,200. Want to bake a coffee cake? The instructions are here for at least eleven varieties, including plain coffee cake with honey-bee topping or almond filling, baking powder crumb coffee cake, and a high coffee cake known in German as *kugelhopf.* You can find out how many calories there are in a roughly 1½-inch-square piece (100) that presumably is not of the variety containing a marzipan center. And if you were to discover, once you'd already greased the pan, that you were fresh out of baking powder, you could (*The Joy* informs you) substitute ¼ teaspoon of baking soda plus ½ teaspoon of cream of tartar.

The Joy can be read as social history, yielding clues about the role of women in American culture. Rombauer advises the hostess to serve hot food from hot dishes, cold food from chilled dishes, and also to "Keep calm even if your hair striggles and you drip unattractively." She's a fan of cocktails: "They loosen tongues and unbutton the reserves of the socially diffident. Serve them by all means, preferably in the living room, and the sooner the better."

My edition of *The Joy* is an artifact of the fifties. For one thing, it's aimed entirely at women; the preface to an entry on sweetbreads calls it "a hush-hush section, just between us girls." Beyond that, its aim is ecumenical, pitched equally to women who can afford to put caviar on their canapés and those who must get by with economy timbales or "mock" oyster casserole. There's a whole section on what to do with leftovers: onions filled with mashed potatoes, waffles filled with flaked fish, tomatoes filled with just about anything, coffee jelly with marshmallows. How to avoid disasters—"Do not put buttered bread in the toaster"—or, failing that, how to fix them by, say, adding a raw sliced potato to soup that has been over-salted. How to do lots of things with ham: ham à la king, ham cakes with eggs, ham cakes with pineapple, ham in tomato cases, jellied ham mousse, ham sandwich spread, ham soufflé, ham loaf, ham noodles, ground ham on pineapple slices, ham rolls with rice, baked potatoes filled with minced ham. How to shop for seafood: "There should be no unpleasant odor." And how to dress a squirrel: "Hold the tail down with your shoe and strip the skin off."

Rombauer offers shortcuts for polishing silver (tin foil, salt, baking soda) and another for getting rid of stains on tablecloths (boiling water poured from a height of two feet); an extraordinarily detailed calorie counter (3 kumquats = 35; 1 martini = 135); instructions for setting the table for a five-course dinner for twelve people or preparing a tray for an invalid: "The recipient is often helpless, finicky, and wanting attention."

Rombauer's tone throughout conveys that there's nothing mysterious about the art of cookery—or, rather, that cookery is not an art but a skill that anyone can learn. It's simply a matter of tying on an apron and getting down to business. She takes food—its preparation and presentation—seriously. It's the glue that holds families, communities, and perhaps whole civilizations together. But (she seems to be saying) the person who fixes the food should never take herself too seriously. The final step in her recipe for steamed crabs is to add "½ cup beer or what have you." It's the languid wave of the hand, the "what have you," that slays me.

The Joy is neither memoir nor autobiography—it lacks personal anecdotes (the mother-daughter exchange in the foreword is an exception)—yet one senses throughout the *interestingness* of the author's experience. "My book reflects my life," she writes in the preface, "and, as you may see by its timely contents, I have not stood still."

Haute bourgeois that she was, her vocabulary is littered with French words and phrases: *bain marie, blanquette, bombe, chantilly, charlotte, sauce espagnole, forcemeat, fumet, galantine, macedoine, maître d'hôtel, nesselrode, rissole, trichina, velouté.* Yet the index, in places, reads like an Appalachian found poem: Rink Tum Diddy Rarebit, kedgeree of lobster, shrimp wiggle, doughnut hamburgers, onion shortcake, vegetarian woodchuck, cheese monkey, hot Tom and Jerry. In her pre-*Joy* life, Rombauer rubbed shoulders with ladies who lunched and complained about how hard it was to find good help: "When our scarcity of domestic service was first making itself felt," she writes, "I was approached by a woman of seventy who asked for help in realizing the ambition of her lifetime—to know how to separate an egg. She died happy." Up until 1929, Irma Rombauer might have found herself in the same pickle. She and Edgar were socially prominent philanthropists and pillars of St. Louis society. Then came the stock market crash. Edgar was something of a delayed casualty, waiting until 1930 to commit suicide. He left his wife and three nearly grown children with less than $6,000 in savings. Irma was fifty-three and hadn't worked a day in her life.

With very little fuss, she set about finding a way to earn a living. A year after Edgar's death, she self-published *The Joy of Cooking: A Compilation of Reliable Recipes, with a Casual Culinary Chat.* Reviews were generally favorable. "It does not insult my intelligence," wrote the *St. Louis Dispatch.* The little volume remained in print long enough for Rombauer to sell the rights to the Bobbs-Merrill Company, now Macmillan. The book was (and still is) a runaway success for its publishers, though it never made Rombauer rich or even particularly comfortable. She negotiated the original contract without the advice of a lawyer, and the terms turned out less than ideal. What she earned instead was cultural capital. Anne Mendelsohn, her biographer (she had a biographer!), calls her "one of the eternal verities of American cooking."

If she didn't find fortune, she did find something like fame. By 1962, the year of Rombauer's death, more than twenty-six million copies of *The Joy* had been sold worldwide, which is twice as many as *Gone with the Wind*. She also found something even more elusive, which was the perfect vessel for her particular intelligence. *The Joy* overflows with offhanded advice for how to go about the tasks of living: how not to be bullied by the butcher, for example, and how to make yourself, as hostess, unobtrusive so your guests can take center stage. She's often very funny, frequently at her own expense. Mostly what one feels, reading *The Joy*, is that hers is the voice of someone one would like to have known in person:

"The soufflé is the 'misunderstood woman' of the culinary world."

"Peanut butter needs enlivening." (To a sandwich, add tomato, bacon drippings, brown sugar, salt and paprika.)

"The chicken is a world-citizen to be found everywhere along with Coca Cola, the Singer sewing machine, the *Christian Science Monitor*, and Hollywood movies."

I went looking for my grandmother's recipe for lima beans in cream sauce and found *The Joy*. Not a bad trade-off, though I'm still looking for the recipe. Superficially, Irma Rombauer and helenka Brice had almost nothing in common. They were born in different centuries and different worlds—the diplomat's daughter to that of a Swiss finishing school, Grandma to Wesleyan College for Women. Rombauer believed in following a recipe; Grandma, not so much. They had a few things in common, though, not least that both their lives were upended in 1930. Whatever path they found themselves on in the late 1920s was foreclosed by the Depression, and they had to make their own way in the world. They did not dither or give in to despair. They did not stand still. Instead, they got on with things—Rombauer to writing her cookbook, Grandma to teaching school in Otter Creek (pop. 1,000).

What would I have done if I'd been in their shoes? Ambivalence is my resting state. I wobble between possibilities, then, at the last possible second, seize on one that is just as often wrong as right. It worries me, this pattern, yet I seem helpless to repeat it—with jobs, houses, clothing, causes, men. Most nights I can't even decide what I want to eat for dinner. What strikes me most about Irma and Helen is that they knew (or seemed to know) their own minds.

Also, this: writing in the minor, domestic keys (cookbook, correspondence), they were their best selves: funny, playful, rueful, generous, warm, wise. They grasped the transcendent power of both food and words. Their writing *cooked*.

For three decades, I told myself I needed to silence my grandmother's voice in order to find my own. I wasn't entirely wrong. But there was pettiness in my resistance too. Delusions of grandeur require an audience; I'd played my part when she was alive. Now that she was gone, I felt free to call her out for the fabulist that she was, and also to move toward center stage in my own life.

The final packet arrived a few months ago. It contained the correspondence between me and my grandmother when I was in college in the eighties. I pick out a letter at random. It's undated and seems to be a response to something I said or wrote earlier, about how we didn't get on especially well during a trip to Anchorage over the winter break. I remember the trip quite well. We stayed at the Captain Cook, the most elegant hotel in town, and we had fancy facials in the ground-floor salon. I'd never had a facial before. Anyway, whatever I'd said seems to have wounded her. (She was surprisingly thin-skinned—as am I, alas.) In the letter, which is typed, not handwritten—meaning, of course, it was dictated to a typist—she says this:

> You were raised in a family that is self-contained in its relationships. Your brothers and sisters and your Mother and Father have always been totally adequate as far as real loving is expressed. It is very difficult for you to go out and throw your arms around someone else just because you yearn to do so. I have never observed you or your brothers or sisters showing active emotion in greeting. It is a thing that I miss. I love to be touched as an expression of love . . . I am always at a loss just how to greet you. My impulse of course is just to grab you and hold you right tight against me for a second or so then go out from this central warmth of gut feeling to enjoying other things.

This is thinly veiled criticism of my parents, especially my mother, for loving me—what?—too well. I wonder what she means by calling me "self-contained"—that I am standoffish or cold or impervious toward her? If so, I can cop to that, especially as the alternative was to be totally annexed by her.

A few weeks later, she writes to me by hand to urge me to take Senator Stevens up on his offer of an internship in Washington, DC. She ends this way: "My dearest Jennifer," she writes, "I have 10 million things to say to you—My heart yearns to see you . . . Of course I can't meet you for Savannah. I want to read what you are saying about coming home—. . . Jennifer, I am suffering fatigue. I miss you. I love you. I depend on you. I will write more fully when I can."

At twenty-two I simply didn't know what to do with this flood of feeling. I judged it more of a performance of love than the thing itself. Now, decades later, my parents are still living, but my mother is lost to dementia, and my father is lost to the full-time work of caring for her. I recoil from melodrama as much as ever. But I also see now, as I did not then, that we are all of us acting, all the time. And the performance of an emotion like love or anger doesn't necessarily camouflage its opposite, or even its absence. Just because something is performed does not mean it's inauthentic.

The last time I saw my grandmother, she'd summoned me to her office for me to make obeisance before she flew to the Mayo Clinic for gallbladder surgery. At that point, it felt to me as if we'd rehearsed her brink-of-death scene seventy-three times, and I fiercely resented giving up even an hour of my day to one more run-through. In those days, I thought of myself as the opposite of my grandmother: self-aware and self-possessed, grounded, subdued, practical, restrained, private, empathetic, cool-headed, sane, *blah blah*. A favorite grad school professor had just returned my essay on Milan Kundera's *Book of Laughter and Forgetting* with no grade, only the comment, "You seem to have written twenty pages on the topic of irony without ever using the word 'irony.'" *That* smarted.

Was there a voice in the back of my mind that day, saying, *This could actually be it*? I'd like to think so, but I doubt it. Nevertheless, *something* told me to pay attention to the spring sunlight saturating her office, alighting on the sickle-shaped desk (behind which she liked to sit and bark orders, like the captain of a ship) and lemony couch cushions. Grandma was wearing her lady executive uniform: crisp white blouse, cashmere pants, thick-soled sneakers (she walked *fast*), Iris Apfel glasses. The blouse had a stain on the front, and her lipstick was crusty at the corners of her lips, probably from eating whatever had stained the front of her blouse. A jelly doughnut, maybe? She was diabetic. A jelly doughnut, definitely.

The form of our exchange that day has stayed with me, even if the actual words have not: the Amazon jungle fussed and preened, the potted plant replied in monosyllables. She presented me with a few odds and ends of antique china—Delft plates, a Limoges jelly jar—sitting atop a filing cabinet. A planned gift or an afterthought? An effort to wring some warmth out of me? It's hard to say. I was to hold onto the china until my daughter was old enough to appreciate it, she said. I pretended not to understand what it meant, this business of giving gifts to a child who would not be born for three more months. I said, *Thank you*. I did not say, *Everything is going to be all right*. I did not say, *I love you*. I'd like to be able to say now that, like Lear's Cordelia, my love was richer than my tongue. In fact, I was just being a bitch.

During the decades when I let her letters gather dust in a box on the floor of my closet, I sensed they wanted something from me. They felt more like an obligation than a bequest, her sticky fingers reaching out to me from beyond the grave. When I finally spread them out in piles, organized chronologically, by recipient, they weren't at all what I expected. Strange to say I could hear her more clearly in her letters than I ever had in life. She sounded ridiculous sometimes (flirting with James Michener! *As if!*) but also perceptive and generous, with a capacity for nuance I'd never credited her with in life. She had illusions, it's true, but don't we all? And how would it feel to have them ripped away? "Let there be truth, and may life perish," writes Nietzsche.

The most surprising thing about the letters, though, is not the vision of my grandmother they contain but the image of my unformed self. My writing (unlike hers) is formal and composed. Stilted, even. The tightly controlled sentences march along the strict lines of my notebook paper, conveying none of the zig-zag motion of genuine thought. They are mortifyingly full of clichés, evasions, and self-congratulation. In one, I gloss over an episode that wounded me deeply. My undergraduate honors thesis about voices in T. S. Eliot's poetry earned a failing grade from one of two professors assigned to read it. The professor's comments were so cutting, I cried until I threw up. I did not tell my grandmother this.

An essay is a thing that cooks. To remember a meal, to try to set it down in words, is a conjuring trick. One of the many things it can conjure is the dead. I've been thinking about Grandma's lima beans in cream sauce along with James Baldwin's essay "Notes of a Native Son." During the funeral for his father—a man who had been, Baldwin notes, capable of extraordinary cruelty—the minister seems to be eulogizing a saintly man who bears little resemblance to Baldwin's father. That kind of irony is too cheap, too easy, for Baldwin, though; he swiftly moves beyond it to say this:

> Every man in the chapel hoped that when his hour came he, too, would be eulogized, which is to say forgiven, and that of his lapses, greeds, errors, and strayings from the truth would be invested with coherence and looked upon with charity. This was perhaps the last thing human beings could give each other.

Amen.

In the course of a life a person could travel widely but could truly open his veins and his soul to just a limited number of places.
　　　　　—David Quammen, "Strawberries Under Ice"

I Am the Space Where I Am

"You're going to love the next one," the real estate agent said. "It just went on the market, and it's really cute."

If I'd known Sue better, I would've told her I don't *do* cute. But the two of us had only just met. Over email a week or two earlier, I'd told her of my plan to fly into Syracuse, rent a car, and drive fifty miles southeast to Hamilton. I was intent on buying a house in a day. So far, she'd shown me one that was perfect except for the location (next to a fraternity house); another that was perfect except for the size of the kitchen (think *Airbus galley*); and a third that was perfect except for the cost—$50,000 more than I could afford on my assistant professor's salary.

Sue was both wrong and right about the fourth house. It wasn't cute, but I loved it. I made an offer on the spot. Three hours later, just as a friend and I were digging into our Caesar salads at the Hamilton Inn, Sue called to say the house would be mine. Three months later, I was moved in and cleaning up the mess left by the former owners when they skulked off to their new home in New Hampshire. (In fact, I hope they read this: *You're slobs! And you never thanked me for forwarding your Jimi Hendrix CD!*)

The new property had little in the way of curb appeal. The yard was barely big enough for a trampoline, and the two-story barn listed ominously. Gray paint on the south-facing wall of the house had begun to blister, an upstairs shutter was missing, and the wrought-iron railing on the front stairs had been jimmied out of its concrete base. The house itself—a long rectangle with a pitched roof and chimney, four double-hung windows facing the street—was as bland as a kindergartener's drawing.

There was nothing bland about the interior. It had had tongue-and-groove wood floors, wainscoting in the great room (it *had* a great room!), ornate molding around the windows and built-in bookcases. Its most cunning feature was a "cupboard" staircase: steep and narrow, enclosed on three sides, hidden like a secret behind an ordinary-looking door. (Of course I'd misheard the Realtor: the word she used was *covered*, not *cupboard*.)

When the owner of the furniture store came to deliver my queen-size bed, he took one look at the staircase, said "Uh-oh," then left. Half an hour later, he came back with two twin-size box springs, which he hauled up the stairs and then rigged side by side on the queen-size frame. Apparently queen-size box springs are to cupboard staircases as Kenworth tractor-trailers are to covered bridges: non-starters.

I grew up in Fairbanks, where houses tend to be low-ceilinged and boxy, often split-level, carpeted from wall to wall, designed more for energy-efficiency than aesthetics. Alaska, which celebrated its sixtieth year of statehood in 2019, does not have a long and distinguished architectural history. It does not have grand houses like the ones in central New York canal towns—houses that date from the late 1700s and have servants' quarters, carriage barns, front and back stairs, and rooms under the eaves that perhaps sheltered runaway slaves on the Underground Railroad. Alaskan houses do not age gracefully. They may get more storied, but the stories are all about busted pipes and permafrost damage. A grand house in Alaska is most likely a contemporary design with an open floor plan, cathedral ceiling, and spiral staircase worn like an exoskeleton. In Alaska architecture (if not Alaska politics, which are as complex and baroque and full of backroom deals as politics anywhere), everything is out in the open.

What is mysterious and changeable, prodigally beautiful and oblivious to utility, is Alaska itself. Seen from the air, the Tanana River shines like molten metal in the morning light. Creeks and tributaries curl around it like a silvery ribbon. To the south of Fairbanks, the mountains read from east to west, like a text: Hayes, Hess, Deborah, then Denali. Light is the most salient feature of this place. In December and January, the crepuscular sky is deepest indigo, never black, and streaked with mango at sunrise, pomegranate at sunset.

When I try to write about Alaska, I use the word *like* a lot, which suggests a failure of imagination, or language, or both; I can approach but never arrive. This falling back on metaphor also suggests that my feeling for this landscape goes beyond language. Alaska is the place to which I have opened my veins and my soul, in David Quammen's formulation. It is where I feel most at home—whatever that means—yet paradoxically most disconnected from myself. Something about the enormous scale of things undoes me; I become a stranger to myself, a raging wilderness of regret and longing and despair. A while back, I theorized that people move to Alaska in search of open spaces as big as the ones in their soul. What does this say, I wonder, about those of us who move away? Who move, in the idiom of the Far North, Outside? Who move, as I did, from the geographic center of Alaska to the geographic center of New York, to a village built around a communal green, with Fourth of July fireworks and houses that were stops on the Underground Railroad?

Is my soul a cupboard staircase?

A couple of days after I moved to Hamilton, around noon, the doorbell rang. I was not expecting company. I had been stripping wallpaper in the July heat, and I was wearing the fewest items of clothes that a middle-aged woman can get away with in the privacy of her own home. Also, I was drinking a cold beer, which I had the presence of mind to hide behind the ladder before going to the door. By the time I got there, a stranger had let himself in. He took in my sweat-streaked face and skimpy tank top, then explained that he lived with his wife in the arts and crafts house across the street. It was the grandest house in the neighborhood, one of the grandest in town. Jack (not his real name) was roughly the same age as my father, who I was missing. A few days earlier, he and my mother had flown out from Fairbanks to help me move. For them to give up even a weekend of summer in the Far North was a great-hearted gift. Greater even than the $5,000 they'd given me toward the down payment on my first house, post-divorce. But the U-Haul was barely unloaded when I drove them to the airport for their return flight. They left saying, *You'll be fine* and *Call if you need anything.*

Because this stranger in my entryway put me in mind of my father, I nearly handed him my heart, which is something I tend to do more often than is healthy, and which can create some awkwardness when I have to ask for it back. Jack did not want so much as a glass of water from me though. He'd been watching me since move-in day and wanted to be sure that he and I got off on the right foot (his phrase). Getting off on the right foot meant the following: I should always back *my* Toyota minivan into *my* driveway in order to avoid colliding with his Lexus SUV as it backed out of *his*. I should join him in a complaint to the village police about another neighbor who had just adopted a dog that barked its head off all day long. I should trade my Virginia license plates for New York ones at my earliest convenience. I should cut my grass at least once a week (but never on a Sunday). I should recycle ostentatiously. I should scrape and redo the blistering paint on my shutters. I should prune my shrubs.

I would like to say that I took a slug from my Corona before replying. I cannot say it, though, because I was a coward then as now. Also, I was trying to figure out the rules for living in this place that Americans who are not from Alaska regard as the North. The rules for living in the Far North are not a mystery to me. Alaska is the only state where a plurality of voters would like to legalize pot and outlaw abortion. Where the strongest claim to authority on any subject, from Sarah Palin's intelligence to subsistence hunting, is length of residency in the state. Where a failed candidate for attorney general cracked to *Vanity Fair* that "a liberal is someone who carries a .357 or smaller." Signs on the University of Alaska campus remind students it is illegal to carry concealed weapons there—meaning, of course, it's legal to carry them just about everywhere else. Alaska's motto is "The Last Frontier" but it might just as well be "Live and Let Live" or "Busybodies Shot on Sight." In Alaska, ornamental gardening is not a competitive sport, and *prune* is a noun, a dried fruit that old people gum with their oatmeal.

"What shrubs?" I asked Jack.

My early days in Hamilton were a study in perpetual motion. I knocked down spiderwebs, mucked out storage rooms, painted floors and walls and closets, bought a lawn mower and learned to use it. My daughters were spending the summer in Alaska with their father, which freed me to throw away clothes and toys they'd outgrown and to paint their bedrooms in subtler colors than they themselves would have chosen. In the late afternoons, I strapped on my sneakers and walked the ski trails that crisscross the densely wooded hills above Colgate University. One time I got lost. When I realized there was no one to miss me—no friends yet in this new town—I felt doubly lost. In a detached way, I inventoried my emotions. Anxiety, of course. And a smidgeon of fear. But not the quaking terror I've felt a time or two in the Alaska wilderness, which is vast beyond vast, and filled with bears. I am wildly, irrationally afraid of bears. People do not die in the Alaska wilderness so much as disappear forever. By comparison, Hamilton's woods are as tame as Central Park. (In fact, much of Colgate's campus was designed by the same man, Frederick Law Olmstead, who designed the park after New York City officials drove out the free Black inhabitants of its predecessor, Seneca Village. As my mother likes to say, "Pretty is as pretty does.") A poet friend describes Hamilton as a Lionel train set town. It's hard to be too scared when you're lost inside a child's plaything. Mostly, I felt resolute: *I will find a way out.* For the next couple of hours, I walked in the direction of the sunset, and downhill.

When the town's emergency siren went off—a two-minute ululation pitched to a place deep inside the chest, a howl of loneliness and terror—I turned toward it. A few minutes past 10:00 p.m., I stepped into a clearing that adjoins the college cemetery. A safety officer was parked there. He started his engine and turned on his headlights, pinning me in their glare, then—seeing nothing more alarming than a wild-haired woman—swept down the drive toward the heart of campus.

Another day, I walked in the woods for an hour or so, then headed home. As I turned onto Broad Street, just across from the oak-lined drive to campus, I found myself a few yards behind a man in a black suit and a woman in a billowy white gown. They were walking hand in hand by themselves: no bridal party, no friends or family. I followed them past the fraternities and sororities on the west side of Broad Street, past the Baptist Church and village green on the east. It seems now, in my memory, there were no cars—just the green expanse of fertilized lawns in dappled sunlight, waving ferns, and nodding peonies. The couple never turned around, so I never saw their faces. They were as anonymous as figures atop a wedding cake. I turned onto my street before they reached their destination—most likely the big white inn at the top of the village green. The whole scene felt both staged and real, like a vivid dream set in the last small town in America.

In the years that followed, I knit myself into the community inasmuch as such a thing is possible for someone who is geographically and temperamentally an outsider. I serve on the village's pedestrian safety committee. I'm on a first-name basis with the mayor and the mailman. To newcomers, I've told the deathless joke about car windows and zucchini that an old timer told me when I first moved here (keep them rolled up if you don't want any). I have not (thank goodness) been asked to join the Rotary or the Optimists. The other day, I let myself into a friend's empty house, knowing she wouldn't mind if I put some leftover steak bits for her dog in the fridge. My daughters play on the high school soccer team, and I bring carafes of hot chocolate to the games, which the parents' group sells to raise money for an end-of-the-year banquet. Sometimes the other parents talk to me; other times they talk over my head about camping trips or church dinners to which (it almost goes without saying) I am not invited. Once Jack, my neighbor, realized I wasn't going to throw any wild parties or sell drugs out the back door, he loosened up a bit; one time, when I locked myself out, I asked him to boost me through the laundry room window, which he did cheerfully.

Besides the zucchini joke, the other one you hear is about socks, which are just about the only thing you can't buy in the village proper (a wonderful phrase—as if there could possibly be a village *improper*). There's a bookstore, a bike shop, a chocolatier, a movie theater, a gas station, a clothing boutique, a couple of wine shops, delicatessens, and hardware stores, and several each of galleries, hair salons, pizzerias, and bars. When I cross the threshold of the apothecary shop, the woman behind the counter reaches for my prescription, saying, "Just one today, Jen?" (All of my life I've given my name as Jennifer; in central New York, it always comes back as Jen.)

One of the first people I called when the university gave me tenure was Sue, the Realtor. She helped me sell my gray clapboard house with its cunning cupboard staircase and under-insulated walls. (That first winter, I discovered I could stand in the middle of the kitchen on blustery mornings and tell which way the wind was blowing.) Sue found me a bigger house with less charm—more farmhouse than Victorian—and thicker walls. It has a central staircase, a garage, and a spacious yard, and it is two blocks closer to campus. To liven it up, I had it painted white with pea soup trim and shutters. The pale lavender house across the street is owned by a professor in the psychology department. Like my former neighbor, she drives a Lexus SUV, but she has never asked me to back into my own driveway on account of it. Next door to *her* lives a professor of philosophy. A painter in the art department lives to the south of me and, a few houses to the north, across the street from each other, live the English department's two medievalists. One of the medievalists fixed a fabulous dinner for my whole family on move-in day. She and a couple of other neighbors are churchgoers, but none of them has a hang-up about me mowing the grass on a Sunday.

When I left for a semester-long sabbatical in Alaska last January, I forgot to arrange for lawn care after the snow melted. I didn't remember until I was already on a plane back to New York in late May, mentally inventorying the work that needed to be done on the house and yard. By the time I pulled in the driveway that night, the sun had already set but I could smell the newly cut grass. My neighbor to the north is a freelance house painter and all-around nice guy who rides his bike everywhere and plays the drums in his garage.

"Don't mention it," he said, when I tried to thank him. "You'd have done the same for me." When I told this story to my friend Meredith, a descendant of Hamilton's original settlers and a childhood friend of my neighbor, she laughed and said, "Of course he mowed for you. Rich is a good central New York boy."

Not to dwell overlong on what was meant to be a lighthearted, not profound, remark, Meredith set me thinking more seriously than before about this place where I've alighted, and about the connection between where and how one lives. Is geography really destiny? Is there such a thing as an internal, metaphoric landscape that responds to the external, literal landscape, as the nature writer Barry Lopez has suggested? Or is it the other way around: do we dream our homes into existence?

More questions:

What do we mean when we say, "I belong here"?

What do we mean when we say, "I don't"?

Last spring, when I was on sabbatical in Fairbanks, a tiny redpoll mistook the reflection of trees for the real thing. It careered into my mother's kitchen window. For a while afterward, it crouched, hunched and shivering, feathers puffed up for warmth, on the bottom shelf of the feeder. The strength of my desire to save it surprised even me, who would cheerfully throttle a human being most any day of the week. My mother, who knows about such things—wounded birds and difficult daughters—scooped it up and set it inside an open paper bag, where it would be warmer. The bird panicked, attacking the paper walls. We took it out of the bag and put it back on the feeder. Sometime during the night, it fell off. The next morning, heedless, I let the dog out to pee. Daisy swooped up the redpoll in her mouth, crunched once, and swallowed.

Is this story an allegory for what happens when one mistakes one's true home for a false one? Mistakes the homing instinct for home itself? I'm not sure. Probably it's just a story about a bird that hit a window, died, and got eaten.

A friend who grew up in England and is raising her family in Fairbanks says that, on visits home, she sees the landscape around Devon as a stranger might, like images on postcards. The first time she traveled there with her young sons, they drove past fields of white cows. "What are those?" she asked the boys. "Polar bears!" they cried.

When I was a teenager in Fairbanks, I went cross-country skiing after school nearly every day. Nordic skiing, it would be called now, to distinguish it from skate skiing. Moonlight on snow creates an optical illusion: you are not skiing in the grooves but straddling them. The body feels as if it is right where it belongs, but the eyes say not.

Nearly everyone you meet in a college town is from somewhere else. When we are introduced at a party, we ask, Where is home for you? When I tell people where I'm from, people say things like this:

"*Alaska!! Really?!* I've always wanted to go there. Tell me all about it."

"Alaska. Wow. I had a brother/uncle/cousin who served in the military up there. It was brutal. I could never do that."

"You're from *Alaska*? And you left? What on earth are you doing *here*?"

I always flub my reply—partly because I am not socially adept, and partly because I regard Alaska with roughly the same amount of distance as I regard my mother, which is to say, not much. What would *you* say to someone who implied you were a nutcase for leaving home? People live where they live for all sorts of reasons, don't they?—not just because of climate or topography or the nearest IKEA. The obvious answer in my case is that my work brought me to Hamilton, New York. And I like my work, which mostly involves talking about books with smart undergraduates. It's work that, on the best days, feels as if it makes meaningful headway against confusion and darkness—my own and that of my students. Even on the worst days, it distracts me from the arthritis in my left foot. But loving one's work is not the same as loving one's place. For my first six summers in Hamilton, I focused on fixing up my new houses on the inside. The outside I merely maintained by mowing the grass and shoveling the driveway. I did not thin the day lilies or prune the shrubs. I did not plant bulbs. I did not put down roots.

Aspects of the central New York landscape appeal to me, even if my soul doesn't keen to them as it does to mountains and glaciers and wild rivers that run so thick with silt they sound like snare drums. The Adirondacks remind me of Alaska, but Hamilton is not in the Adirondacks; it is farther south, between Binghamton and Syracuse, in farm country. That move from interior Alaska to central New York was a move from the sublime to the pastoral. From tundra to cornfields. From Mahler symphonies to Bach partitas. From the sprawling novels of Tolstoy to the domestic ones of Jane Austen. After Alaska, being in New York is a little bit like being on Prozac: the highs are not as high, the lows not as low.

I find sweetness in this civilized landscape—in gardens that spill daffodils and tulips and hyacinths in spring, then peonies, hydrangeas, and lilies through summer. In ponds my children can swim in. Fireflies flashing in the night sky. Big barns and little lambs. Holstein cows lying among yarrow and Queen Anne's lace. Yard sales. The scent of lilacs in the rain. Cafés with outdoor tables instead of drive-through espresso stands. Hand-lettered signs with missing punctuation and letters: "Rhubarb come to house," "Aspargus Lebanon St." Long before moving here, I dwelt among these rolling hills in my imagination nearly every time I opened one of my favorite books: *Little Women, Jack and Jill, The Leatherstocking Tales, The Last of the Mohicans.*

A confession: When I visit Alaska, I am a curmudgeon. Actually, a curmudgeon is much better than what I am. In Alaska, I am mean, mean, mean. I curse at slow drivers in the left lane and treat chatty people with contempt that borders on risible. God help the perky soul on the elevator who asks, "What floor?" *I can push my own damn button, thank you very much.* Fairbanks is twenty times bigger than Hamilton, yet every time I visit, I bump into people I used to know and ought to recognize. Schoolmates or friends from church. When they see me at the farmers' market or the fair or the grocery store, they give me a warm look that suggests we have some catching up to do, right there in front of the Tilt-a-Whirl or the produce section. I look away, feigning interest in bananas.

It's true that Alaska brings out the worst in me. The things that fill me with the most rage happen only there: being mistaken for one of my sisters or one of my cousins. Being mistaken for my mother. Being asked, "Which Brice are you?" (*Why, Jennifer Brice,* I am tempted to say, but I do not, because like many rage-filled people, I am also—see above—a coward.) The news that the walk right/pass left rule applies in the supermarket has not yet reached Alaska, and this, too, fills me with rage. So do people who assume that one is not really looking for a book at Barnes & Noble but a date. The very worst, though, is the cashier who asks for a driver's license, sees that it is from New York, then does the tourist shtick: *Oh, you're from New York? What do you think of Alaska so far? Have you gone on the* Riverboat Discovery?

"On by" is what mushers shout when they want their dogs to ignore something in the path: a skier, a snowmachiner, a moose, another dog team. Alaskans rarely apply the "on by" rule to human relations, while New Yorkers intuitively do. This is not to say New Yorkers are not friendly or helpful. I'm thinking of the homeless man in New York City who let me know without a single obscene gesture that I was driving the wrong way on a one-way street. Or the taxi driver, also in the city, who dispatched his elderly father to the restaurant where I was dining with friends to return my wallet, which I'd left in his cab.

In Hamilton, a person can't walk half a block without bumping into a friend or acquaintance; the unspoken rule is to smile and say "Good morning," pet the dog, then walk on by. There is no expectation to renew a relationship that has lapsed, or to form a new one, although that can certainly happen. At core, the friendliness of New Yorkers seems to be about drawing boundaries—*This far will I go, and no farther*—while the friendliness of Alaskans is about breaking them down.

I'm fascinated by research that shows that people are more likely to talk to strangers across space—across an empty seat in an airplane, say—than to those who are smooshed up against them in a crowded subway car. Obviously this research was carried out in the continental United States, because Alaskans talk to *everyone*. One New Year's Eve, I flew first class (thanks to my parents' largesse with mileage) from Fairbanks to Seattle; so freely were drinks and conversation flowing, I felt as if I were perched on a barstool at the Ritz. Judging from the racket in coach, I'd say it was like a bar back there too—Tommy's Elbow Room or the Hideaway. To say that every Alaskan is friendly is a gross exaggeration, of course. It's a lie that may have a basis in an evolutionary truth, though: a small number of organisms, finding themselves in a large, potentially hostile, environment, huddle together for safety; a large number of organisms in a smaller, gentler environment need space in order to thrive.

It would likewise be reductive to say that Alaska brings out the worst in me, and New York brings out the best. Even so, a couple of years ago, I felt a jolt of recognition when I came upon a *New York Times Book Review* retrospective on Norman Mailer. The author of the article observes that people with porous boundaries tend to protect them most ferociously: "[Those] who have the gift of melting into another nature usually need to assert themselves all the more so as not to melt away altogether." *Yikes*, I thought, is this my problem too? Is the wildness that seizes me in Alaska the response of a weak nature to a strong place? Is my (relative) serenity in New York about the way that everything—even the weather, which comes in four distinct seasons—is *bounded*?

In *The Poetics of Space*, his wide-ranging book on architecture and philosophy, Gaston Bachelard quotes George Sand, who believed that "people could be classified according to whether they aspired to live in a cottage or in a palace." A cottage person likes to be cocooned in close, low-ceilinged spaces. A palace person yearns to stretch out, even if that means feeling dwarfed by her environs. Bachelard sees human nature as more complex. "When we live in a manor house we dream of a cottage," he writes, "and when we live in a cottage we dream of a palace. Better still, we all have our cottage moments and our palace moments."

I wonder if the cottage-palace metaphor applies to landscape as well as architecture. Can it be that our dreaming of a cottage or a palace says less about what is lacking in our lives than about what is already here—that, chameleon-like, we take our colors from our surroundings? To dream, it occurs to me, is not necessarily to yearn or to pine. In its noun form, a dream can be a serene thing too.

The word *nostalgia* is born from the Greek for "return home," the German for "homesickness." As recently as the late 1800s, nostalgia was regarded (and dreaded) as a medical condition; soldiers who claimed to suffer from it could be sent home from the front. The best way to prevent nostalgia, of course, was never to leave home—a fate that parents wished for fervently. In 1919, in his "Prayer for My Daughter," W. B. Yeats writes:

O may she live like some green laurel
Rooted in one dear perpetual place.

Nearly eighty years later, in his "Prayer for Our Daughters," Mark Jarman sings back to Yeats:

May they find a place to love, without nostalgia
For some place else that they can never go back to.

I love these poems separately, but I love them best in conversation with each other: Yeats's gorgeous laurel metaphor, and Jarman's sly suggestion that one can find a place to love without being from it. Also, that love is not the same as nostalgia, that sepia-tinted, soft-focus image of the past that owes more to invention than memory.

This summer, when I returned from my sabbatical in Alaska, my best friend came to visit for a few days. "Why don't you have a garden yet?" she asked, genuinely puzzled. We got in the car and drove to the nearest greenhouse, where I wrote an enormous check for hydrangeas, summersweet, azaleas, daisies, lamb's ears, vinca, mint, Russian sage, and a lilac tree. The next morning, we went to work with shovel and trowel to soften the symmetry of my inherited garden plot and transplant the perennials. A few hours later, we stood on the sidewalk, admiring our handiwork from the vantage of strangers. What both of us knew, neither of us said: we had just planted something bigger than a garden.

The next time someone asks me what on earth I was thinking when I traded Alaska for New York, I will answer bravely. I will say that I love both places. I love them separately, but I love them best when they sing back to each other: wildness and quietude—that palace made of sky, my cupboard staircase home.

Already flowers are often so infinitely much to me . . . and I look at
everything more quietly and with greater justness.
—Rainer Maria Rilke

I'd rather have roses on my table than diamonds on my neck.
—Emma Goldman

My Essay on Flowers and How Things End

A

Alstroemeria [devotion]

They're the corps de ballet, the workhorse, the spinster aunt, the tilapia-not-sea-bass of blooms. One day they were nowhere, the next everywhere. Inexpensive and unshowy, they seem to have been conjured simply to serve as the supermarket avatar of the beautiful *idea* of flowers.

I adore them wildly and beyond all reason.

Fifteen dollars at the local Price Chopper buys three big bunches, and flowers in every room of the house is my best trick, a bit of dinner party trompe l'oeil, meant to divert attention from dingy windows and scuffed furniture.

In the Alaska of my childhood, store-bought flowers were as rare as rattlesnakes. That my father wooed my mother with yellow roses (meaning: friendship) and a Tiffany diamond ring is part of my family lore. A big part. He was working in those years, the early sixties, as a mechanic for Pan Am and was pretty close to penniless. Apparently, the daily delivery of roses softened up my mother, who eventually put on the diamond ring, married my father a month later, and gave birth to me a year after that. Fast-forward to the Seven Sisters education and graduate degree (for which they footed the bills), which elevated me to the lofty academic perch from which I can safely survey my family lore with the arched brow of a deconstructionist critic.

Between college and grad school, I worked my way up from receptionist to reporter at my hometown newspaper. Then (as now), I was nobody's idea of a beauty; I did not sparkle. This is not false modesty. A photo of the features staff in 1987 or so recently made the rounds on Facebook. I showed it to my daughters and my partner. None of them could find me in the photo. Even I struggled to recognize myself in the startled-looking woman standing in the doorway.

Here's a thing about fairy tales: read enough of them as a child, and eventually you come to believe that you are a princess in disguise. Someday your prince will come. He will see beneath the unpromising surface—glasses, frizzy hair, acne, matronly bustline—and fall in love with the true you. I tell you this so you will understand what I mean when I say that the first time a bouquet of pink Peruvian lilies landed on my desk in the middle of the workday, I accepted them as my due. The card, from an anonymous admirer, pleased and delighted me; it did not surprise me. *Of course* I had an anonymous admirer. Plenty more where *he* came from.

The bouquets kept on coming. Not every day or even every week, but once or twice a month, always alstroemeria swaddled in tissue paper, delivered by a tight-lipped florist. Unsigned cards piled up in my pen drawer. It's embarrassing to admit, even now, that I lack the most important quality for anyone contemplating a career as a journalist, which is curiosity. I can *perform* it when necessary. Left to my own devices I much prefer to dwell in dreamy uncertainty.

Back when people still got most of their news from newspapers, and when those newspapers were published only once per day, there came a moment every day when the staff put the paper "to bed." One day, in the lull that followed the deadline rush, a colleague sauntered over to my desk. Hands pushed deep into the pockets of his khakis. Tipped his chin toward the lilies on my desk, asked, "Know who sent them?" He was a bit of a mongrel, this colleague: an evangelical Christian who was also whip-smart and wickedly funny. Charismatic and confident in the manner of men who've never doubted themselves for a moment. Not exactly handsome—soft stomach, bootstrap beard—but not unsexy either.

"I don't," I said, and it was sort of true, because up until that moment, I hadn't.

The ostensible subject of Annie Dillard's essay "The Stunt Pilot" is a guy named Dave Rahm. He took her flying one day and executed a few barrel rolls, casual as you please. She, too, seemed unruffled. From her perch in the back seat, she writes, "I could see the serious line of his cheek and jaw. He was in shirtsleeves, tanned, strong-wristed. *I could not imagine loving him under any circumstance.*" [My italics.]

"Nope," I said. "No idea at all."

Reader, you will not be surprised by how this story ends. A couple of years later, my colleague met somebody. So did I. He got married, then promoted; he took a job in a new city, raised two kids, stayed married to the same woman. After the breakup of my marriage, I drifted for a few years between insecure academic posts, before landing at a liberal arts college in upstate New York. Facebook dangles my former colleague as a friend prospect sometimes; sometimes I'm tempted, but that's as far as it goes. For one thing, my troublemaking days are over. For another, *I could not imagine loving him under any circumstance.*

Why think of that former colleague now? Whenever I summon a memory of myself in my mid-twenties, a picture of him comes along for the ride. Nothing between us but a whole lot of alstroemeria and my whopping air of entitlement—*More flowers? For* me? *Lovely! Just set them anywhere. Yes, there is fine.*

If I could go back in time, what would I tell that unformed young woman dressed in a skirt she'd poached from her mother's closet? She thought every day was an audition, that real life would commence in a year or two. When it did, bouquets sent by myriad suitors would materialize out of thin air. *(For me? Again? Just set them anywhere.)* To the handsome and the well-to-do, the boot-strapped and the striving, she'd be kind but noncommittal, smiling gently and stretching out her hand to be kissed or perhaps adorned with a diamond ring.

Maybe I would tell her this: there will be admirers, yes, but fewer than you think. Some of them strange. I would tell her that the stories that nourished and sustained her as a child—Cinderella and Sleeping Beauty, yellow roses and Tiffany diamonds—were too anemic to carry her into the next century. I would tell her that graciousness is at best only a stilted performance of self that serves no meaningful use and only disguises the shabby state of one's interior life. *Wake up*, I feel like shouting, from the vantage point of years. *It's better to be bold. At the very least, say "Thank you" to the nice boy.*

I can't tell her anything, of course.

She's going to be so surprised.

B

Bittersweet [truth]

"But you, I adore." That's what A said right before he kissed me for the first time. We'd just left a north London pub, the Bree Louise, and we'd been talking about a mutual friend. "I like her a lot," said I. "Me, too," said he. Then he said the thing about *adoring* me.

"Where does a story begin? The fiction is that they do, and end, rather than that the stuff of a story is just a cup of water scooped from the sea and poured back into it," writes Rebecca Solnit, in *The Faraway Nearby*.

Now it is my and A's faraway nearby: three years on from that moment outside the Bree Louise, and we are back in London, living together for a few months in a light-filled flat near Hampstead Heath. The expiry date on this blissful domestic arrangement is in just a few weeks, when we'll return to our separate homes in upstate New York. But for now, England. And on the table before me, a vase of tulips so purple they are nearly black. A bought them from a greengrocer for Valentine's Day. When he presented them, the color seemed edgy and sophisticated. I'll soon be disabused of this notion, when we take the train to Suffolk to spend the weekend with friends. Tulips the color of bruises or storm clouds spring from stone planters flanking the cottage's front door. The husband in this couple is color-blind. When

I compliment his wife on the tulips, she laughs and says she planted them against her gardener's advice. (So much unconscious privilege in that phrase: *Against my gardener's advice. Against my cook's advice. Against my manicurist's advice.*) What the gardener was trying to say to his client was, Stay away from deep purple tulips, which are all the rage among Suffolk newcomers—and a dead giveaway, like a brand-new set of matching luggage.

A is a few years younger than me. More sentimental, too, though he'd probably use the word *romantic*. He would have liked to celebrate Valentine's Day with dinner at the Bree Louise. Alas, it was not to be because the pub was shuttered, about to be torn down to make way for a new high-speed railway. I would have liked for him to make us a reservation somewhere, maybe at the trattoria I like and keep mentioning, the one near Marylebone Station. *Briciole.* After our respective workdays, we met up in central London. Before we could decide on a plan, it started to rain. We ducked into a burger place near Camden Market. Afterward, we kissed on the sidewalk.

Tulips, I adore.

C

Here's Lady Mary Wortley Montague in a three-hundred-year-old letter: "There is no colour, no flower, no weed, no fruit, herb, pebble or feather that has not a verse belonging to it; and you may quarrel, reproach, or send letters of passion, friendship or civility without ever inking your fingers." She goes on to describe floriography, the language of flowers, in which lovers, or would-be lovers, could carry on entire conversations without saying a word.

White camellia: "You're adorable!"

Candy-tuff: [silence]

Four-leaf clover: "Be mine?"

Striped carnation: "Sorry, I can't."

Red camellia: "But you're a flame in my heart!"

Red carnation: "Alas, poor heart."

Coral honeysuckle: "I love you!"

Chrysanthemum: "You're a wonderful friend."

Cedar: "Think of me?"

Cyclamen: "Goodbye."

D
Daffodil [respect]

After that first kiss outside the Bree Louise, A and I went our separate ways, he to visit his friends in Suffolk, me to travel for a few days in Italy with one of my daughters. I boarded our flight still feeling a bit giddy from the night before. A month earlier I'd turned fifty-two. The bloom was definitely off the rose (as my mother would say, though not to my face). I'd been living on my own for so long it was beginning to feel like a permanent condition. A and I had made a date to meet back up in London in a week. On the appointed afternoon, A left his friends' cottage and tromped two miles across muddy fields to the train station. He arrived at the door to my flat only to discover we were not there: our flight from Pisa had been delayed by several hours. He settled into a corner table at a nearby pub, Angel in the Fields. I wonder what the after-work crowd there made of him—the black sport coat and mud-covered shoes, the wind-ruffled hair, and, alongside his half-empty pint glass, a great fistful of wild daffodils.

E
Endine [frugality]

My first serious boyfriend was not a chocolates-and-flowers kind of guy. For our first date, we went spear fishing after dark on the Chatanika River near Fairbanks. A year later, he left to cover state politics from Alaska's capital. Flights between Fairbanks and Juneau were expensive, so we didn't see each other very often. When we did, we spent most of the time in bed. One Saturday we woke up, showered, and dressed just in time to think about dinner. I was ravenous. I wanted to put on a dress and dine at a fancy farm-to-table restaurant I'd never been to: The Fiddlehead. S drove us to a steakhouse instead. At that point, the end of us went from immanent to imminent, in Frank Kermode's phrase from *The Sense of an Ending*. Over drinks, we carried on our breakup conversation like civilized people. He told me a little bit about the woman he'd begun seeing in Juneau. Like me, she was learning to fly. He thought I'd be amused by an anecdote she'd told him, something about the cargo door swinging open during her first solo flight. *How stupid can you be*, I wondered, *not to check the latch before you fly?* I asked if he thought there was any hope for the two of us. He said he thought there might be, and I thought I agreed—all the way up until the moment our dinner arrived: overdone steak, a few stalks of underdone broccoli, and baked potatoes in tin foil. Honestly, I don't remember feeling as if I was about to cry, and I definitely don't remember starting to cry. All I remember is the sight of my tears splashing onto the tin foil.

F
Flowering dogwood [Am I indifferent to you?]

Seriously, what kind of question is this? A rhetorical one, as in, *Hmmm, what is this ineffable sort-of non-feeling I have in your presence?* Or a real one: *Have you mistaken my resting bitch face for something else? Do I seem indifferent to you?*

"Say it with flowers" was coined during World War I by a group of entrepreneurial florists who struck on the idea of using the nascent telegraph to place orders across the country. It's one of the catchiest slogans of all time, right up there with "A diamond is forever" and

"Just do it." Like 14-carat diamonds and fancy workout gear, a bouquet of flowers exists at the intersection of capitalism and symbolism (or sentimentality, a cynic might say). But flowers are fleeting; after just a few days, they start to droop, and then they die. FTD, the consortium founded by those early entrepreneurs, makes more than a billion dollars a year by translating feelings into flowers.

Like all catchphrases, "Say it with flowers" begs to be deconstructed. If you really can "Say it with flowers" (whatever *it* is), then what are you saying if you *don't* send them?

G
Geranium [stupidity]

"Mind over matter" was one of my mother's favorite sayings, until she lost hers. (Mind, not matter.)

I remember late-evening sunlight streaming through the open windows of my bedroom. The sound of my mother digging in her garden below. The feel of my skin heating up the sheets. I was rarely sick as a child, and on this particular evening, my mother, a registered nurse, was taking a wait-and-see attitude. While she waited to see whether my fever would develop into something interesting, she was doing what she loved. My parents lived, then and now, about a hundred miles south of the Arctic Circle, which means that early summer is the season for transplanting the geraniums, dahlias, marigolds, dusty miller, and lobelia that will eventually explode from the raised beds, planters, and hanging baskets that surround our family home.

Transplanting, Mom once explained to me, is an act of violence: a forcible uprooting into cold and potentially hostile soil. Plants often die from the shock of it. She could be brusque and sometimes cold toward us, her children, who had never been transplanted, not really, though we'd lived in four or five locations in one city, moving every few years into a new, larger house just a few miles from the old one.

My mother prepared the ground by digging a hole then filling it partway with rich black soil, brackish water, and a few sprinkles of fertilizer. Then she turned the plastic six-pack of seedlings upside down and gently squeezed one out, cupping it like a baby chick in her palm. She righted it then tucked it into the prepared hole, covering it with more loamy soil and plenty of water. Then she tamped down on it down with her trowel. The whole time she was doing this, she whispered sweet nothings to the seedlings: *I'm sorry, I know you're scared, but it's going to be all right. There you go: snug as a bug in your new home.*

On this particular night, I was sixteen or seventeen. Old enough to drive, certainly, because those were Mom's migraine years. When she felt one coming on, usually in the morning, she'd pull the shades in her bedroom, prepare a cool rag for her forehead, and climb naked into the king-size four-poster bed she shared with my father at night. Half the time, she rose from her bed a few hours later, showered, dressed, and returned to the world, pale and wobbly but otherwise her usual brisk self. *Mind over matter.* Other times, she summoned me to her bedside with instructions to drive as fast as I could to the Fred Meyer pharmacy, where she had a standing prescription for morphine. I'd return with a pre-filled syringe, and she'd stab the needle into her own thigh. It was an act of desperation. Her body had failed her, and she'd be damned if she was going to reward it with any tenderness.

Three decades later, I'll be living—transplanted—on the other side of the country. One of my daughters will suffer for longer than expected from the aftereffects of oral surgery. The pain will ramp up until it becomes unbearable. She won't be able to keep any of her food down. On a holiday weekend, with the surgeon unreachable, I will call Mom for advice. I will tell her I've tried everything—Advil, hot and cold compresses, sympathy. She will say, "You don't want her to get too attached to the attention. You should name a day—tomorrow or the next day—and tell her that when she wakes up that morning, she's going to feel like her old self." *Mind over matter.*

For once, I will disregard my mother's advice, placing another call to the surgeon's answering service. An hour later, he will meet us outside the door to his office. In golf wear. Quickly and kindly, he will treat my daughter for dry sockets, a painful but easy-to-treat complication of wisdom tooth removal.

That episode is decades in the future on the night that I've been describing, the night when I myself am ill. I listen for the sound of the screen door every twenty minutes or so. Then water running in the kitchen sink. Muffled footsteps on the stairs, then Mom's weight on the edge of my bed, her cool hand on my burning forehead. Three wrist-flicks to reset the mercury, a thermometer jabbing the soft tissue under my tongue: 101.1, 102.6, 103.2, 104.7. Mostly what I remember from that night is the sensation of heat.

What did I want from my mother? Creature comforts: clean, cool sheets; a fresh washcloth; ice in my glass. Also: tenderness. She leaves for a moment, and I hear water running in the upstairs bathroom. She returns, pulls me from under the covers, shucks my pajamas from my unresisting body and leads me naked and shivering to the tub, which is full of water with ice cubes floating in it.

The next day, I am back to my old self.

H
Hydrangea [heartlessness]

When I was forty, I moved with my daughters to a small town in upstate New York. That first winter, dried hydrangeas blew along the sidewalks like wannabe tumbleweeds. I assumed on the basis of this behavior that they must be very hardy, resistant to all forms of neglect short of actual violence. So the next summer, I bought three pots of hydrangeas from a nursery down the road and planted them in my garden. Years passed. The plants grew into bushes. The leaves flourished and multiplied, threatening to take over the garden. But there were no blossoms. Nine years later, I returned to the greenhouse. The owner said: come September, cut the leaves back mercilessly. I did as she advised, and the next summer I got . . . more leaves.

The next summer, I went on a date with a bicycle racer who was an engineer in his spare time. He distracted me from my nonexistent garden. By the time I saw it, the blossom was nearly as big as a dinner plate, its color a seductive blend of pink and blue. The bicycle racer rode for a minimum of four hours a day on the weekends. He subsisted on maybe twelve hundred calories a day, in order to make himself light on the hills. When we went out to dinner, he talked me into ordering just one entrée to share. I gave up alcohol. That hydrangea was a real tart. A lot of people remarked on it, even the mailman. One day, a stranger even crossed the street to ask me for my secret.

By the time school started in the fall, the hydrangea was the size of a child's umbrella. The bicycle racer was so skinny he had to use safety pins to hold up his pants. My hardy mums bloomed then wilted, but the hydrangea kept blooming. At odd moments, I caught myself drafting an acceptance speech for the award I expected to receive from the garden club.

Then, suddenly, the wind shifted. The bicycle racer and I had an argument, our first. The hydrangea stopped growing but kept blooming, even when everything around it died. How long can something beautiful stay on the vine before it becomes something strange or even ridiculous? Our first argument wasn't fatal. Shortly after Halloween, I snipped the hydrangea and placed it in a pottery vase on a table full of books. I thought the blue vase and hardcover books might restore some of its dignity.

A year later, when the romance finally died, I felt hollow inside. To make the sad feeling go away, I tried making myself smaller. My friends told me later they were frightened for me.

Then one morning, I woke up. I felt hollow—as usual—but this time I called the feeling hunger. I cooked myself an egg. Then I cooked myself another, which I ate along with some buttered toast. And half an avocado.

Five years on, there is a new love in my life.

A.

When we go out for dinner, we order our own meals. He likes a rack of lamb or confit of duck. I like mushroom ravioli or salmon. Afterward, we sometimes order a slice of flourless chocolate cake to share, but he lets me eat most of it.

A couple of years ago, I dug up the hydrangeas and replaced them with peonies. They bloom every June.

I

Ipomaca [I attach myself to you.]

The Ides of March. I agree to meet a man at Waterloo station. Reader: I know what you're thinking, and it's not that. He and I had known each other for at least a decade. Now, living on separate continents, we'd grown close over email. It took me days to decide what to wear to meet his train. I imagined all the ways that moment might play out. Then, on the appointed afternoon, it rained. There were mix-ups. He accidentally texted the wrong Jennifer with his arrival time; having heard nothing, I dialed his number then hung up before he answered. At the station, we both spent twenty minutes wandering through the throng, looking for a familiar face. I spotted him first. Black sport coat, backpack, crinkly eyes. He didn't turn until I called his name a second time. An awkward hug. Whatever had been meant to happen in that moment would not now happen.

Now it's three years later and we are living together for a semester in London. The cherry trees have just burst into bloom, seemingly overnight. The smell is just this side of rancid. Branches form a floral canopy over the sidewalk. When the wind blows, it sweeps petals into confetti-like piles. Needing some milk for tea, I put on a windbreaker and boots. I don't actually take milk in my tea, but the man from Waterloo station does. While I run to Tesco, he stays behind in the flat, grading student essays with one eye on what he calls "the football." I don't mind any of it—not the errand, not the football, not even the idiosyncratic article ("the"), which reminds me he is British while I am not. The fresh air feels good, and the pink and white cherry blossoms make it seem as if I'm wading through the detritus of some just-ended bacchanal—a party, a parade, a procession of priests bearing offerings to the Hindu deities.

J

Juniper [protection]

The founder of Mother's Day was never a mother herself. According to myth, Anna Jarvis (1864–1948) once wore a white carnation on the anniversary of her mother's death, and, suddenly, "to Miss Jarvis's delight, Mother's Day 'broke out' across the country and supporters all over were clamoring for white carnations." My source is a Library of Congress blog by Jennifer Harbster, who goes on to quote a 1911 issue of *Weekly Florists' Review* as saying that Miss Jarvis chose the white carnation because "Its whiteness stands for purity, its form, beauty, and its fragrance, love, its wide field of growth, charity; its lasting qualities, faithfulness—all a true mother's attributes."

The reality is more complex. A 2015 *BuzzFeed* article depicts Miss Jarvis as a monomaniacal self-promoter who waged a relentless publicity campaign not merely to establish the holiday (which came about in 1914) but to dictate the terms of it. She railed against anyone she perceived as trying to piggyback or profit off *her* holiday. At one point, she had thirty-three Mother's Day–related lawsuits pending.

According to *BuzzFeed*'s James Oliphint, she was once charged with disorderly conduct for turning up uninvited at a convention of American War Mothers to protest against their adopting the white carnation as the emblem of their organization. In another incident, she ordered salad from a tearoom that belonged to a friend, then dumped it on the floor because the menu described it as a "Mother's Day Salad." In yet another, she took on the Golden Rule Foundation, which gave away funds for needy mothers and children, claiming it was "trespassing on her cause and commercializing the day." The leader of the Golden Rule Foundation was Eleanor Roosevelt.

Speaking of Miss Jarvis, the First Lady told the *Times*, "I think she misunderstands us."

Anna Jarvis lost control of her brainchild, and it nearly drove her mad. In 1908 carnations cost half a penny each; four years later, the "profiteering tradesmen and carnation peddlers" (Jarvis's own words) had lifted the price to fifteen cents. In 2015, the year the *BuzzFeed* article was published, the National Retail Federation predicted Americans would spend about $20 billion on Mother's Day gifts, and that 66 percent of us would buy flowers.

Back in 1911, the *Weekly Florists' Review* had the temerity to suggest that florists promote white flowers for mothers who had died, bright flowers for those still living. "It would be an understatement," writes Harbster, "to say that this was much to the displeasure of Miss Jarvis."

K
King's cup [I wish I were rich.]

On Valentine's Day 2015, I return from Indaba Yoga to find three boxes in the foyer. The biggest is nearly four feet tall. It contains an extraordinary amount of packaging that eventually yields a hand-tied long-stem bouquet of roses and lilies. The medium-size box holds a crystal vase meant to hold the expensive bouquet. Together, they form a gift from the businessman I've been dating for a few months now. The smallest of the boxes, maybe ten inches square, is from an old friend. It holds a miniature rose bush and a planter in the shape of an oversize teacup, white with red hearts—a bit of whimsy that wouldn't be out of place in *Alice in Wonderland*.

The expensive bouquet with its crystal vase is an homage but also a claim—a heavy gold chain around the neck. The miniature rose with its ridiculous teapot is a question. The men who sent these arrangements are on the other side of the Atlantic. They've never met. For now, all I can say in response to both is *thank you*.

Is there a better feeling in the world, I wonder, than to be admired, wanted, wooed by more than one person? To see multiple paths opening up before one? I want it never to end, this feeling.

It will end.

L
Lily-of-the-valley [humility]

In *A Sport and a Pastime*, James Salter's narrator responds to the appearance of a woman in late middle age, thinking she is "in the midst of that last and most confident beauty." It's a phrase that could describe Christine, another fictional character, this one from a story by Tessa Hadley. She is single, a professor, and of a certain age. "The idea came to her out of nowhere," Hadley writes, "that there would be a last time that she brought anyone home to make love in her bed. It was not yet, it might not be for years, but it would come, even though she might not recognize it until long afterward."

M
Marigold [cruelty]

October 2009. I'm reeling from a bad breakup. At work, I put one foot in front of the other until it's time to leave. At home, I put pasta in front of the girls then change into flannel pajamas. Lean heavily on Kleenex and scotch to get through the evenings. One day, a colleague drags me out to a talk by a visiting scholar. (You already know how this ends, don't you?) The talk is unmemorable, the scholar too diffident to make his subject (geology) sparkle. But grief has made me reckless and thin, maybe just a little bit sparkly. After three martinis, the scholar and I start kissing on my couch. He borrows my car to buy condoms at the Sunoco station. While he's gone, I climb the stairs to kiss my sleeping children. Later, in my bed, he asks if I believe in God. I know there is a right answer to this question. *No*, I tell him. "Are you spiritual but not religious?" he asks. Again, I answer honestly.

The next morning, I walk him back to his hotel. He grabs my hand. Because it's early on a Saturday in a college town, and he's still wearing the clothes from his talk, one of us cracks the obvious joke about a pair of forty-somethings doing the walk of shame. Seeing us laughing, an outsider might mistake us for boyfriend and girlfriend. But we are not that and never will be. One of us is neither religious nor spiritual.

N
Night-scented stock [lasting beauty]

That stories unfold in time *and* space is one of those truths so obviously we (OK, *I*) never even pause to consider it. Rebecca Solnit's question, "Where does a story begin?," marries the spatial to the temporal.

The same is true of endings, of course: they unfold in space and time. What's less obvious, and—for me—more interesting is the way these two elements can be cleaved: a story that reaches its temporal end may continue for a while in space, or vice versa.

It's early in the 2000s and a man I've been seeing (you haven't met this one yet) asks if I remember a scene in *Holy Smoke* between Ruth (Kate Winslet) and PJ Waters (Harvey Keitel). Waters has been hired by Ruth's family to extract her from a cult, which he does—at a price— then he falls in love with her. The scene that my boyfriend has in mind is not the obvious one (involving full frontal nudity while peeing) but one in which Ruth forces Waters to be still while she puts makeup on him. My lover would like to know if I would be willing do this for him sometime. *Yes*, I say. *OK, sometime I will do this for you.*

I will not ever. Nope.

O

Oleander [caution]

Valentine's Day began in third-century Rome, when Emperor Claudius II, believing that single men made better soldiers, outlawed marriage for them. A Catholic priest named Valentine continued performing marriages in secret. By all accounts (one of those wonderful hedging phrases!), Claudius found Valentine's sense of conviction impressive at first, then he wearied of it. The priest was arrested, convicted, and sentenced to death. It's hard to say where, if anywhere, the story veers into myth, but right here is one possibility: while waiting for the sentence to be carried out, Valentine befriended his jailer's blind daughter and, drawing on his faith, restored her sight. By all accounts the relationship between the two was platonic, their affection described as *agape*, not *eros*.

Just before Valentine was beheaded, on February 14, 270 AD, he supposedly wrote a farewell letter to the jailer's daughter, signing it "from your Valentine." A couple of centuries later, Pope Gelasius set aside the day to honor St. Valentine. A few centuries after *that* the holiday became associated with love and romance, on account of the belief that birds begin mating in mid-February.

The oldest extant valentine was from Charles. It was from Charles, Duke of Orleans, to his wife, Bonne of Armagnac. Captured at the Battle of Agincourt, Charles was locked up in the Tower of London. He was twenty-one, Bonne a few days shy of sixteen. The story, if it were to end here, would be romantic, no? It turns out his "valentine" took the form of a poem titled "Farewell to Love," a poem that repeated (three times) the line, "I am already sick of love." Charles remained a prisoner for twenty-five years, during which time Bonne died, childless, her date of death (her ending) unrecorded. Charles, on the other hand, survived a comfortable captivity, was eventually ransomed, and returned to France, where he remarried, fathered three children, and died at seventy-one, a renowned poet and patron of the arts.

Valentine's Day is one of those holidays (the Fourth of July is the other) that brings out my inner crank. It's not the commercialization I resent so much as the coercion. When my daughters were young, we had to purchase valentines in bulk from Target or Walmart, then sit up late—after school, after practice, after dinner, after homework—painstakingly filling out, then addressing a card to every student in every class. A note would have been sent home a few days earlier reminding us parents that no student was to be left out. But what is love if it doesn't leave somebody out? Is a gift not freely given but actually expected, even punished in the breach, still a gift?

One of my oldest friends is a mathematician in Alaska who every year sends me a red heart that is clumsily cut from construction paper. It's always about the size of my palm, and it's always inscribed in ballpoint pen with some anodyne saying: "Be mine." It sort of means something, but I'm not sure what. I suspect John sends these Valentines to dozens of women every year. (*Hundreds, my dear*, I can hear him say. *Hundreds*.)

P
Peony [good luck]

Flowers held symbolic meaning in ancient Greece. The practice of sending messages with flowers—floriography—spread from the Mediterranean to Europe during the Crusades, then surged again during the Renaissance. It peaked during the Victorian era, when a dozen or more flower dictionaries were published. The most definitive, *The Poetry of Flowers*, ran to 522 pages.

Last June, a beloved uncle died in a plane crash, and I flew to Alaska for the funeral. While there, I kept seeing florist vans emblazoned with peonies. I asked my father about them, and he said peonies were Alaska's new bumper crop. According to an article in the *Anchorage Daily News*, the "delicate yet decadent" and "showy but elegant" blooms actually *need* cold weather to flourish. During the June to September wedding season, Alaska is one of the few places in the world that supplies peonies to the rest of the world, at about five dollars a stem. Here are the names of the some of the farms that have sprung up to meet the demand: Alaska Peony Patch, Alaska Perfect Peony, Arctic Sun Peonies, Boreal Peonies, Frosty Acres Peonies, Howling Downs Peonies, Northern Bloom Peonies, North Pole Peonies, Pioneer Peonies, and Polar Peonies.

Q
Queen Anne's lace [haven]

It's April 2018, and Prince Harry will marry the American actress Meghan Markle next month. Among the ways I've found to distract myself from my work is looking at news stories about the royal romance. In a photo taken outside the church on Christmas Day, Meghan wears a wren-like ensemble of brown coat and brown hat—an outfit that shouts, *Please, no one look at me!* Instead, one's eye is drawn to the queen, who is busy casting shade in a coat-and-hat combo that brings to mind a tequila sunrise, somewhere between peach, apricot, and coral. Valspar's "pomegranate punch" paint color comes close. It's an outfit that cries, *Don't you dare put Lizzie in the corner!*

A vase of tulips sits on the table in front of me. It's early morning, my favorite time to write. A will sleep a while longer (so many student essays; a couple of drams of whiskey). The morning light fingers each of the tulips in turn. I look up their color on the paint chart, which suggests many possibilities beginning with the word *world*: world beauty, world favorite, world fire, world legend. I declare their color to be "the queen's Christmas suit."

R
Rhododendron [danger, beware]

I also declare that, in the history of the world, no one has ever suffered from a worse case of imposter syndrome than I did during college. At Smith and, later, at Harvard, I was shy and studious, tongue-tied in the presence of people (just about everyone, really) who struck me as prettier or smarter, more stylish or confident or interesting. I wasn't a wallflower so much as a wall-clinger. For reasons I can't begin to explain, I was a completely different person when I returned to Fairbanks in the summer: flirtatious and outgoing, at ease in the limelight and in my own skin.

In the summer before my junior year, I was hanging out with friends at a bar called the Feed and Fuel. A boy asked me to dance. A man, really—maybe the first man who'd ever shown an interest in me that wasn't creepy. He was tall and lean with blue eyes and straw-colored hair that he wore in a ponytail. He was very handsome but also very drunk. When he asked me for my number, I made one up.

That January, when I was home for the holidays, I saw him again at a different bar. P was drunk, but not as drunk as he'd been the previous summer, and we talked a little bit. He was studying art at the University of Alaska and living with his parents. His father was an academic, a horticulturist of some kind.

This time, I gave him my real phone number.

The next evening was cold. Fifty below at least. I opened the door to an explosion of roses. Dozens and dozens in every conceivable shade. P was a big man with long arms, but he could barely hold onto them all.

The rest of my family was at a hockey game and wouldn't return for hours.

Come in, I said.

S

Sweet William [Grant me one smile.]

Snapdragon [presumption, deception]

This story begins with a woman out walking. She's forty-five years old, an academic living in upstate New York. For the past couple of weeks, she's been visiting her parents in Alaska. It's February, clear and cold, the temperature around twenty below. She tries to walk three or four miles in a loop every day. She's about to turn back onto the road where her parents live when a flash of color catches her eye. She stops in front of a neighbor's house. It's unremarkable in every way, a seventies-era split-level, painted peach, with a flight of stairs leading to a second-story deck. Set back maybe a hundred feet from the road. The woman has never met the people who live here, a childless couple who are said (by her parents) to be private but not unfriendly. They used to keep their snowmachines locked around a birch tree in their front yard. One day, the man knocked on the neighbors' front door to ask if they'd heard any suspicious noises during the night. Apparently, thieves had chopped down the tree and made off with the snowmachines.

Roses are scarce this time of year. They cost eighty dollars a dozen, if you can even get them. The woman out walking, the voyeur, has the eighty-dollar figure in her head because, a few days earlier, her father had asked her to use his credit card to order yellow roses for him to present to her mother on their anniversary.

From the middle of the driveway, up the stairs, and along the deck of the neighbors' house are strewn dozens and dozens of roses in a kaleidoscope of hues: yellow, pink, coral, purple, red, even white, though only the stems of those are visible in the snow. Roses hang from the banister and sprawl on hay bales at the base of the steps. (Why hay bales? The woman has no idea. They just are.) The roses glint like jewels in the snow.

The woman stands there gawking, trying to make sense of what she's seeing, trying to turn a paradox into a story. Were the roses tossed out the front door in a fit of anger? Arranged in an act of love? Are they saying, "I'm sorry I hurt you"? Or "Fuck off"? Just then, a black F-250 pickup turns into the driveway. The engine cuts off. Then, for long seconds, nothing. The woman waits for the driver to get out, but he (she's sure it's a he) doesn't. He's waiting for her to walk on. Whatever is about to transpire, he doesn't want a stranger for a witness. The woman walks on.

The next morning, she heads out on another walk. She wills herself not to look in the neighbors' yard, but of course she does. The roses are gone. The pickup is still there.

I dip my cup back into the sea.

T

Tuberose [dangerous pleasure]

In Victorian times, a nosegay made up of assorted blooms was called a tussie-mussie, and a tussie-mussie was, essentially, a letter in flower form: *You're adorable* (white camellia). Please *forgive* (purple hyacinth) *my excessive ardor* (dragon root) and *relieve my anxiety* (Christmas rose) by saying you'll *dance with me* (ivy geranium) at tonight's ball. In exchange for a yes, I can promise *everlasting love* (lemon leaves).

A tussie-mussie that arrived upside down meant exactly the opposite of what it meant right side up.

If two people were to meet in person, they could speak using flowers rather than words. A single blossom extended with the right hand meant yes; with the left, no.

The meanings that the Victorians ascribed to certain flowers resist twenty-first-century interpretive strategies. A mignonette meant "Your qualities surpass your charms"; flowering reed equaled "Confide in heaven"; and eglantine, or sweet briar, asserted "Poetry, I wound to heal." "Death is preferable to a loss of virtue" declared a dead white rose.

Like the word *cleave*, which can mean either "to cling" or "to cut," a petunia could be read in two ways that might be seen as conflicting: either "resentment or anger" or "your presence soothes me."

Pity the poor cowslip, which bends under the burden of so many meanings: "rusticity, winning grace, healing, youth, and pensiveness."

Pity the poor recipient of the cowslip!

U

Ursinia [gentleness]

In February 2016 I went into the hospital for a routine operation that quickly became complicated, and I nearly bled to death. For Christmas that year, A gave me a collection of Jorie Graham's poems. *Fast*. The speaker in one, "Prying," has just awoken from surgery, a circumstance she describes as being on "the other side." In her room, she sees "cut flowers still in their paper stapled up. Undelivered."

Undelivered: that one-word sentence is haunting in its indeterminacy. How can a bouquet of flowers simultaneously be sitting in the speaker's hospital room and also be "undelivered"? What—or who—is undelivered here? There's someone else in the room, and that person says, "you get a little extra life to live now—here—can you still live it."

The poem ends there, not with a question mark but a period. An astonishment.

V

Venus flytrap [caught at last]

In Prague, the man I've been dating for a while is starting to get on my nerves. It's July 2003, and we are only one city into a tour of European capitals that he has thoughtfully arranged and paid for. Trying to check into our hotel in Vienna, he tests out his college German on the desk clerk. My boyfriend is a corporate lawyer, a tax specialist, who likes for people to know that he majored in philosophy at a prestigious Quaker school. The clerk answers him in English. The weather in Vienna is unusually hot, even for July. We go to a museum where the guards reproach me for the size of my handbag, and I am ridiculously offended by this. In the evening, we have tickets for a concert at the Schonbrunn Palace. The audience seems to consist entirely of Japanese tourists who have been disgorged from buses, and us. The orangerie where the concert is held is sweltering, like the greenhouse it was meant to be, and after the second or third Strauss waltz, they start to sound exactly alike. Which is probably the point of Strauss waltzes. I am barely holding it together when a slightly pudgy ballerina appears onstage to perform a solo to the tune of a Strauss waltz. *What the fuck?* I hiss to my boyfriend, who shushes me. After it's over, the Japanese tourists and my boyfriend give the orchestra and the ballerina a standing ovation. My boyfriend informs me that I am a snob for staying in my seat. I reply in a way that does not, shall we say, *open up* the conversation.

This quarrel is not the end of us.

The next morning, we rise early and take turns in the shower. I put on a skirt and a cotton shirt, then spend a few minutes absorbed in the task of transferring my things into a bag that's likely to pass muster with museum guards. When I look up, I realize that my boyfriend has decided not to put on his usual khakis and polo shirt but a pair of white satin basketball shorts and a wife-beater.

My eyebrows shoot up.

What? he asks, defensively. *It's too hot for long pants.*

The next thing I know, I am on the phone with American Airlines. To change my ticket and fly back to Philadelphia today, by myself, will cost $250.

"Do you take American Express?" I ask.

W

White hollyhock [female ambition]

April in London is cherry blossom season. Branches bend under the weight of blossoms, turning bus stops into impromptu bowers. The slightest breeze sweeps the petals into piles of confetti.

It's teatime now, and A and I are working on our laptops. He's on the couch, facing me, while I'm at my desk, facing the wall.

"What are you working on?" he asks.

"This weird abecedarian essay on the language of flowers." I don't bother to turn around.

"Oh?"

"Actually, I'm stuck on W."

"Withered delights," he says, instantly.

I turn around.

A is a medieval historian and a Brit who attended the University of Pennsylvania for one year back in the eighties as an exchange student. There (he tells me now) he witnessed what he has always thought of as a quaint American custom: a lover who wanted to break up would signal her or his intention by sending a bouquet of dead flowers. Hence the phrase "withered delights."

"That's a crock," I inform him.

So he texts a couple of friends from his Penn days. Amazingly, they back him up. Next, he noodles around on the Internet until he finds the website for a company that promises to send wilted roses (a "heart-wrenching arrangement that lets 'em know how you feel") anywhere in the country for $24.99 plus shipping.

The name of the website is ThePayback.com—which is not, I observe, the same as "Withered Delights." I turn back to my laptop, fingers poised for competitive googling.

"Don't do it," he warns me.

"Why not?"

"Because you don't know how to clear your browsing history."

This is true. Like backing up my hard drive or using the TV remote, it's something I prefer not to waste any brain space on.

"All right, give me a hint. What did *you* find?"

"Mature women with working holes."

X

Xeranthemum [argument]

I once dated a Scotsman whose last name sounded like a particular kind of fish. He had a foot fetish, which I kind of liked, and sweat that smelled of metal, which I did not. For New Year's Eve, I prepared a hot artichoke dip in a hand-thrown pottery dish and took it to a party at his house. Most of the guests were, like him, recreational bird watchers. They had a lot to say, none of it very interesting to me, about a phenomenon called the Christmas Bird Count. Hours later, when I went into the kitchen to say goodbye, I spotted my beautiful dish on the counter amid all the other detritus from the party—chip bags, salsa jars, plastic cups. The man I was dating offered to wash it out for me, but I said not to bother, I'd pick it up the next time I saw him.

I knew there would be no next time.

Ten years on, I remember the way that bowl felt in my hands, its smoothness and heft, its saturated, swirling greens and blues. It came from a gallery a couple of blocks from my house, so I could easily replace it, but I won't. The permanent loss of it feels like appropriate penance for a small act of cruelty toward a man whose last name I can't even remember. What *was* the fish it rhymed with? Salmon? Grayling? Trout?

Y
Yew [sorrow]

My friend P is what people sometimes call a "live wire"—a brilliant filmmaker with beauty and verve to burn. Also, a Tinder connoisseur. She swears she can tell, within five minutes of meeting someone, exactly why the two of them will eventually break up. At first I don't believe her. Then I do.

A lovely man—tall, gentle, distinguished; a psychiatrist nearly twenty years my senior—turns up for our second date bearing an enormous bouquet of yellow roses. It's his way of saying he's read my memoir, or at least the part at the very beginning where I describe how my father wooed my mother with yellow roses and a Tiffany diamond. My parents have been married nearly sixty years.

After our date, I rearrange the florist's bouquet, separating the roses from all the filler, which goes straight into the trash.

I *hate* baby's breath.

Z
Zephyr flower [love]

Critics talk about closure in terms that range from the *tactical* (Greek: "to order or arrange") to the *tactile* (Latin: "to touch"). They describe it as *hard* ("Reader, I married him") or *soft* ("So we beat on, boats against the current, borne back ceaselessly into the past"). Endings and closure are similar but not the same. An ending is a thing that happens—a door opens, or it closes; closure is the way one eventually comes to feel about that event—the longing I feel from time to time for the beautiful pottery dish I left behind as a false promise to return. And then there is *disappearance*, a word that resists all of our epistemological strategies. When someone disappears, without a *trace* (Latin: "path"), those who are left behind end up in a kind of limbo, that borderland of the imagination and of the heart.

"The schoolgirl who caught a cab to oblivion" blared a 2018 headline in the *Guardian*. Ruth Wilson was sixteen, "a good girl from a good family" living in a village in Surrey. One winter morning in 1995, she left her house on foot. Instead of going to school, she ran a couple of errands in the village then caught a cab to a scenic outlook atop a nearby hill. She hasn't been heard from since, and, despite scouring the area with cadaver-sniffing dogs, no one has ever been able to find her body.

A few years ago, a reporter named Martin Bright teamed up with a detective, thinking the two of them might solve this cold case. Was Ruth a runaway? Or was she kidnapped? Is there any chance, slim though it might be, that she's still alive? Ruth's "good family" declined to talk to the men, saying they'd moved on and didn't want to reopen old wounds. Her friends, now grown women, were more forthcoming. They told Bright that shortly before Ruth disappeared, two significant things happened: she broke up with her boyfriend, and she learned a family secret. Ruth had been raised by her father and stepmother after her mother's death when Ruth was a toddler. Ruth had always been told that her mother died in a tragic accident. Recently, she had learned that her mother had not broken her neck in a fall down some stairs; rather, she had hung herself.

The two-man team of reporter and detective never did figure out what happened to Ruth on the day she disappeared without a trace. If anything, they deepened the mystery by discovering one previously undisclosed fact. On the morning of her disappearance, one of Ruth's errands was to the local florist shop. There, she picked out a bouquet, paid for it, and requested delivery for two days hence.

To her stepmother.

What did it mean, I wonder? *A zephyr wind has come along and blown me out of your life, but I will love you forever, nonetheless?*

We would walk a million miles to see one of mum's smiles.
—Epitaph on a headstone at London's Highgate Cemetery

Irene, Goodnight

One morning in 1974, spring sunlight glinting off stale snow, my mother drove the family car into the side of a moving train.

The family car was a Travelall, an SUV prototype built by International Harvester, the tractor company. It was egg-yolk yellow with faux-wood paneling and an empty weight of just over two tons.

I was eleven. My parents were working long hours then—Dad at the helm of the family construction company, Mom as a public health nurse and cofounder of a struggling nonprofit for the prevention of child abuse and neglect. They leaned heavily on me for help with my younger brothers and sisters, ages ten, nine, six, and five. Some random memories from that year include getting my first period while on a weekend trip to Juneau with my grandmother and her buying me bullet-sized OB tampons from the airport gift shop. I had no idea where to put them. The whole family went to Disneyworld, where an old lady saw me shepherding my younger siblings into an ice cream parlor and praised me for being such a good mother. What she couldn't see: the insides of my middle sister's arms, bruises the size and shape of cat prints.

My mother's name is not Irene, like the woman in Lead Belly's song, who had a big urge to jump in the river and drown; it's Carol Ann, like the little girl in *Poltergeist*. She was born in Bronxville, New York, on July 10, 1936. When she was four months old, her parents—a Harvard-educated surgeon and his socialite wife—took a trip to England together. That year, and the most stylish way to cross the Atlantic was aboard the *Queen Mary*, with its white-tie dress code, fancy restaurants and cocktail bars, swimming pools and squash courts, grand ballroom and even a hospital. The surgeon and the socialite left both of their daughters—my toddler aunt and my infant mother—back in New York City, with friends. Baby Carol Ann cried inconsolably. The friends took her to a doctor who diagnosed a strangulated hernia and rushed her into surgery. Her parents heard the news via ship-to-shore radio.

To be injured or ill or otherwise in desperate need, and simultaneously to be separated from or abandoned by the people who ought to have loved her the most: this state has always been my mother's psychic home base. She can take any set of facts, no matter how disparate or stubborn, and patiently arrange and rearrange them until they fit this pattern of loss plus abandonment. It is both a cry for help and, weirdly, the help itself.

Like radio static in the brain. That's the phrase psychologists use to describe "high place phenomenon": the impulse to jump off a cliff, to jerk the steering wheel into the bridge's guardrail or oncoming traffic, to open the plane's emergency hatch at thirty thousand feet. The more you live inside your head, the more susceptible you are to high place phenomenon, which, according to scientists, afflicts roughly 50 percent of the general population and 100 percent of writers. A psychologist named April Smith describes it this way: "It could be the case that when you're up somewhere high, your brain is basically sending an alarm signal—you know, be careful. And that could actually lead you to take a step back, or notice your surroundings. Then that more deliberative process kind of kicks in and you start to think, *Why did I just take a step back? I'm totally fine. There's no reason for me to be afraid. Oh, I must have wanted to jump.*

When we were kids, my brothers and sisters and I took horseback riding lessons every Saturday morning. Our middle sister, the one with the bruises on her arms, turned out to be a fearless rider who won lots of ribbons and broke more than a few bones. During one of our Saturday lessons—trot, stop, canter, stop, turn, stop and repeat—our instructor, Janice, must have sensed reluctance in the set of my shoulders. *Looks to me like you'd rather be anywhere but here right now,* she observed. *Maybe next week you should just stay home and play with your dolls?* She meant to be snarky, but I thought this sounded like an excellent plan. When the person in charge of paying for our weekly riding lessons (Grandma) learned of it, though, there was a bit of a scene. The following week, I was forced back into the ring, where Janice apologized through gritted teeth.

The year of the accident would have been the first when all five of us kids were enrolled in public school. It would also have been the year that Carol Ann returned to working full-time. She hired an elderly woman to do some light housecleaning and to be there when we got home from school. We called her "Grandma Fowler" to her face, "Fowler" behind her back. She spent most of her time in the recliner in the living room watching what she called "so-poppers" on TV. I was in college before I realized they were actually soap operas.

At work, Carol Ann administered vaccines and STD tests, and she visited new mothers at home. The home visits were usually the best part of her job, except for the times when she got bit by dogs. The worst part was going into dive bars like The Hideaway and Tommy's Elbow Room, wearing her blue polyester nurse's uniform and penny loafers, to notify the partner of someone who'd been diagnosed with gonorrhea.

On the day of the accident, Carol Ann spent too long with the first new mother on her list, which meant she was running behind for her appointment with the second. To get from one end of town to the other in a hurry, she cut through the railroad industrial area—a wasteland of low-slung cinderblock buildings, orphaned train cars, tie cranes, and steel tracks. Anywhere else in America, it would be off limits to vehicular traffic. In Fairbanks, Alaska, people tend to take a libertarian attitude toward ordinary danger. That railroad crossings might be marked only by stop signs—not flashing lights or electronic gates—would not have struck anyone as untoward back then.

On my father's rare weekends off, we'd load up the Travelall with tents and sleeping bags and the makings for s'mores, and we'd all go camping on a gravel bar in the Salcha River, or somewhere in Denali Park, or alongside Liberty Falls in the Wrangell–St. Elias Mountains. The FM radio stations petered out within a few miles of town, leaving only KJNP, "King Jesus North Pole." We entertained ourselves by singing: "Michael, Row the Boat Ashore," "My Darling Clementine," "Amazing Grace," "A Hundred Bottles of Beer on the Wall" (*that* got us down the road!), and "Goodnight, Irene."

The day before the accident, my mother moved us from a three-bedroom house on Farmers Loop, in the country, to a five-bedroom house on the outskirts of town. The sale of our old house and the purchase of our new one coincided (collided?) with our father's sojourn in the Arctic, running a Cat train from one job site to another. So there she was, on the morning of the accident, a thirty-seven-year-old woman with five children under the age of twelve, trying to hold down a full-time job while simultaneously moving us all into a new house, without help from her husband. It was a lot to manage. Was it too much? Sometimes I wonder.

At a writers' conference a while back, I heard my friend Brock Clarke read from the opening of his novel-in-progress, *Who Are You, Calvin Bledsoe?* Calvin is an orphan, we learn, having lost his father a long time ago, his mother—a salt-of-the-earth type and Methodist minister—more recently. Somehow the family car, with her in it, had ended up on the train tracks in the path of an oncoming you-know-what. The reading shook me. Afterward, I asked Brock how to interpret the death of Calvin's mother. Was it an accident or suicide? "I haven't figured that out yet," he said.

I'm fifty-eight now, twenty years older than my mother at the time of the accident. I think of this decade as my desert of not-knowing—an endless stretch of negative capability without a glimmer of horizon or even the compensatory gift of creativity. I feel both stupider and more empathic, and I find some comfort in William James, who asks, in "What Makes a Life Significant," "If we cannot gain much positive insight into one another, cannot we at least use our sense of our blindness to make us more cautious in going over the dark places?"

When I was eleven, playing with dolls was my favorite thing to do, and my favorite dolls were based on *Little Women* by Louisa May Alcott. Each doll cost about fifty dollars, which was a lot of money for my family back then. I collected them at the rate of one or two a year—one for my birthday or Christmas, another as a reward for earning all A's on my report card. Getting a new one was kind of a big deal. My mother would telephone FAO Schwartz in New York City to place the order, then I would have to wait a month or longer for the enormous Wedgwood-blue box to appear in the mail. I collected the four sisters first—Beth (the one who dies of Scarlet Fever), Amy (the flighty one), Meg (the steady one), and Jo (the aspiring writer). By April 1974 the only ones I lacked were Laurie, the neighbor boy who falls in love with Jo but marries Amy, and Marmee.

My younger siblings were not allowed to touch my dolls, let alone to play with them. When I wanted to play with them, I set them up in a corner of the living room, where everyone could watch me, then positioned them to act out all of my favorite scenes. Which was really just one scene: "The Valley of the Shadow."

Jo: "More than anyone else in the world, Beth, I used to think I couldn't let you go; but I'm learning to feel that I don't lose you; that you'll be more to me than ever, and death can't part us, though it seems to."

Beth: "I know it cannot, and I don't fear it any longer, for I'm sure I shall be your Beth still, to love and help you more than ever."

My mother in her thirties suffered from Ménière's disease, an inner-ear disorder that presents as vertigo. The attacks came on suddenly, like bad weather, lasted twenty or thirty minutes, then passed just as quickly. My mother referred to this ailment familiarly, like an old friend who'd just stopped in for tea: "I'm unable to do anything right now, I've got my Ménière's." This might explain why, in my mind, Ménière's got tangled up with those other *m* words: *menses, menstruation, menopause. Mother.*

Between her job and our ballet lessons, riding lessons, piano lessons, French lessons, sewing lessons, and hockey practice, my mother spent half her waking hours behind the wheel of the yellow Travelall. She filed her nails at red lights and used the rearview mirror to apply lipstick. The five of us kids and two or three extras would bounce around in the back seats, screaming and pinching and singing and fighting, untethered as a bunch of electrons. One time, when my youngest sister was three or four months old, Mom herded us all into the car then drove ten miles before realizing that Rebecca was still strapped in her car seat, sitting in the driveway. A few weeks after we adopted the four-year-old orphan who became my youngest brother, my whole family went to Kentucky Fried Chicken to celebrate. An hour or so later, the Travelall pulled into the driveway and Mom counted us into the house: one-two-three-four-*oh shit*. Careening back into the KFC parking lot on two wheels, she saw Ben's tear-stained face peering out of the restaurant's frost-rimed front door. "As long as I live, I'll never forget the way he looked at me," she used to say, "as if he'd been abandoned all over again."

Since her diagnosis, she has forgotten a lot of things, including the look on Ben's face.

It's 1974 again, and I'm riding in the rear-facing pop-up seat of the green Plymouth station wagon that replaced the Travelall. Red lights blossom in the rear window. "*Mahhhhm!*" She curses, glides to the shoulder, says, "Tell your father about this and I'll knock you into next Sunday." That was how things usually played out when the police stopped her for speeding. Then, this one time, she just kept on driving. In my memory, she drove the length of College Road—three or four miles—with what must have looked like a VIP police escort. When she finally pulled into the parking lot of the ballet studio, where I was due for my lesson, an officer materialized at her rolled-down window. I don't remember what he said, or what my mother said in reply, only the tone of their voices. His, incredulous; hers, imperious. My mother had a capacity for imperiousness in the face of authority. In fact, she had a capacity for imperiousness in the face of just about anything. A person could truthfully say that imperiousness was my mother's resting state. She might have looked in her nurse's uniform like a factory worker or harried housewife, but beneath that disguise, she was the daughter of a Harvard-educated surgeon and his socialite wife—*quality* people, the kind of people who left their children in New York while they traveled to England on the *Queen Mary*, the kind of people who outsourced the work of raising their children to camp counselors and dorm mothers. She herself was a proud alumna of the Emma Willard School for Girls in Troy, New York, and Columbia-Presbyterian School of Nursing in New York City. The diamond solitaire on her left hand originated at Tiffany's on Fifth Avenue. Fifth Avenue in *New York City*, Officer. New York City, as in the East Coast of the Lower 48. *Just in case you've never heard of it.* That particular ticket turned out to be extra expensive, as it included not just speeding but also failure to obey the direct order of a police officer.

Anger was a sin in our household. If anyone talked back or yelled or slammed a door, they were punished. I should rephrase that: When *I* talked back, yelled, or slammed a door, my mother punished me. She preferred the word *discipline* or, better, *consequences*. The consequences for slamming a door were being forced to close it quietly ten times while suppressing tears of impotent rage.

Marmee: "I am angry nearly every day of my life, Jo; but I have learned not to show it; and I still hope to learn not to feel it, though it may take me another forty years to do so."

My father turned forty in November of 1974. He spent most of that spring in the Bush, leading a Cat train across the Arctic. Then, and now, the only way to move heavy equipment—bulldozers, backhoes, scrapers—between job sites was to drive it in winter over frozen tundra. Leading a Cat train was cold, dirty, dull, arduous work. Every day was long, and at the end of it, the only pleasure to be had was that of climbing down out of the cab of the D-10 and frying a steak on the engine manifold. Afterward, the men slept under the stars, with northern lights for their blankets. Whenever my father returned from running weeks or even months on a Cat train, it would be with his beard grown out, his eyes red-rimmed with exhaustion. His Carhartt insulated coveralls would be so stiff with grease and grime, they could stand up all by themselves. The only way to send word of my mother's accident was via "Trapline Chatter," a public message service of KJNP radio. He received it two days later, when the Cat train pulled into a village that happened to have a radio tower.

"It must be very disagreeable to sleep in a tent, and eat all sorts of bad-tasting things, and drink out of a tin mug," sighed Amy.

*"When will he come home, Marmee?" asked Beth, with a little quiver
in her voice.*

*"Not for many months, dear, unless he is sick. He will stay and do his
work faithfully as long as he can, and we won't ask for him back a minute
sooner than he can be spared."*

Luckily (or not) for my mother, the train she struck was only moving
freight in the yard. It was going very slowly. She broke a lot of bones
in the accident—an arm, a collarbone, her pelvis. She spent a few days
in the hospital, then a few weeks propped in the recliner in the living
room, surrounded by moving boxes. Fowler moved in to help during
the day. Mom's casts were heavy and hot, and they itched. At night, my
brother Sam and I took turns sleeping on a mattress beside her chair.
Several times, she'd wake us with her moans, needing pain medicine or
a bedpan. Worse was when she woke us with her screams, reliving an
accident she could not recall in her conscious hours.

*When they got up on Saturday morning, there was no fire in the kitchen,
no breakfast in the dining room, and no mother anywhere to be seen.*

"Mercy on us, what has happened?" cried Jo, staring about her in dismay.

*Meg ran upstairs, and soon came back again, looking relieved, but
rather bewildered, and a little ashamed.*

*"Mother isn't sick, only very tired, and she says she is going to stay quietly
in her room all day, and let us do the best we can. It's a very queer thing
for her to do, she doesn't act a bit like herself; but she says it has been a
hard week for her, so we mustn't grumble, but take care of ourselves."*

In the years after the accident, Mom's episodes of Ménière's became
less frequent, then faded away altogether. The Resource Center for
Parents and Children became a thriving enterprise, and she quit nursing to become an advocate for children. Around the time I left for college, she went back to graduate school, earning a degree in counseling.
I think of this as her Lanz nightgown and Birkenstock sandal phase.
She started to work as a family therapist and a consultant to the court

system in child welfare cases when it was contemplating terminating or restoring parental rights. She became a founding member and, later, chair of the Alaska Children's Trust. More than once, a family dinner was interrupted by a phone call from the governor, who wanted her opinion about one thing or another. Plaques multiplied on her office wall, awards and citations for her tireless efforts on behalf of children and families. She'd become the go-to person in the community for everything child-related: how to manage blended families, how to talk to children about divorce, how to handle an angry adolescent. (Her mantra was "Never give up on a child.") She testified in court about whether parental rights ought to be terminated or restored. (She was almost always on the side of restoring them.) When the largest day care center in town was struck by an epidemic of biting, she was called in to consult. (Her advice: Stop giving the victims so much attention. It worked.) The building that houses Head Start in Fairbanks is now named the Carol H. Brice Center in her honor. In family photographs, she is fit and radiant, secure in her sense of herself as a problem-solver extraordinaire.

My father's company took off at roughly the same time as Mom's career; it flourished and was eventually purchased for a princely sum by one of Alaska's wealthy Native corporations. Now he and Mom split their time between a home in Fairbanks, a vacation cabin in McCarthy (the Jackson Hole of Alaska), another place on the Salcha River, and a Key West condo that belongs to one of Mom's cousins.

My parents have never been drinkers. Dad swore off alcohol in high school, after three of his friends were killed in a drunk-driving accident. He can be goaded into a glass of Bailey's Irish Cream at Christmas but, really, it's the sweetness he likes, not the booze. Mom went through a phase where she drank a glass of white zin every night but gave it up when she felt it was becoming a habit—that she was looking forward to it too much.

The French phrase for the sudden impulse to do oneself in is called *l'appel du vide*: the call of the void, which sounds more alluring than high place phenomenon.

In the early 2000s, Mom's office was in the former music room of our house, and Dad's was in a building a few miles away, in a newer industrial area. On days when Mom didn't have many appointments, the two of them would meet for lunch. Sometimes they went out to eat, but usually Mom just fixed a couple of meat and cheese sandwiches for them to eat at Dad's office. One April day in 2006, she followed her usual routine, first backing her Volvo sedan out of the garage, then taking Valley Hi Drive to Ballaine Road, turning right onto Farmers Loop, which becomes University Avenue. After half a mile or so, she took a left onto the Johansen Expressway, vaulted over the old railroad industrial area, and exited onto Peger Road. From there, it was pretty much a straight shot for a couple of miles to the door of Dad's office. She'd made this drive, conservatively speaking, about a thousand times. This time was different. She was on Peger Road, not far from the site of her old accident with the train, when everything went dark. She didn't pass out, exactly—she just lost her bearings completely. Later, she told me it felt as if she'd suddenly driven into a tunnel. She didn't know where in the world she was, or what she was meant to be doing. She knew she was behind the wheel of a car, but not whose car it was. Her first impulse was to hit the brakes, but she was sensible enough not to do that. Instead, she just kept driving, trusting that the road would eventually carry her back to herself. Which it did.

The day after the accident with the train, a police officer paid a call on my mother. She was still in the hospital then. He asked her to tell him how it was that she had failed utterly to see a slow-moving freight train that was right in front of her. *The sun was in my eyes,* she said. Had this been her first offense, the officer said, he would have been able to let her off with just a warning. As it was, he was forced to write her a ticket for failing to stop at a railroad crossing.

In June or July, a few weeks after Mom moved out of the La-Z-Boy in the living room and Fowler moved back into her double-wide trailer, and most of the moving boxes had been unpacked, a big blue box arrived in the mail. The doll that emerged from layers of tissue paper wore a maroon dress with a white apron over it and a voile cap on her head. Marmee. It was my mother's way of saying thank you.

She got behind the wheel for the last time one spring day in 2017. I was two thousand miles from home, in my office on the campus where I teach, when my youngest sister called. Apparently, Dad had woken up that morning with a bee in his bonnet. He wanted to take his camper van to the mechanic's. He wanted to leave right away. Without waiting for one of my siblings to become available, he asked Mom to follow him into town in the Honda Pilot. *Sure*, Mom said. *I can do that.*

And she did. For about three miles. At a stoplight on Peger Road, he checked the rearview mirror. No Honda Pilot.

Oh shit, I said to my sister. *Shit, shit, shit.*

How long till we call the police? my sister asked. Underneath that question was another question: What will happen to Dad if we involve the police?

Since her dementia diagnosis in late 2006, my formerly fastidious mother has gotten fat. She gets up in the middle of the night to eat whatever she can lay her hands on: uncooked English muffins, jam, bologna, ice cream, cookies, leftover pasta, frozen Hot Pockets. She and my father still spend a few months a year in Florida, where she spends her mornings picking up seashells. If someone hands her a bucket or a plastic bag, she uses that. If not, she uses the pockets of her elastic-waist shorts, filling them until they fall down around her ankles. She is unflustered by this, simply resting a hand on my shoulder while I kneel in the sand to pull them back up. She spends her afternoons sitting at a little table on the balcony of the condominium, sorting and washing her shells, talking to them and fussing over them as if they are her children.

Every morning, regardless of whether she's in Fairbanks or McCarthy or Key West, she wakes up early in the morning, puts on her bathrobe, fixes a cup of black coffee, then goes back into her bedroom for an hour or more. She opens the closets and drawers and studies their contents, runs her hands over all of her clothes and jewelry and scarves, picks up her hairbrush and puts it back down, behaving for all the world as if the touch of her own things can conjure her own self.

Half an hour after she went missing in the Pilot, Dad got a call from the secretary at St. Matthew's Episcopal Church on First Avenue. He and my mother have been parishioners for half a century. Apparently, Mom had materialized at the door to the church office and greeted the secretary by name. *Hi, Hillary. I've been running errands all morning, and I'm plumb exhausted. Is it OK if I rest here awhile?*

The thing I have been asking myself, of course, is whether Mom drove the Travelall into the side of a moving train by accident or on purpose. Or is that even the right question, assuming as it does that a bright line can be drawn between our conscious and subconscious actions? I've withheld until now a strong piece of evidence that tilts toward the accidental: Mom wasn't alone in the Travelall that morning. A fellow nurse was in the passenger seat, and she, too, suffered serious injuries. It's not hard to imagine my mother contemplating suicide; it's nearly impossible to imagine her acting on those impulses if doing so meant harming someone else as well. And yet. I've felt it, too, when my kids were strapped behind me in their car seats and the thruway stretched out in front of me. The siren call of the swerve.

When I got tired of acting out scenes from *Little Women* (which seems unbearably treacly to me now), I liked to dress my dolls in one another's clothes—Jo in Amy's more frivolous yellow dress, Amy in Meg's more somber purple-and-white gingham. For reasons I can't now explain, the only dolls I never undressed were Laurie and Marmee. This wasn't out of a sense of propriety—deference to Laurie's gender and

Marmee's age—but, I think, out of a sense that their identities were fixed, immutable in some way the sisters' were not. Was it possible, I wondered, to temper Jo's brashness by dressing her in Beth's demure pink frock? What if Jo were the one dying of scarlet fever instead of Beth? You realize, right, that the bruises on the inside of my sister's arm could not have been explained away by a fall from a horse? After playing with my dolls in this way, I'd wash each tiny item of clothing in cold water and Woolite, then lay them out to dry on a towel beside the radiator. Afterward, I'd iron them, then put them back on their rightful owner. I could kill a whole afternoon in this way. My sister never told anyone how often, and how badly, I hurt her.

The title of Dr. April Smith's article about high place phenomenon is "An Urge to Jump Affirms the Will to Live." The gist of it is that we would not fear the void if we did not love life even more. The impulse to leap or to swerve or to drive into the side of a moving train is like our own evolutionary warning system, reminding us that we humans were never meant to travel at high (or even low) speed inside two-ton steel cages, or to fly at thirty-three thousand feet inside steel bullets, or to strap a bungee cord to our ankle and leap into a gorge.

A few months ago, I drove from my home in upstate New York to Boston, to visit one of my daughters. I offered my friend Jane a lift to *her* daughter's home in Hartford, Connecticut. The most direct route was to travel due east on the New York State Thruway, which turns at the state border into the Massachusetts Turnpike. A few miles east of Albany, though, I missed a crucial turn and headed due south, on I-87 toward New York City. I didn't realize my error until I'd driven us hours out of our way, onto the Tappan Zee Bridge in Westchester County. How did I manage this? By being so wrapped up in conversation with my friend that I paid no attention to my surroundings.

When my father was in the Bush for long stretches, he wrote me letters. Recently, I came across one that was posted from Livengood (which looks, on the page, as if it ought to be pronounced "livin' good," though, in fact, the *i* is long, as in *enliven*).

Dear Jennifer,
Daddy was pleased with the papers you brought home from school. He believes that you can do even better if you would stop and think before you answer some of the questions.
I think you are getting to be a very lovely young girl. Daddy expects you to be a lot of help to Mother while he is gone.
Love, Dad
P.S. Give all my love to your Mother.

The letter is dated June 1969. I was six years old.

Just Magic

I am a divorced woman with twenty-eight dollars in my checking account and a mink coat in my closet. I've never worn the mink, probably never will. The story of how I came to own it begins a long time ago, and, yes, I am going to tell it here. In 1985, after graduating from college, I returned home and took what I thought would be a stopgap job as a receptionist on my hometown newspaper. The previous four years had been intellectually demoralizing and socially perplexing. My honors thesis psychoanalyzing the voices in T. S. Eliot's *Waste Land* had barely passed muster with the graybeards in the Smith College English Department. Their critiques of it—"Considering the fact that this thesis represents a semester's work on the part of the student, I'm sorry to say that it is very unsatisfactory," wrote one—flayed me. After graduation, I packed my trunk and fled. Now that a graduate program in literature was off the table, it wasn't clear what my next move would be. Law school at the lowest-ranked program to which I'd applied, and the only one that accepted me, was a possibility, but not an alluring one. I grew up in a place where winter temperatures often dipped below minus fifty, and I was a middle-of-the-pack ski racer in high school, so I'd been cold a number of times in my life, but the world Outside (as we Alaskans called the Lower 48) was metaphorically cold in a way I'd never experienced. It was the coldness of not fitting in—of never having the right shoes or the right haircut or the right words at mixers with boys from Dartmouth or Williams or West Point. I didn't know how to swing dance or tailgate, and I never in four years found my tribe—which I realize now was probably less a function of my personal failings than simple bad luck.

Anyway, I returned home, moved back into my childhood bedroom, raided my mother's closet for work clothes, and poured myself into cut-throat Scrabble tournaments with my parents. I got a puppy, an Australian shepherd named Zach, which was probably the first sign that I wasn't going anywhere come fall. No one was more surprised than me to discover, a few weeks in, that I actually liked the drama of the newsroom and also the cast of characters it attracted: the bald, phlegmatic city editor who presided over everything in short sleeves and a tie that he yanked off as soon as he hit the threshold at the end of the day; the platinum blonde tough-as-nails city reporter; the acne-scarred, Camaro-driving graphic designer destined to die young of AIDS; the sports guys who turned up around 4:00 p.m. and worked until the wee hours, subsisting, as far as I could tell, on Coke and testosterone; the features staff, mostly women, who cracked wise all day long behind the windows of their glassed-in suite. I quickly developed a crush on a guy my age who'd earned a journalism degree from an Oregon college and who was, partly on account of that journalism degree and partly on account his Y chromosome, already working as a reporter, while I was making lists of marriages, divorces, zoning permits, and DUIs.

What did my colleagues make of me? In those days (as now), I was nothing special to look at: brown hair, blue eyes, average build. My favorite outfit was a shapeless black jumper I'd bought at Urban Outfitters in Cambridge. I was then (as now) paralyzed by shyness, which is—a wise person once told me—just self-consciousness in its pathological form. Possibly people mistook my shyness for standoffishness. I said little about myself, so I shouldn't have been surprised when my colleagues turned out to know nothing about me. Six months or so into my time there, the blonde city reporter pulled me aside to fill me in on a piece of juicy gossip: the publisher's secretary was about to retire after roughly half a century on the job, and if I played my cards right, I might be able to move into *her* job. A few weeks after that, I bumped into one of the guys from the copy desk when I was out for brunch with a friend. Tom was a decade or so older than me, handsome and self-assured (and soon to be fired by the publisher for allowing his hair to grow long enough to touch his shirt collar), and I was generally tongue-tied in his presence. The waitress brought me a hurricane glass holding a daiquiri with whipped cream, fresh strawberries, and two red plastic straws. "He sent it," she said. When I went over to his table to thank him, he said, "I told her to bring you the sluttiest drink on the menu." He seemed to think this was hilarious. I didn't get it.

The newspaper job came about as a result of my grandmother's friendship with the managing editor. He was younger than she was—closer to my parents' age, maybe a little younger. Bobbing in the sea of uninteresting middle age. He was divorced and far-sighted, possessed of Coke-bottle glasses and a deceptively shambling gait. K (I'll call him) was a demanding task master who would, in a couple of years, resign his post to become a taxi driver in Seattle. Go figure. The newspaper went to press between 11:00 a.m. and noon every day. By the time the staff returned from lunch, K had read every story and every headline, had analyzed every editing and design decision, and had rendered his judgments—positive as well as negative—in the form of underlining, circling, arrows, and marginalia, all in thick red ink. He often supplemented these markups with typed notes stapled to the appropriate pages. Sometimes he placed these critiques in people's mailboxes himself; other times, he left the task for me. The last thing in the world I wanted was to become secretary to the publisher who'd just fired Tom for letting his hair grow half an inch longer than regulation. What I wanted most in the world was to someday be on the receiving end of one of K's typed messages telling me I'd done a good job.

One winter day about a year before K's surprise resignation, I was standing at the narrow table behind my desk, sorting through newspapers and discarding ones from the previous print run. It was shortly after noon, and nearly everyone on the staff was at lunch already. K came out of his glass-walled office and stood beside me, reading the copies that were, true to the cliché, still warm from the press. This was not an unusual occurrence. I kept quiet so as not to distract him. One of the papers he was reading was open—or maybe he'd opened it—to a full-page ad for Gerald Victor Furs. The women in the ad wore a variety of colors and styles, including stoles, jackets, and full-length coats. They were hand drawn in the style of Simplicity patterns or the J. Peterman catalog. The look was retro in a way that seemed more dated than chic.

"I'm sorry, what did you say?" K was soft-spoken at the best of times, and I didn't think I'd heard him properly.

"I said, could you ever imagine yourself in one of these?" he said, pointing to one of the drawings.

"Me? No way, I would never wear a fur coat." And that was the end of that.

Whatever *that* was.

(To be clear, my life since then has taught me few lessons more important than this: sometimes people speak unguardedly. Words sometimes get cut off from their intended meaning. While it's true that some people are intentionally provocative, even cruel, more often they are simply careless. They say things that make them writhe with shame in their beds at two o'clock in the morning. Did K mean what I thought he meant by asking me whether I'd ever wear a fur like one of the ones in the Gerald Victor ad? The more years that go by, the less sure I am. Journalism is a field that attracts inquisitive people. Maybe all K was interested in was sussing out the kind of woman I was. Perhaps we all appear to others as more of a cipher than to ourselves.)

◆ ◆ ◆

Linda: "Well my first was a Conservative and my second is a Communist."
Fabrice: "Just as I guessed. Your first is rich and your second poor."
Linda: "How can you tell?"
Fabrice: "The fur coat. Though it is a hideous color still it usually betokens a rich husband somewhere."
       —Nancy Mitford, *Love in a Cold Climate*

♦ ♦ ♦

The story of K and me doesn't have anything to do with the gorgeous mink that currently hangs in my closet, but it *is* the story of the first time in my life that fur got linked to anything but utility. What I am doing here is working out a handful of questions about fashion and pop culture, about the politics of place, of power relations between the sexes, and—perhaps—my desire never to feel cold again. What I am *not* doing here is exploring the ethics of wearing fur. It's not that I'm uninterested or even ambivalent. Truthfully, it's one of the few subjects on which I'm *not* ambivalent. Because I was born and raised in the Far North, I know and like many people who make their living as trappers. They eschew steel-jawed traps in favor of snares, and they check them regularly. They kill quickly and cleanly, and they use every part of the animal: meat, hide, and fur. Not for anything would I cast aspersions on these people, who live in (what I think of as) right balance with the natural world.

As for myself, I could never hunt or trap a living thing, and I'm even squeamish about fishing. I stay away from fabrics with hunting themes—camouflage as well as animal prints—though I do wear leather boots, and I once owned, quite happily, a suede jacket. The closest thing to a phobia that I have is a weird aversion even to thinking about interior scaffolding. I turn faint at the sound of cracking knuckles, and I once passed out when confronted with an X-ray of one of my daughter's broken bones. The older and more health conscious I get, and the more I read about the ecological horrors we've visited upon ourselves, the more I tend toward vegetarianism, especially when I'm cooking for myself at home. The chances of my buying or, heaven forfend, commissioning a new fur coat are about as remote as the chances of my voting for Ivanka Trump.

And yet. I am a person who feels the cold like the princess feels her pea. Joining the cross-country ski team way back when was partly an act of rebellion against my mother, who thought my time would be better spent on ballet or the violin. It was an act of rebellion that cost me dearly and also literally in terms of flesh. The cutoff temperature for racing, which we did in skimpy Lycra one-pieces, was thirty below zero. The cutoff for *practicing* was fifty below. At that temperature, Coach Carlson had us run up Ester Dome (elev. 2,364 feet) to take advantage of the temperature inversion. The fact that I have on several occasions frostbitten nearly all of my toes and fingers, the tips of both ears, and (I strongly suspect but could not possibly confirm) my bottom—repository of most of the ten extra pounds that coach often compared to a sack of potatoes—means that to this day, I get cold faster and stay cold longer than most people. The older I get, the less stoic I feel on upstate New York days when the temperature can be measured in single digits and the wind in double digits. "You're from Alaska, how can you be cold?" my friends ask, incredulously, witlessly, as if my shivering puts the lie to my origin story. What I want to say to them is this: being from Alaska means, if anything, being less tolerant and more frightened of the cold than other people. It means I am more attuned to the signs of frostbite and hypothermia than others, and therefore more adept at seeking out sources of warmth. One of the best sources, of course, is fur.

The story of the mink in my closet goes back even farther, though—maybe to the fall of 1967, when my parents put most of their belongings into storage and packed just enough clothes to get their burgeoning family—with three children under the age of four—through several months in what was called the Bush. Our second stop, after Noorvik, was Wainwright, another Inupiat village, this one on the northernmost coast of Alaska. At five hundred souls, Wainwright is now the third-largest village in the North Slope Borough, but it was even smaller back then. My father's company was building a new runway, and my mother tagged along with us kids partly to cook for the crew, partly to keep us all under one roof and to avoid paying rent in Fairbanks. Before leaving town for what they expected to be an indefinite period, they put everything they owned except a few items of clothing in storage. On our first day in Wainwright, three elderly Inupiat women walked into the tiny house that we were renting. They didn't knock first, and they didn't say anything by way of greeting. They simply entered, then took seats alongside each other on a bench against a wall, watching us white people from the big city as if we were a nature documentary. Roseanna, Nannie, and Mae were their names. My mother was juggling a lot, what with cooking meals and doing laundry for the crew, cleaning up after the three of us, and washing out my brother's and sister's cloth diapers. Sam was old enough for toilet training but had resisted it. After a few days of silent observation, the old women indicated to my mother that they would like to take over the Sam project. They stripped him from the waist down and let him run around half-naked, all the while keeping a close eye on him. Whenever he seemed likely to do something, one of them would rise swiftly from the bench, grab him under the arms, and plunk him down on the toilet.

It worked. With Sam's toilet training accomplished, the elders turned to the project of keeping us warm. A few months earlier, when we were in Noorvik (pop. 600), the warehouse where my parents had left all of their furniture and wedding gifts, and our out-of-season clothes, had burned to the ground. We turned up in Wainwright in September with little more than the clothes on our backs: in the case of us kids, that meant flimsy windbreakers and Keds. The Inupiat ladies gave my mother a list of supplies they needed from town, and Mom sent it to her sister-in-law in Fairbanks. When the fabrics, thread, and rickrack arrived, they shifted from their usual spot on the bench to the floor, each one sitting in her own parka with the hood thrown back, and with her legs scissored out in front of her. Then they went to work conjuring parkas for each of us kids and our mother. Unlike her, they didn't pin their paper patterns onto fabrics. Instead, they simply called one of us over every so often to check the size. Eventually, four corduroy parka shells emerged: garnet for our mother, styled with a drop waist and deep flounce; teal, sapphire, and aquamarine for us kids. Each one had deep slash pockets that extended from collarbone to hip, and the pockets, hems, and sleeves were trimmed with row upon row of brightly colored rickrack.

The next day, the ladies turned up with armloads of fur. They set to work lining the parkas with Arctic hare and wolverine; lastly, they stitched wolf ruffs onto the hoods. Next, they turned their attention to our feet, tracing our feet on sheets of paper then constructing caribou fur mukluks with sealskin soles that we pulled on and secured with sinew laces.

One of the reasons my parents took us to Noorvik and then Wainwright was to keep the family together during what would otherwise have been a long fatherless stretch. Another was that they were penniless. Despite the owner's assurances to the contrary, the storage facility that burned down was uninsured. There was no money to pay the ladies for our parkas. I don't know exactly what kind of arrangement my mother worked out with them, but I do know that every Christmas for years after she sent them an enormous package with yards of fabric, rickracks, zippers, needles, and thread.

My brother's parka and mine zipped up the front, but Hannah's pulled on over her head. Sometimes on the way in or out, she would get stuck for a few seconds, an experience that so undid her that she began howling every time the parka was produced. In a photograph from that time, though, we're all smiling for the camera held by our beautiful thirty-year-old mother, who made dozens of copies of the photo, pasting them into handmade Christmas cards she sent to friends and relatives on the East Coast.

In another photograph from that time, two men slide a walrus-skin boat over snow-pocked sand, toward a frothing Chukchi Sea. The man at the bow is my father, age thirty-two. He wears a Carhartt cap and jacket, no gloves. In just a moment, he will be up to his knees in freezing seawater. The man at the stern has on gloves and mukluks, a parka with a wolf ruff. He is Weir Negovanna, an Inupiaq elder and employee of my father's. Every few days, the men take the walrus-skin boat across a small inlet to Liz-3, a DEW line site with a radio phone, which they use to order supplies from Fairbanks. On the day the photograph was taken, my mother had left us with Nannie, Mae, and Roseanna—

Weir's wife—while she went with the men—"just for a change, for me to see other people."

"On the way back, a storm blew up from the Arctic Ocean," she told me. "The waves kept getting bigger until we couldn't see over them. When the fog lifted just enough to see the shoreline, your dad aimed straight for it. He rammed the umiak up on the beach and tried to find some rocks to anchor it. After a few minutes, we gave up and ran for the village."

After that scare, Mom said, she and my father stopped traveling together in the Far North. That way, if something happened to them, my brother and sister and I wouldn't be orphaned all at once.

What do I remember from that time? An old lady's hand brushing my hair from my forehead and crooning in a language I didn't understand but that soothed me nevertheless. The clink of coffee cups and grownup voices speaking in the dark, after the village generator had been turned off for the night. The smell of our kerosene lamps and stove. By September in Wainwright, it was so cold indoors, you could set a bowl of liquid Jell-O on the floor at night, and it would be solid by morning. I remember the feeling of fur worn next to the skin, soft and warm, like an opulent secret. The objective correlative of kindness.

◆ ◆ ◆

In Russia, even very plain women look beautiful in fur.
—Jasmine Bailey, a poet, in conversation

◆ ◆ ◆

More than twenty years on, I find myself on the Aleutian Island of Unalaska, driving an off-road dump truck for my father's company, which is blasting rock from the side of a mountain and dumping it into the bay. The aim is to increase the island's footprint so the Chinese-owned companies processing bottom fish aboard enormous ships can build facilities on land. It is 1989, the year the Cold War thaws and the Berlin Wall tumbles down. For the first time in decades, Soviet fishermen plying the international treaty waters of the North Atlantic are welcome to set foot on American soil, an invitation they eagerly accept, bobbing ashore in giant orange lifeboats. Once here, they set off alone or in pairs for the Alaska Commercial Co. store in Dutch Harbor. I stop in one day when the fishermen are there and see seven or eight of them crowded around the nail polish display, looking stunned and bedazzled. One of my compatriots, a guy who sometimes offers lifts to the fishermen, tells me about their crackpot theory: the shelves of the A.C. Store are stocked specially for their visits; normally, they are picked bone-clean, like the shelves back home.

To procure the American dollars they need in order to buy the electronics and batteries and nail polish they yearn for, the fishermen hit on the idea of selling their fur hats. These are extraordinary hats, towering concoctions of mink, marten, wolf, wolverine, bear, and beaver— as otherworldly and magical to me, perhaps, as that rack of OPI nail polish is to them. And they are extraordinarily cheap, ranging from $50 to $100. I want one desperately. Partly I want it as an artifact of this moment, when the first sign of geopolitical warming appeared on a remote, wind-scoured Alaskan island. Mainly I want it for the warmth and glamour. I think it will make me feel, for a fleeting moment, as confident and exuberant as Julie Christie in *Dr. Zhivago*.

Setting aside for now—maybe forever—the question of beauty, I have never been a woman to whom the word *glamour* attaches naturally. I rarely wear high heels or jewelry, and I gave up on dyeing my hair in my early forties. (On a recent trip to New York City, I stopped at the Macy's makeup counter to ask about the best lipstick to wear with gray hair and was told to seek the opinion of a hair colorist.) We are all of us different people at different stages in our lives, of course, but the difference between me in my twenties and me in my fifties is more marked than at any other period. I was shyer then, deeply inhibited, but also full of yearning—for clothes, adventure, beauty, romance. I found it easier to risk my life at the controls of a small plane than to talk to a stranger. Whenever I spied a fisherman on Unalaska with his thumb out, wanting nothing more than to trade his fur hat for enough American dollars to buy a few bottles of nail polish for his wife and daughters, I sped up. *For Pete's sake*, I want to shout at myself, across the distance of years: *What are you so afraid of? You're behind the wheel of a twenty-three-ton articulated dump truck. No one is going to embarrass you without your permission.*

In the late twentieth-century Far North version of America that I grew up in, yoga and vegetarianism were fringe pursuits. Only cranks questioned the use of animals in experiments, and nonconsensual sex inside of marriage was legal. A fur coat was a symbol of a certain kind of success, the kind enjoyed by corporate lawyers and cardiologists, men who took their women to the theater or the opera and then to dine at restaurants with heavy décor: wood paneling, chandeliers, gilt mirrors, weighty linens, and cigar smoke. The fur coat slipping off the shoulders of the woman and into the hands of the hat-check girl signified the economic power of the man, of course, as well as the beauty and desirability—even if both were long fled—of the woman. A man gave a diamond to the woman he wanted to marry, a fur to the one he wanted to sleep with. Sometimes the diamond and the fur went to the same woman. Sometimes not.

What about the woman in this image I carry around in my head? The mink she's half-wearing is a sign of the bargain she has sought or struck, or perhaps just acquiesced to. If she was ever self-sufficient, a woman of independent means, she is now a kept creature, someone whose value, like that of an animal in the zoo, is mostly ornamental and, frankly, sexual. In twentieth-century literature and pop culture, the wearing of fur was a sure sign that a female character was a villain. I'm thinking here of Cruella de Vil in *101 Dalmatians* (with her insatiable appetite not just for fur but for the fur of *puppies*) and the White Witch in *The Lion, the Witch, and the Wardrobe*, both of them the animating spirits of their respective works, and both of them dripping in furs they seem to have procured all by themselves, with no male provider in sight.

Irresistible digression 1: Researching this essay required me to re-watch Disney's *101 Dalmatians*, the ur-film about going to extremes in pursuit of fur. (Cruella de Vil: "I live for fur, I worship fur. After all, is there a woman in all this wretched world who doesn't?") I'm talking about the animated, not live action, version, of course, which I saw once a year when it cycled around to the Lacey Street Theater in Fairbanks. Now, watching on the small screen with the ability to pause and replay scenes, I see it doing two things at once—playing to the kids for laughs while nudging their parents in the ribs. Example A: When Cruella de Vil learns of Anita's impending marriage to Roger, she tries to head it off: "More good women have been lost to marriage than to war, famine, disease, and disaster." Example B: "Stop being such a sycophant!" Cruella screams at one of her hapless henchmen. "What kind of sycophant would you like me to be?" he replies.

Irresistible digression 2: I loved *The Lion, the Witch, and the Wardrobe* as a child, but when I tried reading it to my daughters, I found it didn't hold up. The Christian symbolism seemed overt and heavy-handed, the worldview too Manichean: goodness was treacly and evil was insane. Compared to, say, Marisa Coulter in Phillip Pullman's *Golden Compass*, the White Witch of Narnia has no backstory, no depth or complexity beyond the paradox of surface beauty masking a profoundly murderous nature. ("I have no interest in prisoners," she says. "Kill them all.") Somehow my lack of enthusiasm must have conveyed itself to my daughters, who lost interest before we got through the first book. Early in my romance with the Englishman, when we were living an ocean apart and courting (that old-fashioned word!) over email, he confessed he was a fan of the C. S. Lewis biopic, *Shadowlands*. One evening, despite my allergy to biopics and also to watching movies by myself—the definition of loneliness!—I poured myself a glass of red wine and curled up on the couch to watch. It moved me more than I expected, and not just on account of Anthony Hopkins and Debra Winger, actors of a caliber to breathe life into an ottoman. The question that hangs over the whole film is one that cuts to the heart of the human condition: *Why love, if losing hurts so much?*

Also—the point of my digression!—there's a marvelous scene near the beginning in which C. S. Lewis's male friends interrogate him about the portal to Narnia, which is at the back of an unused wardrobe full of fur coats. The scene takes place inside a noisy bar, so it's not always easy to tell who is speaking. The gist of it is this:

> Friend: "In the book you describe the house as belonging to an old professor who has no wife, and yet you say that when the little girl enters the magic wardrobe, she finds it full of fur coats."
> Lewis: "It's simple. It belonged to the professor's old mother. Simple."
> Friend: "Aha. So, to reach the magic world, the child must push through the mother's fur."
> Lewis: "I won't have that, John. There's none of your hand-me-down Freudianism."
> Friend: "But the imagery is Christian, surely."
> Lewis: "No, Harry. It's what it is. Just itself. It . . . It's . . . It's just magic."

If the rest of the movie were truly terrible (which it is not; we've already established this), it would be redeemed by that one snippet of dialogue. It gets at the essence of creature comforts like fur, which possess the quality of determinate *being*—solid, soft, substantial, safe, luxurious—and indeterminate *meaning*. They shimmer with possibility. They transport us out of our quotidian lives, into a world where absolutely anything can happen.

They are, as Lewis's character asserts, before fleeing the pub, *just magic.*

◆ ◆ ◆

My lover and I are holding mittened hands and walking briskly, heads down against the wind, from our hotel near Times Square to Café Fiorello, near Lincoln Center. It's early January 2017, blustery and cold, with snow falling heavily enough to erase our footprints. We'd hail a cab if we could find one, but we can't. Instead, we duck into bars to snatch a few minutes of warmth. In the second, we perch on barstools in front of the plate-glass window, sipping our fourteen-dollar Irish coffees and watching the Manhattanites as if they were extras milling about in a Woody Allen film. I am wearing my $300 Patagonia parka, thin in places from too many washings, and my lover his ancient Italian wool coat from J. Crew. We could do better in the way of outerwear—we are tenured faculty members at a reputable college, after all—but we are the sort of people who, having discovered something we like, wear it until it falls apart. Outside the window, it seems as if every woman who rushes by is wearing a full-length fur coat and fur hat. In this century, unlike the last—to state the semi-obvious—a woman wearing fur is just as likely to have bought it for herself or to have inherited it as to have received it as a gift from a lover. Even though I'm the one who's indoors, hands wrapped around a warming drink, I want desperately to be one of those women. Their furs mean they don't have to seek refuge in bars, like a couple of vagabonds stretching out their sleeping bags beside heating vents. Their furs signify lives of privilege led in ninety-eighth-floor apartments with jewel-toned walls, roaring fires, and kitchen drawers that slide back into place at the touch of a finger. Is envy the most corrosive emotion? I think it must be, as my lover signals for the check and rummages in the torn lining of his pocket for the Mastercard he pays off in full every month. *You must change your life*, Rilke said. And I want to. Oh, how I want to.

◆ ◆ ◆

My mother has owned a fur for each of her identities. She married my father in February 1962, wearing an ivory silk ballgown topped by a stone marten stole. Her bridesmaids wore red velvet cocktail dresses and carried rabbit fur muffs in place of flowers. Like us kids, she had a parka with a wolf ruff and bear trim handmade for her by the elders in Wainwright; unlike us, she had hers made over several times—in royal blue velvet, then red corduroy, and lastly, in a deep purple paisley. On dressy occasions in Fairbanks—dinner at Club 11, say, or an election— she reached for her mouton, a phrase she spoke with hushed reverence: *Tonight, I'm going to wear my mouton.* In the parka she was one thing—

scrappy frontier wife and mother, someone savvy enough to have embraced the customs and costumes of her adopted home—and in the mouton another—*grand dame* of Fairbanks society, member of the League of Women Voters and the Farthest North Bridge Club, and a lector at St. Matthew's Episcopal Church.

I was in my thirties, possibly my forties, before it dawned on me there is no such beast as a *mouton*—it is simply French for "mutton." Also known as "beaver lamb," mouton is actually sheepskin that has been processed to resemble a more luxurious fur. It's not so much fake as, let us say, *aspirational.*

◆ ◆ ◆

Carol Brice: "My parents gave me that mouton coat when I was in boarding school. I hated it. I hated anything that made us look rich. I only wore it when my mother was standing right there.

"It went in the fire."

Me: "It couldn't have gone in the fire, Mom. You had it made over at least once, and you still bring it out for fancy occasions, like Hannah's wedding, or when you and Dad go out to dinner."

Carol Brice: "That's right. I must have confused it with the stone marten stole. *That* went in the fire."

◆ ◆ ◆

An October evening in 2007, and my Aunt Care is talking on the phone, a landline in the kitchen of her home in Wilmington, North Carolina. She just finished unpacking from a weekend with girlfriends in someone's cabin in the Blue Mountains. It's getting late. I have a picture of her in my mind then: tall, large-boned, effortlessly chic, with the rare gift of paying attention, deep and authentic attention, to whomever she's with. If she'd been born to less privilege, she might have pursued a career as a psychoanalyst. Up till now, her attention has been one of the greatest gifts of my life. Always a night owl, she's indulging in a cup of tea (she hates coffee but loves coffee ice cream) and light gossip with one of the women from the weekend trip. Her husband, Bill, my mother's younger brother, and her son, Trip, have already gone up to bed.

Then, mid-sentence, Care's voice falls silent. Assuming they'd been cut off, her friend tries calling back, gets a busy signal, tries again, then gives up and goes to bed.

By the time Bill pads back downstairs to check on Care, and by the time paramedics negotiate the labyrinthine streets of their gated community, it's too late. The shell of her will spend a few days connected to life support in the ICU while those of us who love her get used to the idea that she's not coming back. She was young—not even seventy yet—and seemingly in excellent health, an avid gardener and golfer who'd only recently given up tennis on account of a bum knee. The only warning was the death a few years earlier of her older sister Jane, whose heart attack came while she was at the dressing table in her Bronxville bedroom, getting ready for lunch with friends.

I was a little bit in love with Care. She and Bill were still living in Connecticut during my college years, and she was a cross between a cool mom and a wise girlfriend. Now that I think about it, *she* was the tribe I yearned for. The weekends I spent in their old house in Wilton, Connecticut—starting with a stop at Scoops, the ice cream parlor she owned with a friend, and ending with Bill's tearing up my bus ticket and driving me all the way back to Northampton in his Volkswagen Scirocco—were among the happiest of my life. During the day, I'd do my schoolwork then iron all of Bill's shirts—a task Care hated but I loved. After dinner, she and I would stay up until midnight playing Trivial Pursuit and talking. Even though I had a car, she offered in the spring of my senior year to drive me to law school interviews, so we went on a road trip together, first to Ithaca, New York (rejection), then to Georgetown, Washington, DC (waitlist), then to Charlottesville, Virginia (waitlist).

Care taught me by example to be kinder than you have to be—to your partner, your children, your neighbors, your customers, your niece. To scoop a little more ice cream onto the cone than strictly fits the definition of "small." It's a lesson I've absorbed unevenly. I have a capacity for coldness that sometimes frightens me, and I have been less than generous on occasion to students whose work disappointed me.

My beloved aunt and I disagreed about only one thing, but we disagreed about it fiercely. She died just a couple of weeks before a presidential election in which she certainly would have voted for John McCain, a choice that seemed unconscionable to me then, when Donald Trump still seemed like someone's idea of a bad joke. At the funeral, I overheard two of my Republican uncles leering over Sarah Palin. "Wouldn't you like to park your slippers under *that* bed?" said one to the other.

A few weeks later, Bill called. He was sifting through Care's belongings, and he felt certain she would have wanted me to have something. How about her mink coat? Surely it would come in handy during upstate New York winters? All I had to do was say the word, and he'd drop it off tomorrow at the UPS Store.

I'd been hoping Bill would offer me some small thing to remember Care by—a tea towel or hand-painted mug, even the half-empty bottle of Jean Naté that I'd seen in her bathroom in Wilmington, and which had made me break down in tears all over again. But the prospect of owning a mink coat made me faintly nauseous. I didn't want such a thing in my house, let alone on my back. Not wanting to hurt Uncle Bill's feelings, I hedged a bit, telling him I'd *love* the coat, but he shouldn't spend a fortune shipping it to me. We'd see each other soon enough, if not this Christmas, then next, and he could give it to me then. A year went by, then two, and Bill moved from the big house in Wilmington to a rancher in The Villages. He began dating again—no surprise, given his full head of hair, his air of bonhomie, and his financial solvency. The women he met were golfers and bridge players, the widows of military men, representatives of a class of women who have their hair done on Mondays and their nails on Tuesdays, and who own what's known as "cruise wear." I began to think—to hope, really—that eventually Bill would forget his offer to me and give the mink to one of them instead.

He didn't forget.

I asked my friend Julia for advice about what to do with the thing that now takes up fully one third of the space in my winter clothes closet. She'd spent the last few months combing through and cleaning out her mother's three-story, antiques-filled Victorian in Cambridge, Massachusetts. She's a corporate lawyer and a life coach, two jobs she holds down simultaneously, and she is my go-to person when it comes to assessing the value of everything from a piece of jewelry to a new friendship. "What do you need a mink coat for?" she asked. "These days, you can't even give away those things on eBay."

What do I need a mink coat for? The question seems inextricable from a much larger one, which can be elegantly phrased as, "Who on earth *am* I?" Middle-aged, gray-haired, twenty pounds heavier than when K proposed (or did he?) to buy me a fur coat in exchange for who-knows-what. Heir to Carol Heeks Brice and Lucia Bell Page and Daisy Maree Bell, women whose worth was (and for Carol, still is, to some degree) measured in silver and china, fur and pearls. Owner of a full set of monogrammed silverware, silver chafing dishes, and a silver tea service, more crystal than you can shake a stick at—champagne glasses, wine goblets, vases, candy dishes—several sets of pearls, not one but *two* full sets of Tiffany china, some Blue Onion plates that are (according to the grandmother who bequeathed them) "priceless," and now a full-length mink coat. The mother I had before Alzheimer's took her away would have said that accepting the gifts that come your way—even the unsought ones; especially the unsought ones—requires good manners. I might go a step further and say that accepting a gift you don't really want and can't get rid of, a gift that reveals a kind of willful blindness on the part of the giver, can sometimes be a kind of grace.

◆ ◆ ◆

We found a large amount of very cheap, mislabeled, real fur being sold and described as fake fur. People don't imagine that real fur could be that cheap.
—From a 2018 BBC exposé of the fur-trimmed bobble-hat fad

An afternoon in late June, temperatures soaring into the high eighties. The transatlantic pen pal who became my lover, and who went with me to New York City in midwinter, has become my partner, and he has just sold his house and moved into my slightly larger one. The question of what to do with our combined inventory of books, furniture, artwork, heirlooms, and teabags looms large. He's unpacking upstairs, in what will be our shared bedroom, while I am working downstairs, at my desk. Suddenly he appears with the mink coat in his arms, a question in his eyes. Wordlessly, I stand up, strip down to my bra and panties, and put it on. It enfolds me like a hug. A really good hug. Sexy, even. I step into the bathroom to weigh myself in the coat. Seven whole pounds. In front of the mirror, I turn from side to side, hunching my shoulders against an imagined squall, a January dash through Central Park, a ride in a sleigh across the Russian steppe. I think, *If I wear this, will I get shouted at or spit on or splashed with red paint?* I think, *Goddammit, why didn't I buy a fur hat when I had the chance?*

Plunging my hands into the pockets, I find—surprise!—a pair of mahogany gloves, soft as butter. Aunt Care was six inches taller than I am, and her gloves are at least a size larger than I would ever buy for myself. (She despaired all her life at the dearth of attractive shoes for women with big feet. *Brogans*, she used to say, dismissively. *Boats. Penny loafers. That's all that's available in size 11.*) I bring the gloves up to my nose and sniff. They smell like leather, of course. Also—can it be my imagination?—a little like Jean Naté. Just magic. I resolve to wear them every winter for the rest of my life.

◆ ◆ ◆

Reader, I lost them.

There was a version of you that was too selfish and there was one where you weren't selfish enough and you were constantly waking up from one into the other and that was why you weren't sure if you were looking down at yourself or you were looking up.

—Jenny Zhang, *Sour Heart*

That Kind of Woman

The romance of becoming a nun went on longer than it should have, starting in adolescence and running through my solitary, surreptitious churchgoing habit in college. Even now, in my fifties and no longer a believer in anything but the world that is here and now, I find myself irresistibly drawn to the word *cloister*. A life behind convent walls was always a big part of the fantasy (though I realize modern nuns often forego it), as was the habit (ditto), the ritual, the clear delineation of power from a Mother Superior all the way down to a novitiate. As a young girl, listening to the sermons of our parish priest, the marvelously named Donald Purple Hart, who was educated at Williams College then Harvard Divinity School, I felt the first stirrings of intellectual life. And then of course there was the vaulting storyline of Maria, the would-be nun in *The Sound of Music*. Mostly, though, my becoming a nun would have been perfect response to—and revenge upon—my mother, who has always accused me of being her most selfish child.

When I was a teenager and in thrall to metaphysics, Mom bought me pop-culture books on life after death: *Into the Light* and other such grotesqueries. Did I ask her to buy them? I don't think so, but maybe I did. My mother had certain fixed ideas about me, about all of her children, really, that were hard to resist. In my teenage years, she decided that angels were my guiding spirits, and I ought to start collecting figurines of them. Over the next few decades, she gave me angels made of porcelain, clay, stained glass, molded plastic, tin, and even corn husks. Whenever I unpack my Christmas ornaments, I'm struck by two things, the first a factual observation (*Wow, that's a lot of angels!*), the second a question (*What kind of point was my mother trying to make, exactly?*).

There used to be five kids in my family, three girls and two boys. A few days after Christmas 2010, a friend knocked on my youngest brother's door and got no answer. By then, I had outgrown my slender interest in the possibility of angels or an afterlife. Ben was barely alive, and then he wasn't, having succumbed to the congenital heart failure his doctor had warned him about. You could call it suicide by binge drinking. He was only forty-three. At the memorial service, his ashes rested in a makeshift shrine near the altar of St. Matthew's Episcopal Church in Fairbanks, which is where I and all my siblings were baptized and confirmed, and where I and my sisters were married. (Ben was single, and my other brother married a Catholic.) His ashes were not in an urn but in a cardboard box because our mother had decided that Ben's favorite song was "My Favorite Things," which contains the line "brown paper packages tied up in string." To see Ben's earthly remains on display like someone's unclaimed dry-cleaning tore at my heart, tore at everyone's heart except Mom's. But my siblings and I were all parents ourselves by then, and we grasped that for a mother to lose a child, even an adopted child such as Ben, whose life had been troubled from the get-go, violated the natural order of things. Our mother could be formidable at the best of times. *Is* still formidable, in fact, despite the ravages of age and dementia. A force to be reckoned with, as the saying goes. None of us dared call bullshit on her made-up *Sound of Music* story.

My mother is one of those rare people who has never felt—or perhaps I should say she has never given in to—the wobble of ambivalence. She wore clip-on earrings her whole life because, when she was growing up in Bronxville, New York, only "fast" girls pierced their ears. She never shopped at yard sales or secondhand stores, even when she was broke, because she was afraid of the germs that might lurk there. And even though she was a devout Episcopalian, not Christian Scientist or Jehovah's Witness, she has always been repelled by the prospect of donating or receiving someone else's blood. For decades, she and my father went to church every Sunday at 8:00 a.m., where they sat in the second pew on the left. She has never cursed, chewed gum, or used slang; she always says *police* instead of *cops*; *dollars*, not *bucks*. (Once, when I was ten or eleven, I asked her what the word *thespian* meant. She looked around to be sure no one else could hear then whispered, "A woman who likes other women.")

Mom moved to Alaska in the early sixties, straight out of nursing school. A decade later, she cofounded (with the Rev. Donald Purple Hart) the Resource Center for Parents and Children, with the idea of decreasing child abuse and neglect. A decade later, she returned to graduate school, earned a master's in counseling, and became a highly sought-after family counselor. A protégé of the Harvard pediatrician and child-rearing guru T. Berry Brazelton, she focused on parent-infant bonding and its implications for healthy, durable bonds later in life. She was a founding member and, later, the chair of the Alaska Children's Trust. She did all of these things while raising us five kids (including Ben, who was such an agent of chaos he should have counted at least double) with a partner, our father, who was often gone for long stretches, working on civil construction projects. Before she was forced to retire, Mom won every citizenship award in our small city, where there is even a building named in her honor.

About the time her career was peaking, my marriage began to un-ravel. I had three children and an adjunct teaching job that paid about $8,000 a year. I used to cry in the shower every morning because that was the only chance I got. A friend suggested a therapist, and I made an appointment. The therapist asked me about my marriage, of course, and then she asked about my parents.

"What did they say when you told them your marriage was ending?" she asked.

"My mother said, 'No one ever thinks of the children anymore,'" I told her.

No one ever thinks of the children anymore. The three of us—my father, my mother, and me—were standing in front of their garage when she said this. She refused to look at me while she said it, and he groaned in a way that could have been interpreted (by her) as assent or (by me) as a reproach for the sucker punch. Later, he'd come find me out on the ski trails near the house to say that both of them had been caught off guard in the moment; what they'd meant to say was that they were so sorry to hear this, and that they would do anything in their power to help. But in the moment, I felt betrayed. Worse, I felt banished—as if the blazing spotlight of my mother's love and attention had finally been withdrawn from me forever and henceforth would shine brightly on someone who was less selfish and more worthy.

Weeping, I told the therapist I couldn't bear to stay in my marriage, on account of my husband, but I couldn't bear to leave it, on account of my mother.

Quietly, venomously, the therapist began to speak. All these years later, I don't remember her name, and I wouldn't write it down even if I did. She was a decade or so older than me, a bit on the dumpy side (as my mother would have observed). She'd been practicing in Fairbanks for long enough that several close friends had vouched for her expertise and kindness. She would also, in the course of her long career, have had many occasions to see my mother, family therapist to the Volvo crowd and civic leader *par excellence*, in action.

While I sat across from her, crumpling wet Kleenex in my fists, the therapist warmed to her subject. She went on at some length. I don't recall her exact words, only the gist of them. And her tone when she uttered them. There was no nuance in her counsel. She offered no insights to assuage my grief or serve me in the long run as I faced the prospect of parenting my daughters alone with no clear job prospects. She told me that my mother's treatment of me had been not just wrongheaded but cruel. That she was as wrong in this instance as she had been in many others, blinded as she was by arrogance and ham-fisted morality. I realized I was in the presence of someone who'd fumed in silence for years and who wasn't going to fume one second longer. She was horrified not by me, the soon-to-be divorcée, but by my mother, who'd withheld not just her permission for me to live my own life but also her love. I found it liberating and more than a little bit scary to be in the presence of someone who was angrier on my behalf than I had ever allowed myself to be. I left the therapist's office that day and never returned.

A few years went by. I found refuge in a temporary teaching job at a women's college and moved to Virginia with the girls. On the phone, my mother and I fell back into the old companionable grooves of our relationship. Even though I'd left Alaska and taken up with someone else, I hadn't yet gotten divorced, and I think she held out some hope, faint though it might be, that my husband and I would eventually reconcile.

When the Virginia job ended, I flew to New York City for interviews. The post I really wanted was at a well-regarded liberal arts college a few hours north of the city. My interviews coincided with a large academic conference, and they took place in a fancy Manhattan hotel. Even though I'd already published one book and had another underway, I felt, as always on such occasions, hopelessly out of my depth: provincial, frumpy, clueless as to the customs of my tribe. I feel like a fraud when I wear anything but blue jeans. I was dressed that day as one ought to be, in a black wool suit and high black boots. Stepping in a side door of the hotel, I had to pause for a moment to adjust to the dim interior light. The lobby was teeming with black-suited supplicants, every single one of them looking more chic, confident, and put together than I was. In fact, one of them was walking in my direction as if she meant to greet me. I felt a flutter of panic. Had we met before? Was I meant to know her name? She was a little older and very poised. She looked as if she belonged. *I bet she's a writer, too, and I bet she's interviewing for the same job as me,* I thought. *She'll get it.* The woman continued to walk toward me, more briskly now, gaze locked on mine and lips slightly parted, as if we two were already in mid-conversation.

I raised my hand in a weak wave, then realized *she* was waving too—at someone just behind me.

Excuse me, I said as I bumped into my reflection in a floor-to-ceiling mirror.

Even though every sentient being moves through the world in the present tense, first-person singular, we're often obliged out of politeness to pretend this isn't so. The personal essayist (especially if she's a woman) often makes an apologetic moue, saying, essentially, *Forgive me for intruding in your line of vision* and *If you could just hold still for one more moment, I might be able to see my reflection in your eyes.* We career between the guard rails of narcissism on the one side, excessive (or, worse, false) modesty on the other. I'm dead serious when I say that an essayist is someone who suffers occasionally from the delusion that she's invisible.

Because I grew up in a household where selfishness was regarded as a sin—in particular, it was the sin that was assigned to me by my parents—and because I stumbled straight out of college into a career as a journalist, the first-person singular still smacks to me not just of loosey-goosey subjectivity but of sabotage, subversion, immodesty, even that old-timey word, *vaingloriousness*. (I once caught hell from an editor for a story I wrote about the tenth anniversary of *Roe v. Wade*; in it, he felt I did not sufficiently suppress my own opinion. I chafed at his criticism because, at that point, I honestly didn't *have* an opinion.) Even now, a quarter-century later, I'm conscious of how tentative and friable is my sense of self. How risky, too, the business of trying to catch that self in an opinion.

One of the students in the first writing workshop I took as a graduate student was a handsome, slouching man with hair that flopped down over his forehead. He looked to me like a real writer, and I wanted desperately for him to look at me and see the same thing. A few weeks in, I turned in my first attempt at a personal essay, a piece that had grown out of a newspaper assignment to drive the length of the trans-Alaska pipeline. In the essay, I floated the first-person singular like a trial balloon, trying to probe what *I* thought about environmental activism. It was a cause embraced by newcomers to the place where I was born. I sometimes thought of them as ideologues, demagogues, blinkered scolds. That night, after the workshop, I couldn't wait to read my classmates' written comments. In the car, I rifled through the manuscripts for the one from the man I wanted to impress. He'd written almost nothing. In the right-hand margin of one particular page, where I was plumbing my yes-but ambivalence toward environmental activism, he'd scrawled two words: "*Fuck this!*"

Alexandra Fuller's memoir, *Don't Let's Go to the Dogs Tonight*, about growing up in Rhodesia was a bestseller that wounded her mother deeply. There was all the drinking, for one thing. And also the accidental drowning of Fuller's toddler sister. So Fuller wrote her family's story again, this time—in *Cocktail Hour Under the Tree of Forgetfulness*—from a third-person point of view that hewed closely to that of Nicola, Fuller's mother. Both memoirs stand on their own. Read in sequence, they tell a story about the existential threat that daughters pose to their mothers by becoming an *I*.

One morning in my twenties I woke up and knew I didn't want to be a journalist anymore. Over Scrabble that evening, I told my parents this, and I also told them I wasn't sure what I wanted to do next. It was ordinary, angsty stuff. A few days later I got a phone call at work from their insurance agent, an Australian named Digby Cook. He asked if I could stop in to his office to see him. This wasn't unusual: I was covering the business beat, and every businessperson in Fairbanks was either a friend or a friend of a friend of my family. (In fact, Digby's daughter later married one of my cousins.) I went to the meeting expecting Digby to offer up some tidbit of gossip about a rival insurance company or something along those lines. Instead, he started talking about the insurance industry in general—how sales work was a good fit for self-starters and extroverts.

"I don't mean to be rude, Digby," I said, "but are you *interviewing me for a job?*"

"Well, your mother told me you wanted a career change," he said, "and she asked if I'd be willing talk with you."

"I don't want to be an insurance agent."

"Oh."

My mother didn't read my first book, a work of journalism, before it was published. As soon as it came out, I pressed a copy into her hand. She congratulated me, thanked me, and set the book on her bedside table. She's not really a reader, so I thought it was probably just there for show. Then, a week or so later, she presented me with a Post-it note of all the typos she'd found. After my second book, a memoir, was published, my mother wrote me a long, heartbroken letter saying she was sorry for all of the things she'd gotten wrong.

What I'm chafing against—even as I myself am guilty of it—is the way first-person narratives flatten out other people. Point of view is not merely an aesthetic choice but also an ethical, even moral one. When it comes to storytelling, we are all of us keepers as well as kept.

I'm not really interested in litigating my childhood. (My mother might beg to differ. Or she might say I've already done it.) The truth is, my parents did the best they could by their lights, and often in trying circumstances. (My brother Ben!) They raised us in comfort and safety. They had expectations of us, but not impossible ones. Over the years of my single motherhood, they've rescued me more than once from financial ruin. Furthermore, I don't necessarily trust my own memories. (Sometimes I think that's the best definition of a memoirist: someone who writes down her memories because she doesn't trust them.) Yet I find myself wanting to say, over and over, that my mother "often" accused me of being selfish, of putting myself first, ahead of my younger brothers and sisters; that she "often" told me I ought to be ashamed of myself for being selfish. Weaponizing shame: isn't that what all mothers do? Don't the good ones, mine included, also turn pride—*Look at you, Sweetie!*—into a prize? Tilt your head in one direction, and this shaming verges on emotional abuse. Tilt it in another, and it looks like a blueprint for good citizenship.

I could ask the question this way: What kind of harm, and how much, did my mother do, telling me over and over that I was a selfish little girl? Or I could ask it this way: When am I ever going to stop telling this story about *her*?

It's true that when I try to conjure an image of myself as a young girl, I see someone who mostly did what was expected of her: practicing violin and piano, going to ballet lessons, earning A's in school, minding her younger siblings, doing her chores on Saturday. When my mother would send me to the convenience store on my bicycle, I would spend the change. Sometimes late at night, when everyone else was asleep, I'd sneak into the kitchen and eat up all the chocolate. When confronted, I lied. (I was a champion liar. Also, it was possible in those days to get away with anything by blaming it on Ben.) The gap between who I appeared to be, on the surface, and who I really was made me anxious. At the time, I had no word for the feeling of pressure that built and built until it became so unbearable, I went in search of my middle sister and pinched her viciously. (No one ever believed *her* either.)

It's an old story, isn't it?—how the child pushed to be irreproachably, blandly perfect in public, to be *selfless*, finds surreptitious outlets for her desires, her will, her tamped-down aggression. I'm no apologist for right-wing politicians and evangelical ministers who rail publicly against homosexuality then get caught cruising airport bathrooms for gay sex, but *I kind of get it.* They build so many walls to hide from themselves—they don't know who they are when they're alone, only when they're performing—that they end up boxed in and out of air.

The human psyche was forged under the pressure of *seeming*. Nietzsche (and others) tell us the work of soul-making is what makes us deep. It gives our privacy a shape. It is both a spur and a salve to anxiety. And it gives rise to the old saw about still waters. "Being nothing is being invisible and replaceable," writes Yiyun Li in an essay that is partly about her difficult mother. "Being nothing to others means remaining everything to oneself."

As a young girl, I was bossy and loud and gregarious, always staging plays with the neighborhood kids, or picking wildflowers and selling them door-to-door. Then, at some point, for reasons I can't explain— Did my mother praise my friend Carolyn for being "quiet"?—I made the decision to change, to burrow inside myself, to slip from the center of things to the sidelines. To become more watchful and shy and (was I capable of thinking this at the time?) mysterious. Did I do it for safety? For attention? Or did I even do it at all? Perhaps I'm just making up a story after the fact. In my memory—which, to say it again, I do not trust—I regressed from butterfly to chrysalis in the course of a summer, presenting myself on the first day of third grade (or fourth, or fifth) as a mousier version of my former self.

The upside to living inside your own head, inside your own privacy, is that you can build a world to your exact specifications. You can populate it with characters from your favorite novels, furnish it with images from the pages of *House Beautiful* or *Elle Décor*. Children intuit just how this works because they do it all the time. It's why books like *The Little Prince*, *Alice in Wonderland*, and—my personal favorite—*Sam, Bangs and Moonshine*—seem absolutely true. The downside, of course, is that the more one retreats from it, the more bland, shabby, gritty and impoverished the real world seems. And the danger, the real danger, is that you might lose the ability to navigate between the two worlds, and therefore go mad. One of the most acute sadnesses of aging, for me, is that I am less likely to go mad than to lose access to this formerly vivid interior world.

I'm on the phone with my mother who is visiting her older sister at The Villages in Florida. "Today is Sandie's birthday," Mom says. "I don't suppose you thought to tuck a card in the mail?" Aunt Sandie is my godmother. Even now, when I'm in my fifties, she always remembers my birthday with a card and twenty dollars, which she tells me to spend on a nicer bottle of wine than I would normally buy.

"I don't *do* birthday cards, Mom," I say. "I'm not that kind of person."

"Yes, you are!" I can hear the tears in her voice. "You *are* that kind of person!"

My mother remembers her sister's birthday but she couldn't possibly tell you what happened five minutes ago. In fact, she has trouble reading a watch, which is an early sign of Alzheimer's disease. She isn't anxious about what will happen in the next few minutes, as long as my father, her constant companion, is close by. Dementia has granted her the difficult grace of living only in the present moment. Lately, she and my father have been spending the winters in tropical places. In Hawaii or Florida, they get up early in the morning, fix coffee, watch the sunrise from their lanai or their balcony, then head for the beach, where my mother picks up seashells and my father paces in the shade, smoking his pipe. After lunch, she takes a short nap then gets back to work with the seashells. She takes this work very seriously, selecting seashells as if it is a job for which someone is paying her.

On stormy days, when going to the beach isn't possible, Mom picks up trash instead of shells. She's not so far gone as to try to keep the bits of trash; the seashells, on the other hand, she treats like beloved children. Stuck indoors on rainy days, my mother rinses and sorts these bleached and battered fragments, sealing some in plastic bags and arranging the rest on every flat surface in the condo: countertops, tables, and windowsills. It's a form of madness, of course, but madness that's of a piece with who she is now and who she has been her whole life: the dutiful girl going about her chores, hoping to win love or at least plaudits in this world or the next.

The time I helped my parents move from a rental in north Florida to a condo in Key West, there was barely enough room in their convertible for the three of us, their eighty-pound boxer, our luggage, and Mom's collection of seashells, boxed and swaddled in paper towels like precious jewels or Godiva chocolates. Out of her earshot, I said to Dad, "If I were you, I'd just throw these out one day when she's asleep. Either that or take them all back to the beach. She'll never even know they're gone."

After a long pause, he said, wearily (looking after my mother is exhausting), "*You* would do that, but I'm not you."

My mother speaks slowly these days, picking her words like someone who senses their power to expose her. She remarks on the fineness of the weather, or how much she's enjoying this *National Geographic* special on the treasures of King Tut, or how pleased she is to get to spend this time with me, or how delicious she finds the meal that has been placed in front of her. An obese child who slimmed down in boarding school, she used to be vigilant about her weight. Now she has given in to her appetites. When she's hungry, she fixes something to eat, regardless of the hour. The same goes for sleeping when she's tired. Sometimes my father has to stop her from turning in at 8:30 in the morning or 5:30 in the afternoon. In the evening, she and my father and I play cards. We used to play Scrabble or Upwords or, when we could find a fourth, bridge, but not anymore. Mom still wins at simple card games, like rummy. These evening activities force the three of us into a proximity that I try to avoid during the day, scurrying around behind the scenes, or while my parents are out, to buy groceries, prepare meals, change their sheets, or clean the bathroom. When there's a lull in the card play, Mom tries to make conversation by commenting on some aspect of my appearance.

"I like the way you're wearing your hair these days."

Then, two minutes later:

"The length of your hair is so pretty. Is it the longest it's ever been?"

And again:

"Your hair looks so beautiful. How often do you have to color it?"

And again, and again:

"Jennifer, have I told you that I really like the way you're wearing your hair these days?"

"Do you have to color your hair these days? Or is that gray natural?"

In a picture from my wedding day, my mother and I stand side by side at the dresser in her bedroom. We're leaning into the mirror, fixing our makeup. I'm already dressed in my wedding gown, and my hair flows in loose brown curls under a wreath of silk flowers. My mother's dress is a dusty rose chiffon that suits her Irish coloring. Her hair was darker then too—nearly black. It startles me to realize that in the picture, my mother is younger than I am now.

Nearly everything about dementia is sad and predictable, devoid of any useful lessons for living. It's just an endless litany of losses. One of the first things to go is access to your own inner life, the sense that who you are in the privacy of your own mind might be different from how you appear in company with other people, even those you love. In metaphysical terms, you lose your own soul, the thing that, as Montaigne writes, "can be turned upon itself; it can keep itself company." Memory sloughs away slowly at first, then calves like a glacier, in great chunks, until you not only forget what you were cooking for dinner but where your parents lived after the war; which of your friends is still living and which of them died last week. The names of beloved flowers. (*Bougainvillea, Mom. Those are bougainvillea.*) The names of your grandchildren. You lose, humiliatingly, the ability to remain continent. Some days, it may feel as if good manners—the form of human interaction—are all of you that remains. Other days, you ignore the elaborate trap that someone has set beside your plate, with knives and forks and spoons, and you simply shovel your food into your mouth with your hands.

If I wander off script—if I am, say, the tiniest bit brusque in response to the repeated remarks about my hair or my weight, or if I remind my mother that she's already eaten one breakfast this morning—her fragile poise collapses. She rages, she wails, she sulks like a fat baby that's had its sweets taken away.

The word *dementia* comes from the Latin for "madness," "insanity," "craziness," "folly" (think "demon")—all words that seem to suggest that its sufferers behave strangely because they've become strangers to themselves. They've literally lost the ability to distinguish between other and self, outside and in. Either that, or the wilderness of their own subjectivity is all they have left.

In Mom's presence, I find it hard to be still. Partly this is a relic of my childhood habit of secrecy, the old fear of being caught with a book in my hand when there were chores to do. Partly it's fear of engagement. Conversations with my mother start reasonably enough. Her opening gambit is almost always about the weather or what she's watching on the TV. Pretty soon, though, you're forced to decide between acceding to her worldview—becoming hostage to it, really—or challenging it. (*Am* I the kind of woman who sends birthday cards? Or not?) Will my truthful responses inflict violence on her? Or on myself? Sometimes I play along. Other times, I do not. I cannot.

Was I a selfish child? Early on, I learned that in order to keep my self to myself, I had to hide it from my mother. Like all kids, I was a hedonist at heart. I was full of yearning, which is similar to but not the same as being selfish. The struggle of the child to break free, to achieve exit velocity on the way to becoming a separate *I*—is universal and archetypal, also messy and fraught at best; to fail is one kind of anguish; to succeed, another. For the mother, this split is like giving birth, just on a psychic scale. To hold on too hard, for too long, is one kind of monstrousness. To let go is another. The essence of innocence, writes Yiyun Li, in the essay I mentioned earlier, about her truly terrible mother, is the failure to sense where one's self ends and another's starts: "My mother is a child I had to leave behind in order to have my own life."

For better or worse, I've got my own life now, free of any emotional entanglements with my mother. I've been unlucky in some ways, luckier in others, especially in my friendships with other women. A couple of them in particular have done the difficult work of raising me, of teaching me what my own mother was too distracted or busy to teach me about how to be a woman in the world. Even so, there are days when great gusts of grief sweep through me, and I want to curl up on my bedroom floor and cry for the mother I always thought would be there for me—if not now, then someday. She will not be there. Instead, she is disappearing by degrees. Every time I visit, there is more of her body—overflowing the elastic waistband of her jeans—and less of *her*.

I used to ask myself which is worse—to lose a beloved parent suddenly, to a heart attack or stroke, or by degrees, to dementia. I used to think I knew the answer. Now I'm not sure of anything but this: As much as you try to tell yourself it isn't so, you always feel abandoned by the loss of a parent, no matter how exacting or imperfect she was.

It teaches you how to feel, this business of loving and being loved imperfectly, of taking hostages and being taken hostage—then, many years later, being released—by someone else. It sharpens your hunger for closeness as well as space. It makes you suffer, this surfeit of empathy, this embarrassment of awe. It shows you the capaciousness of the third-person point of view; also, how you can both lose and find yourself in the first-person singular. It catches you up, catches you out.

It holds you fast.

Before you know what kindness really is
you must lose things.

—Naomi Shihab Nye, "Kindness"

The Art of Losing

The Alaska State Spelling Bee when I was in the seventh grade. Having prevailed at the school and district level, I felt invincible—surely, I was bound for Washington, DC. There were only four of us left onstage when I drew a word meaning *to bribe or induce someone to do something illegal.*

"S-u-b-o-r-n," I said, and should have stopped right there.

All my life, I should have stopped right there.

"e?"

A piano competition I never expected to win anyway. Tenth grade, I think. My closest competitor the daughter of Korean immigrants and, unlike me, a real prodigy. I had only one gift, which was the patience— my mother would say compulsion—to work my way up and down the metronome for hours at a time. The judge sat behind a screen to avoid being influenced by the way we looked. Afterward, he caught my teacher in the hall to say he thought I had a lot of raw talent, and he hoped I wouldn't let it go to waste.

The ability to play Chopin's *Fantasie Impromptu* from memory.

The ability to play anything from memory.

The ability to play the piano.

The ability to read music.

Blood, nearly three pints of it, during what was supposed to be routine surgery. I was in my mid-fifties. For years the doctor had been brushing off my complaints. "Perimenopause," he'd said, his hand already on the doorknob. *Female problems,* I heard. Also, *Pull up your socks.*

In the history of the world, how many women have died, I wonder, in the act of pulling up their damn socks?

Baby Dear was roughly the size of a newborn preemie, with a cloth body and plastic limbs that ended in curled fingers and toes. I was four, and I carried her everywhere, mimicking the way my mother joggled my baby sister in one arm while putting on lipstick or cooking dinner with the other. Changing Baby Dear from one pink cotton dress into another was my favorite thing to do. Of course I brought her along on the family trip to Southeast Alaska. Within minutes of boarding our ferry from Haines to Juneau, when Dad was distracted and Mom was busy giving Hannah a bottle, Sam clambered over the railing and hung down the other side. He was only three, his tiny feet churning five stories above the Gulf of Alaska. "Hey, Mom!" he shouted. "Look at me!" Mom didn't scream or lunge or toss the baby to a stranger. Instead, she enunciated: "Sam Robert Brice, get back over here right this minute!"

Of course I didn't have words then for what I was feeling—terror giving way to relief, as soon as Sam's feet were safely planted on the deck—just as I didn't leave Baby Dear behind on purpose. Even so, crazy as it sounds, I've spent the rest of my life feeling as if that was an even swap: my favorite doll for my favorite brother.

My other brother, Ben. He was born with a congenital heart defect that made him allergic to alcohol. When he was forty, his doctor offered him a simple choice: keep drinking or keep living.

The shades of meaning between *etiology*, *epistemology*, and *ontology*.

Yesterday's farm share had two bulbs of _____ in it. In England, this vegetable is known as anise, but I will be goddamned if I can ever retrieve the American name for it.

An add-a-pearl necklace on a gold filament chain, a christening gift, that I wore, against my mother's advice, to swim in a cousin's Connecticut pool when I was fourteen.

From the Anthropologie mother store in New York City, the perfect white T-shirt—finally! Our trip from upstate New York had begun badly. On the four-hour drive, the man I loved got pulled over for speeding just north of Binghamton. Then he got stopped again just south of Scranton. The second time he asked me to retrieve his insurance card from the glove box, I pulled out the New York speeding ticket by accident and proffered it to the Pennsylvania State Trooper. He was not impressed.

In the city, we went to see the Matisses at the Met. Afterward, in the gift shop, I went to pay for a print and realized I'd left my wallet at home. The man I loved loaned me the money for the print and, later, the T-shirt. I paid him back, but weeks later he broke up with me anyway.

Earrings, too many to count, including a Mikimoto pearl that was part of a set from another man I dated for a while. This man might have fallen in love with me, but I was never going to fall in love with him, partly because he needed me to believe in God, partly because he wore brown shoes with gray pants.

My temper, too many times to count. Once, I came home from work to find my three teenage girls in front of the TV, watching *Say Yes to the Dress*. My two cats were on the breakfast bar, eating the rotisserie chicken I'd raced out to buy earlier, during a break between meetings, so we'd have something for dinner.

Umbrellas, sunglasses, my wedding dress.

A loden green maxi cape with something called "princess styling." I was in junior high school and would have made a right spectacle of myself, wearing that on the school bus. No matter. I only ever owned it in my imagination. My mother spotted it in a catalog and had known instantly that I would love it. She was just about to order it when my glasses went missing. After a couple of days of frantic searching, Hannah found them in the driveway, where I'd dropped them, and where the family car had driven over them at least twice.

They cost eighty dollars, exactly as much as the loden green maxi cape.

Plane tickets, social security card, immunization records, tax returns, my passport, my nerve.

Stuff was ever the hard currency of my mother's love. An early memory of shopping with her at Woolworth's: In the toy aisle, stitched to its cardboard backing and rustling in its cellophane sleeve, is a tiny pink dress. Perfect for Baby Dear. Waves of wanting overtake me.

Please, please, please, please, Mommy, please?

Without a word, she pays for her items, gathers them up, and drags me, weeping, from the store.

Now I'm being battered by great gusts of grief. It's possible I am crying very loudly. I might even be wailing. I am definitely making a scene. There's nothing my Yankee mother hates more than a scene. Outside the store, she lets go of my arm, turns her cold face to my hot, tear-streaked one.

Why, Mommy, why?

Because you begged. If you had asked just once, I would have said yes.

A half century later, a $1,000 pair of eyeglasses that tipped out of my gray linen bag onto Duval Street, the throbbing heart of Key West.

Friends. To brain tumors, plane crashes, suicide. Three or four still walking around in the world but lost to me forever, nonetheless. Perhaps I presumed too much or, in one case, too little. Perhaps I lied to cover up my own failings. I might have given away their secrets in return for the quick endorphin rush that gossip brings. Once or twice, I might have given away those same secrets in a piece of writing that got published.

The ability to distinguish—in myself and others—between kindness and the performance of it.

Who said, *What you lose is yours forever?* I forget. In the mid-nineties, pregnant with the twins, I fell in love with a house. Charcoal-shingled with an open floor plan, perched atop a mountain in Ester, Alaska. It cost $150,000, which was $25,000 more than my then husband and I could afford. We settled for a three-bedroom farmhouse in a valley closer to Fairbanks and less than a mile from the package store where he stopped every evening on his way home from work.

What's lost is yours forever. My mother cannot tell you the day of the week or the name of the president or even what she ate for lunch, but she can list every item she lost in a fire in the mid-sixties. When I ask where her brown wooden canisters came from, the ones with roosters on the front, she tells me they were a gift from the friends who threw a shower for her after the fire.

For a brief time in high school, I played in the Fairbanks Symphony Orchestra, sitting in the last seat of the second violin section. My mother signed up to help with a post-concert reception. Before dropping off her sterling silver punch bowl at the symphony office, she wrote her name on a piece of masking tape and affixed it to the bottom. A day or two later, when she went to pick it up, she was handed a punch bowl with her name taped to the bottom.

The punchbowl was made of tin.

A few months after the twins were born, I enrolled them in an MIT study that Steven Pinker drew on for his book, *The Language Instinct*. My assignment was to record every word they uttered, which I duly did until they turned two. Then I threw up my hands and told our grad student handler I couldn't do it anymore: they were talking *all the time*. Now everything they said for the first two years of their life is inscribed on a floppy disk from the mid-nineties.

Memory, muscle mass, eyesight, energy.

A whole essay I wrote about the image of the wash basket in *Let Us Now Praise Famous Men*.

The ability to run a half marathon at a pace that earned me a second- or third-place medal in the 50+ age category.

The ability to run half a mile.

Half an inch in height.

The same twenty pounds, over and over. Where do they go, I wonder?

We measure lost height in inches, lost weight in pounds, but what is the unit of measure for lost memory?

My virginity. I was twenty years old and *dying* to get rid of it.

My heart. Over and over again, because after twenty years of waiting for something big to happen, I turned into a leaper.

When Mom was diagnosed with dementia at seventy, Dad said, "We've been so lucky as a family. Never a serious accident, illness, or injury. We can get through this." The second thing he did was sign her up for a drug trial that required them to travel, at their own expense, to Phoenix several times a year, so she could be infused with an experimental drug.

The first thing he did was buy her the convertible she'd been wanting forever, even though she never begged.

A few of the riches that have fallen undeserved into my life: a fifty-dollar bill lying on the ground outside the Howling Dog Saloon; an expensive camera on an otherwise deserted island in Glacier Bay; a friend of twenty years so steadfast that nothing I do or say (or fail to do or say) can cleave her from me.

While rifling through T-shirts in a crowded Honolulu gift shop, I became separated from my toddler daughter. I spent the next few minutes searching for her frantically, shouting her name and shoving aside the racks of clothes, where she sometimes liked to hide when we were shopping. Then I ran outside. Cars and busses whizzed by mere feet from the sidewalk, and bikini-clad tourists eddied and swirled, as if the world had not just ended.

Then I saw her: she was spinning circles on the pavement fifteen feet away, admiring the flow of her blue muumuu against ankles so fat they looked as if they'd been tied with rubber bands.

During a field trip to New York City a few years ago, I parked my students at the Ninety-Second Street Y then taxied to a restaurant in Greenwich Village to meet some friends. I was deep into my second glass of wine and my account of the afternoon's adventures—a bus accident outside of MoMA, the Y's request for passport numbers from all fifty students, the students' dawning realization that they should have brought their own sheets and towels, the maze of construction and one-way streets that made it impossible for my taxi driver to get within three blocks of the restaurant—when a waiter stopped to ask if there was someone by my name in our party. Just outside the front door, an elderly Jamaican gentleman was waiting. He handed me the wallet I'd left behind in the taxi—not his taxi, his son's—meaning, it was found before it was ever lost.

Years earlier, when I was fresh out of graduate school and teaching as an adjunct, a beloved former student stopped by my cubicle. He had glasses and shoulder-length hair and was gawky and geeky in a way I liked. He was ebullient that day, saying he'd met someone, a girl, who'd helped him get free of an addiction. Until then, I hadn't known. I said some supportive things, then we hugged goodbye. A few minutes later, I went down the hall to use the copier. When I returned to my cubby, my wallet lay on the floor beneath my desk, gutted like a fish.

"There are tears at the heart of things" is how Seamus Heaney translates the famous line uttered by Aeneas, on seeing a mural that depicts the Trojan War. In the original Latin: *sunt lacrimae rerum et mentem mortalia tangent.* But who among us has retained the smidgen of Latin we learned in Professor Sinclair's college classroom—distracted as we were by the sight of his blond curls, his Spanish waiter hips, his monogrammed belt buckle?

My innocence, my train of thought, my confidence, my faith, my fear of talking to strangers on the phone.

The ability to turn cartwheels.

My way.

Literary theory is an unavoidable part of studying literature and criticism. But theory—especially when it takes the form of "-isms"—can often be intimidating or else, frankly, boring.

—*An Introduction to Literature, Criticism, and Theory*, 2nd ed., edited by Andrew Bennett and Nicholas Royle

Theory of Life

The Beginning
"When will we have begun?"

A few days before Christmas, 1961. For the third day in a row, the florist's van swings into the driveway of Lucia and Bill Heeks's place in Stamford, Vermont. They call this place a farm, even though it isn't, and Lucia and Bill aren't farmers. They're retirees, he from a career as a doctor, she from a career as a doctor's wife. The story of their life together is one of retreat. After the war, they moved from Bronxville, New York, where Bill worked as a surgeon and where Lucia appeared in the *New York Times*' society pages, to North Adams, Massachusetts. There, Bill served for more than a decade as in-house doctor to the Sprague Electric Company, now the Massachusetts Museum of Modern Art.

They had three children together but didn't see much of them, what with boarding school and summer camp. Once the kids were grown and gone, Bill and Lucia moved north again, just across the border to Vermont, in search of a more bucolic existence. For a while, they toyed with the idea of becoming gentlemen farmers, even going so far as to enroll themselves in a SUNY Cortland course on rearing dairy cows.

Bill and Lucia interest me for reasons I'll get to in a minute. For now, though, it's their middle child, Carol Ann, I'm trying to parse. In December 1961, she would have been twenty-five—the same age my twins are now. If I could apply the armature of literary theory to their lives, I would. But I can't: not enough distance. Not yet.

After graduating from Columbia-Presbyterian Nursing School in May, Carol Ann accepted the first offer she got, for a one-year stint as a public health nurse in Alaska. She was nursing a broken heart from a broken engagement to a medical student whose socialite mother had taken one look at her, said *Ixnay on the brunette with a brain*. She poured herself into her new job and her new community, Fairbanks. Dating then was not like dating now, so Carol didn't find it odd when a man she'd been seeing casually asked if she'd mind attending his older brother's birthday party as that brother's blind date. Sparks flew between Carol Ann and the brother, whose name was Alba, Al for short.

The party happened around Thanksgiving. Three weeks later, just as Carol Ann was about to board an overnight flight to New York to spend the holidays with her family, Al turned up in his Pan Am mechanic's coveralls. He didn't get down on one knee or even try for a public kiss. He just wanted to let her know there was a diamond ring with her name on it at Tiffany's on Fifth Avenue. She didn't have to pick it up if she didn't want to, and he wouldn't necessarily take it as assent if she did. He just wondered if, during her overnight flight, she might give some thought to the possibility of picking up the ring, trying it on for size, and asking herself whether she could imagine wearing it for the rest of her life.

Carol's younger brother Bill picked her up from the airport in New York. She talked him into (1) making a detour into the heart of the city, (2) napping in the car with her until Tiffany's opened at 10:00 a.m., and, (3) afterward, not telling their parents that she'd just picked up an engagement ring from a guy she'd only known for three weeks.

At the farmhouse in Stamford, Carol left the ring—a simple diamond solitaire on a platinum band, in its trademark baby-blue box— in the bottom of her purse, which she buried in the top drawer of her dresser. If anyone were to see it, what would she say about the giver of the ring? That he'd been offered a full scholarship to Yale but turned it down after a chance viewing of *Battle Cry* led him to join the Marines?

That after three years as an electronics grunt, not the fighter pilot he'd imagined (something to do with his peripheral vision), he tried college for a year—Columbia, the University of Florida—but it didn't stick? That he was now working as a mechanic for Pan Am and bunking in a cabin in the hills outside Fairbanks with his parents and his two younger brothers? There was no way to spin it without making him sound like a loser, a nobody. In truth, Al Brice was brimming with restless, frenetic energy and intelligence. He was (and still is) the kind of person who could read an industrial site like a text, who could identify a plane merely by the sound of its engine, who could fix anything from a log skidder to a shoe buckle. He intended to go into the logging or construction business with his family, the sooner the better, and he was willing to work around the clock to realize the dream.

Christmas came and went. Carol said nothing to her parents. The blue box burned a hole in the bottom of her purse. Alone in her room at night, she took it out, lifted the ring from its bed of blue velvet, and slipped it onto the fourth finger of her right hand. In her telling of this story, the ring alone wasn't enough to persuade her to slide it onto her left hand and walk downstairs, an engaged woman. The daily delivery of long white florist's boxes filled with yellow roses did the trick. After the third delivery in as many days, my frugal grandfather erupted.

"For God's sake, Carol Ann, will you please say yes to this guy before he spends all his money on flowers?"

The Uncanny
"The uncanny is not just a matter of the weird or spooky but has to do more specifically with a disturbance of the familiar."

In Hamilton, New York, I share a home with two men, only one of whom is living. The flesh-and-blood man is English, slow to anger, gentle and generous—a rereader of novels and rewatcher of films. A loyal fan of a third-tier English soccer club. A drinker of coffee in the morning, tea in the afternoon, beer in the evening, and whiskey at bedtime. He doesn't believe in ghosts but indulges me when I tell him about the one upstairs. Besides the fact that our ghost is a man, I know, or feel I know, two things: (1) he means us no harm, and (2) he smells bad—reeks, really, of ancient sweat, what I imagine working men used to exude from their pores in the nineteenth century, before Dial soap and deodorant, washing machines and AC units. The smell is acrid and sticks in your nostrils. It settles like a film on your skin. I've tried everything in my arsenal to vanquish it: scrubbing the walls and ceiling with a Clorox-based product. When that failed, I lit scented candles and installed a fan. Even in November, with the windows wide open, the Smell persisted.

I gave up and shut the door to the bedroom.

That seemed to work. The Smell went away, and I no longer felt embarrassed to put overnight guests in that room. After a year or so, I began to forget about it.

Then, a few weeks ago, shortly after the Englishman and I turned our downstairs bedroom into a study and moved to a larger room upstairs, the Smell came back. This time, it settled in the bathroom, in the vicinity of a fixture that (you'll have to take my word here) I keep *very* clean with Mrs. Meyer's multi-surface ultra-concentrated cleaner. As before, the Englishman claims not to be able to smell it. If I'm being honest, I can't either, so long as I'm standing at the sink in the morning, brushing my teeth or putting on makeup. But in the middle of the night, when I shuffle down the hallway then plunk myself onto the cold toilet seat for a quick pee, the Smell wraps itself around me. It's pungent and needy but not leering at the sight of a nearly old woman with pink-striped pajama bottoms around her ankles.

I think it might be grateful for my company.

Hullo, friend.

Readers and Reading
"What do you do when you come across a story like this?"

The Christmas-in-Vermont/Tiffany diamond/yellow roses story got told so often around the dining room table when I was growing up that it became the family origin story. What do you do with such a story if you're a child who lives mostly in your head? When you're very young, you swirl it together with the fairy tales you love: Cinderella, Snow White, Sleeping Beauty, the Twelve Dancing Princesses, the Princess and the Pea, the Frog Prince. Your mother, of course, is always the princess; your father is always the rube who sees her at a distance, falls in love, has the temerity to ask for her hand, gets turned down and tested repeatedly, then eventually reveals himself to be a prince in disguise.

You insist on having your hair done up in ringlets, on wearing frilly dresses and black patent leather shoes every day, on drinking hot chocolate out of translucent Limoges teacups, on calling your housekeeper-slash-babysitter "the maid," and on all sorts of other things the memory of which still, decades later, makes your skin prickle with shame.

As soon as you're old enough to be aware of boys, you start casting about for a rube or two of your very own, a succession of boys you can condescend to. You light first on a red-haired trumpet player whose father owns a lumber company. Next on the counter guy at an auto parts store you frequent while working for your father's company. At a bar when you're home on break from college, you meet a boy with ambitions to become a painter who turns out to be (judging from the letters he sends you afterward) functionally illiterate. After college, when you're working on your hometown newspaper, there's the handsome army private who drives a Karmann Ghia. He dreams of becoming a policeman someday. Reluctantly—he is *so* handsome!—you break things off. A princess can marry a pauper any day of the week, but she can never marry a policeman.

Desire
"For Lacan, we are, in a way, the senseless puppets of desire as much when we speak or write as when we fall in love."

In college, you are dumbstruck in the presence of your friends' boyfriends, who seem like a completely different species from Alaska boys.

One college friend, a debutante from Texas named Dana, dates the best friend of Prince Albert of Monaco. *Her* best friend dates Prince Albert himself. While you may never have met Prince Albert himself—indistinguishable from all the other golden boys at Amherst frat parties—you take an anthropologist's interest in the contents of his apartment, which you visit from time to time, when Dana needs a lift. (Only now are you struck by the oddity of this: despite her family's immense wealth, Dana doesn't own a car—not that your secondhand Plymouth Volaré station wagon with faux-wood paneling is anything to brag about.) Anyway, among the magazines scattered on his coffee table (*Town and Country, Esquire, GQ*) is the Talbot's Catalog for Men. It feels like a revelation, this catalog—not so much about him, a real-life prince, as about you, about the possibilities for your own life. Deep down, you love Alaska and can't wait to move back there after graduation. But you also love Talbot's: polo shirts in primary colors, monogrammed Shetland sweaters, Papagallo purses with wooden handles and button-on covers. On the one hand, you feel pretty sure, on account of your family's origin myth, that you're going to end up married to an Alaska man. On the other, you feel sure there's not one single man in Alaska who (1) owns anything from Talbot's for Men, or (2) would be caught dead with a Talbot's for Men catalog in his possession, let alone displayed for all to see on his coffee table. What you want, you began to intuit, is a creature who probably doesn't exist outside of your imagination: an Alaska man who is also, secretly, a Talbot's man.

Your friend Julia dates another golden boy, not a prince, exactly, but a pre-med student at Amherst. Julia is from Cambridge, Massachusetts, so beautiful and uninhibited she walks around her dorm room naked on Sunday mornings. At parties, her boyfriend brings you gin and tonics and teaches you the jitterbug, dancing so effortlessly he makes you feel as if you, too, grew up in a world where everyone knows that white is the only color to wear on the tennis court. Because your mother is a nurse and your grandfather a surgeon, you regard the medical profession as hallowed. You're mystified when, in the spring of senior year, Julia breaks things off with David, saying she can't see herself as a doctor's wife and, also because, *Buffalo*.

After college, you return to Fairbanks and meet a boy with a brain at least as good and almost definitely better than yours. He's at home in the natural world in a way that you are not. He can recite the names of all the plants and animals in Alaska. His idea of romance is to go cross-country skiing by moonlight. You're hungry to see more of the world; he is content to stay put, believing as he does that no one should travel until they're truly a savant about the patch of earth they call home. You're the restless one in the relationship, the one with all the power. You believe this all the way up until the night—you're in a tent, on a camping trip with two other couples—he breaks up with you.

Rebounding, you marry the next guy who comes along. He's a chemist, an assayer of gold, a builder of houses, a climber of mountains (including Denali—twice). He shares your love of traveling to far-flung places. Together, you spend months in Central America, Southeast Asia. He teaches you how to roll a kayak in Class V rapids. Together, you have three children.

Nine years later, when you leave the marriage, you try out several versions of the story of what went wrong between you. When you say them out loud, none of them sound plausible. Eventually, you stop trying.

Racial Difference
"Invisibility is the condition of racial otherness."

I visited my daughter Emeline in Yaoundé, Cameroon, a few years ago, and the locals found the two of us in our straw hats and linen sundresses a baffling sight. When we shopped for fabric in the market, children in school uniforms followed, shouting in astonishment: "Les blanches! Les blanches!" and "La mère blanche!"

I'm rewinding nearly thirty years now, to 1971 or '72, the tail end of a family camping trip. We stop for gas in the middle of nowhere, along the Edgerton Cutoff on the way back from Copper Center. The owner of the filling station, a Black man, gases up the Land Cruiser and talks with my father, who is puffing on a pipe. This is in the era before self-serve gas stations, when the owners of the business often live a stone's throw from the pumps. The arrival of a car with two adults and five children is an event.

Mom opens the back of the Land Cruiser and shoos us out.

On legs gone rubbery from sitting for so long, I climb out then, almost instantly, trip over the gas hose, splitting open my forehead on the car's bumper. There is blood. A lot of it. My mother does her best to staunch it with paper towel. Hearing the ruckus I've caused, a woman comes through the door of the log cabin that's set back from the pumps. She's wearing jeans and a flannel shirt, an apron tied around her waist. I register that she is very beautiful, this woman roughly my mother's age, with her pale skin, freckles, and mass of red curls pinned up in a loose bun. Together, she and Mom usher me into the house, where they wash the cut with cold water then wrap gauze around my head.

A few minutes later, we're back on the road. It's unpaved, full of deep ruts and treacherous potholes. The Land Cruiser's shock absorbers are shot. I'm up front now, between my parents. Mom uses her left arm as a brace to prevent me lurching into the dashboard and re-opening my cut. She tells me we'll go see Dr. Deely when we get home, and he might give me stitches. I imagine myself starting the school year in a few days with a bandage wrapped all the way around my head, like one of the soldiers Florence Nightingale treated during the Crimean War. Drifting off to sleep with that delicious image in my head, I hear my mother say something I don't understand and won't for many years.

What she says, sotto voce to my father, is this: "They *have* to live all the way out here."

Me

"How am I a hog and me both?"—Mrs. Turpin in Flannery O'Connor's "Revelation"

"Mrs. William Garland Heeks Enlists Help of Young Women for Bassinet Dinner Dance" is the headline in the *New York Times'* society section, above a studio photograph of Lucia wearing a low-backed evening gown, gazing over her left shoulder at the photographer.

Did it pain Mrs. William Garland Heeks that her middle daughter, Carol Ann, had to shop at Lane Bryant and Chubettes? Maybe so, but not nearly as much as it pained Carol Ann herself.

At the Emma Willard School in Troy, New York, Carol Ann discovered portion control and field hockey. Then, in nursing school, she took up smoking. By the time she married my father, she had a classic fifties hourglass figure. Then she gave birth to three babies in three years and wound up in the hospital for minor surgery. In those days, patient charts still hung on the end of the bed. Carol Ann peeked. The first three words on her chart were, "Obese white female."

The Text and the World
"Is an author an inhabitant of the world or a creation of a literary text?"

In the mid-seventies, we moved from a house in the country to one in a brand-new subdivision closer to town. For the first time, I could ride just about anywhere on my bike, getting myself to music camp at the university and running to the grocery store for my mother (always buying myself an Almond Joy, then tossing the receipt so she wouldn't find out). At the same time I was roaming farther from home, I began to hide more things from my mother: my inner life, for one. Our house in the country had been set in a copse of trees, out of sight and earshot of neighbors. In the Teal Avenue house, I felt unseen eyes on me all the time. On rainy days, I'd walk around the block in a T-shirt and jeans, my face uplifted to the torrent, imagining myself as a Brontë heroine ranging the moors. I must have looked very strange. I *was* strange.

One night, a year or two after we moved, I was lying in bed, in that liminal state before sleep. I don't know how to explain what happened next except to say I saw an explosion of color behind closed lids. It took me a second to realize that what I experienced as a phenomenon of sight was actually sound. My bedroom window had shattered. Glass was everywhere, including on my coverlet. I sat up in bed, screaming.

The Alaska State Trooper who answered my mother's call rang the doorbell and stepped inside, standing stiffly on the rug in his pressed uniform and hardware. He refused to go upstairs to look at the damage. "In my experience, people don't just throw rocks through windows for no reason," he said, to no one in particular. Then, looking at me in my Lanz nightgown and pink foam rollers, "Is it possible you did something to provoke this?"

I looked at him blankly, so he elaborated. "Are you in the habit of putting on shows for the whole neighborhood every night?"

Someone threw a rock through my bedroom window at ten o'clock one night a decade or so before I started identifying as a feminist, several decades before #MeToo. The phrase *victim shaming* hadn't entered the lexicon. On the night the trooper came to our front door, I was just a confused twelve-year-old girl in a floor-length flannel nightgown. Even then, I was old enough to sense a rhetorical trap. To say, *No, Officer, I'm* not *in the habit of shucking my clothes in front of a backlit window* would make it seem as if I'd actually thought about doing it. (I hadn't.)

In the end, I didn't have to say anything. My mother drew herself up to her full height of five feet five inches, then asked the trooper in a low voice how *he'd* feel if someone came into *his* home and accused *his* daughter of being a slut. Before he could reply, she said, through gritted teeth, that he was an idiot who was unworthy of wearing a badge and a gun, and she'd be calling his supervisor in the morning to say that very thing to him.

After locking the door behind him, she turned to me, folding me in arms that suddenly felt like a pair of enormous wings.

"Oh, Jennifer," she said. "I'm *so* sorry."

Monuments
"The word 'monument,' we may remind ourselves, originates in the Latin monere, *to remind."*

Is there anything in the world more potent to a child than a symbol? Whenever my mother got ready to make something with her hands—

pie crust or meat loaf—she'd slide off her Tiffany engagement ring and set it on the windowsill. She never removed her wedding band. The rings, she told us, symbolized the love she and my father felt for one another. I found it hard to reconcile these professions of love with the times when she lost her temper with him, usually for wearing dirty boots in the house or crossing rivers in the Land Cruiser. She never swore. The way she said his name was almost worse, drawing out the first syllable then popping the second: "Al-*BA*!"

One time when he was running a bulldozer on a scree slope, the rocks started to slide. Fearing the dozer would roll in the avalanche, crushing him, he tried to jump free. Somehow his wedding ring caught on a jagged piece of metal and nearly took his finger with it. After that, he stopped wearing it. *Too dangerous*, he said.

Decades later, in the early aughts, I had as a student a young woman whose father had, on the morning of 9/11, ridden the train from their home in Westchester to his office in the World Trade Center. In the frantic days and weeks after, her mother provided searchers with photographs, a description of everything he was wearing and carrying on that day, even his dental records. But no trace of him ever emerged from the rubble. Long after he was declared legally dead, his widow held onto the slimmest of hopes, not that he was alive (she wasn't a fantasist), but that some piece of him might someday return to her. Meanwhile, she kept wearing her rings on her left hand.

One spring day in 2006, two Homeland Security agents rang this woman's doorbell. They had a box roughly the size of one used for cigars. Inside was a plastic evidence bag, and inside it was a gold wedding band, twisted and charred almost beyond recognition.

"Did this belong to your husband?" one of the men asked, gently. The widow put her hand to her mouth and wept.

The next day, she slipped her own rings from her left hand and strung them on a chain around her neck. She added the ring the agents had left with her and fastened the clasp around her neck. From that day on, she wore the necklace under her clothes, the rings resting against her heart and absorbing the heat of her skin. I like to imagine she began to think about dating again.

The story doesn't end there.

In the last paragraph of her essay, my student revealed what her mother had realized the instant she saw the mangled piece of metal presented by the officials who came to her front door. It was a man's wedding ring, all right, and its owner had clearly perished in the World Trade Center on 9/11. But he was someone else's husband.

Character
"Our lives, our real *lives, are governed and directed by the stories we read and write."*

One day in fourth or fifth grade, I decided to become a quiet girl. I made a conscious effort to stop talking so much, and I also made an elaborate show of listening to other people, widening my eyes like the heroines in my favorite Louisa May Alcott novels were said to do.

The trick worked better than I thought it would.

By the time I was in high school and realized that quiet girls don't get invited to any parties, it was too late to change either myself or my reputation. The habit of stifling my inner—clamorous, conflicted—self proved hard to overcome. I joined the cross-country ski team but quickly discovered it was a mostly solitary sport that attracted other oddballs.

For reasons I still can't fathom, one of the popular girls picked me as a friend. Laurel was tall and pretty and talked so much it didn't matter to either of us that I hardly spoke at all. Laurel had a glamorous older sister who wanted to become an actress or a model and a beautiful but eccentric mother—divorced, which was almost unheard-of back then—who was training for a hiking trip in the Ozarks. After work, she tromped around the house in hiking boots and a sixty-pound backpack.

I wasn't Laurel's only quiet friend. Ann (not her real name) was a little bit chubby, with an unflattering, too-short haircut, and oversize glasses. She wore a lot of brown and seemed to me as drab as a robin. Unlike me, she also seemed at peace with not being invited to parties, perhaps having settled on invisibility as the best strategy for surviving high school. But maybe I misread her.

Sometime during the summer between our sophomore and junior year, Ann disappeared. The new girl who took her place was twenty pounds lighter, with grown-out hair, Farrah Fawcett-style, contact lenses, makeup, all new clothes, and an effervescent personality. A school counselor spotted her in the hallway, walking alongside Laurel—who was, of course, her Pygmalion—and asked if she was new to West Valley.

My name, she replied, *is Annabel*.

The Tragic

"The apocalyptic or revelation at the heart of the tragic has to do with the idea that there is no God or gods looking down on the world to see that justice is done, or that, if there are gods, they are profoundly careless, indifferent, even sadistic."

I'm driving west from the tiny town of Hamilton, New York, to the even tinier town of Aurora, New York, where I'm to give a reading this evening. It's late October, a golden time of year in upstate New York. My route takes me on back roads, some of them unpaved and skinny as a driveway. I pass farms and silos, towns made up of a single gas station and a clutch of gray Victorians. At one point, I crest a hill, then swoop down toward a farm on the valley floor. As I descend, white cotton balls in the field on my left resolve into sheep. I *adore* sheep. They're my favorite farm animal: phlegmatic and serene, except when they're *gamboling*—that marvelous word. I could watch them all day long. When I'm having a bad day, my daughters sometimes joke that they should just drive me to the nearest farm and plop me down among the sheep. For now, I lift my foot from the gas pedal to savor more fully the feeling that all is right in my world. It's a gorgeous fall day, with fluffy white clouds and fluffy white sheep; I'm on my way to someplace new, where I'm likely to be regarded as a person with interesting things to say; also (unbelievably, really, for me), I left the house in good time this morning, so I'm likely to arrive ahead of schedule.

The sheep are nibbling grass in evenly spaced clusters of four or five. Except for one, which is off by itself in the center of the field. It's not grazing. In fact, it's not moving at all. *Oh. my. god.* It's lying on its back with its legs in the air, like an upside-down kitchen table. Like those sheep in *Far from the Madding Crowd* that ate a poisonous plant and were on the verge of death when the handsome itinerant farmer Gabriel Oak came along and jabbed a hole in their stomachs to release the gas.

I've never seen a dead or dying sheep in real life, and I don't know what to do about it. How can I claim to love a certain type of animal, then not help an individual of the species when I see it in distress? I tap the brake, cast about frantically for another human being, a tractor in a neighboring field, anything. Nothing. What about a farmhouse? I don't see one of those, either. Desperate, I try honking the horn. It's what I tried years ago, in Alaska, after a moose ricocheted off the hood of my Toyota station wagon. Then, as now, I was on a sparsely populated road with no house in sight. Then, as now, honking accomplished absolutely nothing. It didn't even make me feel better—it just made me feel ridiculous.

The rest of the sheep continue grazing calmly, seemingly aware of and unfazed by death in their midst. My car coasts to the foot of the valley. Decision time: Do I hit the brake and pull over, or press onward with my journey?

A few miles down the road, my cell phone rings. It's my mother. She's calling to say that my beloved Aunt Care seems to have suffered a massive heart attack. She's in a coma in the hospital in Wilmington, North Carolina, and the doctors are running tests, looking for any sign of brain activity. It's not looking good. In her gentlest voice, my mother tells me to brace myself for bad news. I say goodbye and hang up, then press on the horn for a long time.

Voice
"When the mind is like a hall in which thought is like a voice speaking, the voice is always that of someone else."—Wallace Stevens

I'm on my way home from my job as a newspaper reporter, my Toyota Tercel stopped at a red light downtown, when a stranger appears at the driver's side window, startling me. She's a few years older than me and a little disheveled. This is Fairbanks in the mid-eighties, long before the era of stoplight panhandlers. She's mouthing some words, trying to tell me something. When I roll down the window to hear her better, she unleashes on me. *You fucking bitch!* she screams, then accuses me of driving with my foot on the brake for the last quarter of a mile. She says I must have been doing this on purposes, to annoy the drivers behind me, to annoy *her.*

I try to placate her, saying I'm sorry but also pointing out that we've been driving in stop-and-go traffic. This only succeeds in enraging her more. She curls her hands into fists, banging them on the side of the car to punctuate her words. I sense that she wants to throttle me. With shaking hands and in slow motion, as if in a nightmare, I start to roll up the window. She grabs it with both hands and tries to push it back down. She is not finished with me yet. *I'm calling the police on you,* she said. *You think you own the whole road, but you don't. You can't drive like you don't give a shit about anyone else, in your fancy car your daddy bought you.*

It did not occur to me to point out that (1) I'd purchased the car with my own hard-earned money from working summers as a forest fire fighter (plus a small loan from my grandfather, which I repaid—every cent), and (2) a Toyota Tercel is not exactly a fancy car. Instead, the light turned green, and I drove off. I felt embarrassed and rattled, doubtlessly guilty to some degree of what she'd accused me of, but mostly blown backward by the force of a stranger's verbal assault. It was wildly disproportionate to my offense, for one thing; so nakedly *personal*, for another.

Like all the other stories spilling out of me here, liberated by the framework of theory, this one has stayed with me for longer than it should have. Over the years, it keeps unfurling new questions. Is it possible that the stranger was actually a seer (a see-er?) who saw something in me that I couldn't see for myself—that I moved through the world oblivious to my own privilege, worrying not a whit about the inconvenience or damage I might be trailing in my wake? Or was the encounter about race, with me standing in for all the white girls who acted as if they owned not just that stretch of road but the whole highway, the whole town, the whole *state* of Alaska, which wasn't even a concept before my ancestors sailed in, saw her ancestors feasting on *muktuk*, and thought, *Raw whale blubber? Ewww. Let us civilize you.*

A few years later after the incident with the crazy lady at my car window, I left my job at the newspaper to start graduate school. I'd never been a particularly good reporter, so I was surprised when a former colleague stopped me on the street a few years later to ask me what I was thinking. "Why do people have to go to graduate school to learn to write?" he asked. "It's like, '*Ooh, I have to find my voice*'?"

I laughed him off and said something anodyne, the anger that was throttling my vocal cords detectable only to me (not that he was paying attention). But on the inside, a wild animal was struggling to get out. I wanted to scream, *You smug asshole. You think you're so smart, but really, you're just a white guy walking through the world with way more confidence than brains.*

That woman who appeared at my window and shouted at me for being such a bad driver? She had a voice, and she was willing to use it.

The Colony
"*As some linguists like to say, a language is a dialect with an army and a navy.*"

My God-and-country-music-loving sister is fond of such folksy expressions as "The Lord willing and the creek don't rise." The deeper our mother sinks into dementia, the folksier she gets, too, saying *divil* for *devil*, *piddle* for *pee*. When we get pedicures together, she says, "I haven't done that in a coon's age." She remembers that she's not supposed to use the word *pickaninny* anymore, but she forgets why. "It's such a pretty word," she complains.

The last time we went to the nail salon, we got there early. We sat on a banquette in the waiting area across from a young woman with a squirming toddler. My mother's opening gambit in such moments—in every moment, post-diagnosis—is flattery. She's desperate to connect with strangers, with people who don't know there's anything wrong with her. She started by complimenting the little girl's yellow sundress, then her white sandals, then her hair, done up in dozens of braids and clipped with brightly colored barrettes. Then she turned to the little girl's manners, sitting patiently in her own chair, swinging her legs. The grown woman acknowledged each of these compliments with a nod that was courteous but not encouraging.

I was cringing inwardly, because my mother's next move, when rebuffed, is to move from flattery to condescension.

"I can tell that you're a very good mother," said my mother, the retired family counselor.

"Thank you," the woman said, stiffly. "I'm actually not her mother. I'm her aunt. Her mother is getting her nails done."

That shut Mom up for half a minute. While she plotted her next move, I scanned the room desperately. The technicians were all busy helping other people. No one was going to save us from what was coming: *I think "pickaninny" is such a nice word . . .*

Mom cleared her throat and inched forward on the banquette, toward the toddler and her aunt.

"Hey, Mom," I said brightly, standing up quickly and pulling her with me, "let's go pick out your color!"

Figures and Tropes
"Truths are illusions about which one has forgotten that this is what they are."—Nietzsche, "On Truth and Lie in an Extra-Moral Sense"

I prefer peonies, the blowsier, middle-brow cousin of roses. Also spring blossoms that have to be forced from bulbs: daffodils, tulips, hyacinths, iris. Cottage garden favorites like Russian sage, rhododendrons, hydrangeas, lilacs. My house is furnished partly with heirlooms from my grandmother, partly with pieces that strangers left on the curb. Nothing is comfortable: the chairs too spindly, the tables a little too low or wobbly, the couch cushions chucking up their innards. All of it covered in a fine layer of dog hair.

As a hedge against despair, I cut a few peonies from the front garden and arrange them in vases.

Waterford crystal, of course.

Laughter
"Is there something about laughter that, in a profound if ticklish way, puts it in touch with death?"

A Sunday afternoon in August, our second full day back in Fairbanks. For the next two weeks, home base for me and my teenage daughters is my parents' five-bedroom house on the outskirts of our hometown. As usual, after a few months away, I'm hyper-alert to any changes in Mom's condition since the last time. I've already noticed that she rises later in the morning, around 7:30. And Dad no longer goes into the office every day. Instead, he rises an hour or so earlier than Mom, puts on a pair of frayed khakis and a white T-shirt, fixes himself coffee, then heads into the backyard to start patching the bare spots in the grass.

Technically, Dad is now retired from the construction company that he founded with his father and his brothers, and that was recently purchased by an Alaska Native corporation. Even so, he usually goes into the office a few hours a week to work as a consultant for my brother Sam, who is the new president of the company. I'm still getting used to this version of my father, whose former passion for bidding specifications seems to have been displaced by a mania for lawn care.

By the time he and Mom wake from their afternoon nap—another new habit—I've got Scrabble set up on a card table in the living room. It's an obsession with us. For years, we've kept a running tally of our points, playing with a ferocious, single-minded, take-no-prisoners style that has us timing each other's turns and whipping out the dictionary to challenge every questionable play.

When he sees the game board, Dad rubs his hands together. "Oh *ho*," he says, gleefully, as if we're getting away with something by starting so early in the day.

"Has anybody seen my glasses?" Mom asks.

Three plays in, Mom challenges my use of "aa"—a frivolous gesture on the part of someone who used to know all of the two- and three-letter words in the dictionary. An ancient truck belches its way up the driveway. It's the guys from Lemeta Pumping and Thawing. They are here to pump the septic tank. Earlier today, the system backed up, dumping three inches of water into the basement. Working together with push brooms, my mother and I spent a couple of hours herding the smelly water into a drain beside the washing machine. We had a system because the septic system used to overflow a couple of times a month, back in the eighties, when my brothers and sisters and I still lived at home. The recent influx of teenagers—my daughters—who started taking showers and doing laundry on top of Dad's round-the-clock sprinkler use, tipped the fragile system over the edge.

The man who owns the pumping company is an old friend. He and his workers don't even bother to come to front door before unwinding an enormous pipe and wrestling it over to the pipe head in the backyard, just outside our window. While this is happening, Dad and I retain our laser focus on the Scrabble board. Mom gets up to peer out the window.

"Al, who are those men in our backyard?"

"Those are Hank's guys. They're here to pump the septic tank."

"Oh, I didn't realize it needed to be pumped. That's nice of them."

She sits down and stares at the board. Within seconds, she's fidgeting with her reading glasses, lining them up alongside the scorepad, throwing glances into the backyard.

"Will they want a check from us today, or will they bill us?" she asks.

"I don't know, Carol," Dad says. "When they finish pumping, we'll find out."

We continue with our game. I am losing badly, having drawn a board that consists entirely of *u*'s, *v*'s, *k*'s, and an *x*. My mother picks up her iPad and begins to play five-card draw, a profound breach of Scrabble etiquette that my father, inexplicably, ignores.

Suddenly, Mom looks up from the iPad as if she just remembered something important. "Al, will they want a check from us today, or will they bill us?" she asks.

"I don't know, Carol. As soon as they finish pumping, we'll know.

"It's your turn."

Mom used to be the one in charge of paying bills. This was partly on account of Dad's work, which took him away for long periods, but also on account of Mom's reputation for being more on top of things than he was. One of the earliest signs that something was wrong came when Visa notified us that the bill was being paid two or three times every month.

"Alba?"

"Yes, Carol."

"Will they want a check from us today, or will they bill us?"

A definitive diagnosis of Alzheimer's disease is not yet possible without a brain autopsy. One of the most reliable indicators, in a living patient, is something called the clock test. When she was sixty-nine, my mother went to a neurologist. He showed her a clock with the small hand pointing to the three, the big hand to the six. "What time is it?" he asked. "Six fifteen," she replied.

"Al?"

"Yes, Carol."

Before it happens, you might think you have some idea what you're getting into with Alzheimer's. You don't. Along with her memory, my mother—always the family trickster—has lost her sense of humor. She frustrates easily and is quick to accuse people of stealing whatever she herself has misplaced: reading glasses, lipstick, purse, car. She can still drive, follow a recipe, and shop for groceries, but the manager of the nearest Fred Meyer, a family friend, recently called my youngest sister to say that Mom was beginning to turn up there several times a day. That a concerned Fred Meyer employee might eventually call social services to report my mother is one threat to her independence. The arthritis in her knees is a bigger one, but not for the obvious reason. The pain isn't particularly severe (though it will get much worse, with time). The problem is that it's constant, just enough of a nuisance for Mom to reach, half a dozen times a day, for the Tylenol, not realizing that she just took some.

"Al?"

"Yes, Car—"

I cut in. "Hey, Dad?"

"Yes, Jennifer?"

"Will they want a check today, or will they bill you?"

The Performative

"'I confess my ignorance.' Chambers Dictionary gives this as an example of a performative statement."

I'm teaching creative writing in London. My second-floor classroom overlooks a courtyard in Bloomsbury, near the British Museum. Property in the area runs about $190 per square foot, meaning the flats are occupied by professional people: international bankers, barristers, psychiatrists. The kind of people who are rarely at home at ten o'clock on a Tuesday morning, which is when my class begins.

I'm in London for the semester, leading a study group for fifteen English majors from the university in upstate New York where I normally teach. We've rented classroom space in a historic building that is a bit anomalous in this largely residential neighborhood. My seat at the head of the table faces a large Palladian window that mirrors windows in the flats across the way. On the morning of our third class, I sense movement outside the window. I look up. A woman in the flat across the way is staring at us through her own window. From a distance of thirty or forty feet, I guess she's roughly my age—late forties—or maybe a bit older. She seems to be wearing one pink towel around her body and a second wound turban-style around her head. She starts to water the plants in her windows. Watching idly, I feel a surge of something—

sympathy? empathy? protectiveness? *Poor thing,* I think, *she doesn't realize we can see her.*

"Do you know why T. S. Eliot thought *Hamlet* was a failed play?" I ask my students.

The towel drops.

My mouth gapes. Following my gaze, the students look out the window. The woman across the way is completely naked except for her turban. She continues to water her plants.

She's not looking at us, but I can't stop looking at her. Heavy breasts and thighs, a belly that has probably been pregnant once or twice. Not exactly the Venus of Willendorf, but not a body you'd be likely to see on TV either.

After ten minutes of gawking, we return to our text. Over the next half hour or so, I glance up a few times to see if she's still there waterboarding her plants. She is.

The next Tuesday, on the stroke of ten, Pink Towel Lady is back, and things unfold exactly as they did the week before. She potters around semi-clothed for a few minutes, drops her towel, then continues gardening in what the Brits call her *altogether.*

After class, I stop in at reception to speak with the woman in charge, the same woman who told my students, during orientation, not to smoke or drink in the courtyard and also to modulate their voices and generally do their best not to act too conspicuously American.

I ask the woman in charge if anyone else has complained about an exhibitionist living in the flat across from the classroom. She acts surprised by my question—meaning, her surprise strikes me as an act.

What can the lady in reception do? Nothing. The exhibitionist continues to appear every Tuesday at ten. My students' interest in her wanes, even though I continue giving them updates: "emerging from the shower," "commencing to water," "dropping the towel." I can tell they think I'm a little unhinged. I *am* a little unhinged. The crazy woman is making *me* crazy!

By the second-to-last week of the semester, I'm the only one who's still looking at Pink Towel Lady. It occurs to me, not for the first time, that her body and mine have a great deal in common, both of them scarred and sagging, in need of scaffolding—underwire, Spandex—before presenting themselves in public. Seeing this woman naked is oddly reassuring (*I'm not the only woman who looks like this*) but also a little embarrassing. I, too, feel stripped naked, exposed to the pitiless gaze of my students with their perfect skin and gym-toned twenty-year-old bodies.

In May, I returned to the States, and a few years went by. In the spring of 2019, I spent a few weeks with my parents in a rental house in New Smyrna Beach, Florida. Mom's behavior was getting more and more erratic. We had to lock all the doors to keep her from wandering off in the middle of the night. For the most part, she was able to make herself presentable to go out in public: matching her sandals to her outfit, applying lipstick and brushing her hair, and in the evening, putting on her favorite bracelet, a chain of forget-me-nots made of ivory and gold nuggets. She liked to touch and be touched, and any set of hands would do. When I was young, I used to rub lotion into her feet and brush her hair and scratch her back. After her diagnosis, to my shame and horror, I couldn't bear to touch her anymore. Instead, I outsourced the touching to paid caregivers, hairdressers, and nail technicians.

We left the beach early one day in order to get to an appointment on time. I reminded her of this while we used the spigot outside the rental house to rinse the sand off our feet, then again once we were inside, loading the washing machine with beach towels. "Oh, good," she said. "Let me just change my clothes and we'll head right out."

She went into her bedroom, closed the door, and stayed in there so long I began to worry she'd lost the thread. "Mom?" I said, rapping on the door. "Everything OK in there? Need any help?"

"No," she said, a bit tetchily, her tone warning me not to come in. "I'll be right out."

A few seconds later, she emerged. She'd brushed her hair and put on lipstick as well as her forget-me-not bracelet. She was wearing white slacks and white sandals. On top of these, she wore a cotton floral jacket with a zipper that no longer worked because she'd gained too much weight. Under the unzipped jacket, her exposed breasts sat atop her chest like a pair of sad little birds.

"*Oh, Mom,*" I said.

The End

"The future can only be anticipated in the form of an absolute danger."
—Derrida

I'm perched on the edge of the gynecologist's exam table, wearing only a thin cotton gown. My teaching clothes are folded neatly on the chair beside me, and I'm pretending to read a new Tessa Hadley story in *The New Yorker*.

Eileen Fisher trousers, Dansko clogs, jade-rimmed reading glasses, the latest *New Yorker* or *London Review of Books*: the accoutrements of my new middle-aged, middle-class life. I've staged myself thus in order to convey to the doctor that he's dealing with more than just a body—in particular, a body that, having outlived its ability to bear children, no longer has any truck with the part of his practice focused on obstetrics.

I sit there for roughly twenty minutes, long enough for my back to slump and my feet to swell. Like my mother, I suffer from bad circulation—at least, that's what she says whenever I complain of cold feet or hands. Having enjoyed rude good health for most of my life, it used to make me feel interesting to think I suffered from *something*, even a condition as dull as sluggish circulation. Now, at the age of forty-eight, I have some annoying symptoms to discuss with the doctor. On the hour-long drive up to his office in North Syracuse, I'd gone over the script in my head, reminding myself not to be too hyperbolic or to take up too much time in the telling. The gist of it is that my body, which used to do pretty much anything I asked of it, has taken to behaving as if the smallest demand—take the stairs rather than the elevator at work, say—is the equivalent of slogging up a mountain with a seventy-pound pack on my back, arthritic fingers and toes scrabbling for purchase on bouldered terrain.

Friends my age and older reassure me I'm not the only one who feels this way. Ten years ago, when we bumped into each other on the playground or on the sidelines of a soccer game, we talked about our children's teachers or the best clubs for travel sports. Now we get together over white wine and crudités and speak in low voices about which of our other friends might be having an affair, and whether our own relationships can cross the Saharan years between romance and retirement. We talk about books sometimes, too—but with less urgency than before, as if it doesn't really matter whether we're all reading the same Elena Ferrante Neapolitan novel or whether one of us has forged ahead. We wonder about women we know who went through menopause without ever coming off the Pill. Is *that* the best way to get through this long tunnel, we wonder? Sort of like our mothers experienced childbirth under general anesthesia?

Sometimes the conversation interests me. Sometimes it bores me so much I want to grab a handful of red-hot coals from the grill and burn my eyes out. *We're just fucking getting old!* I want to scream. Once, I risked saying these words out loud, the stem of my wine glass wobbling between my fingers. My friends nodded their expertly coifed and highlighted heads sagely: *Ah yes, excessive rumination and triggerless rage are major symptoms. Have I considered hormone replacement therapy?*

I've considered it, yes, and that is why I'm seeing the doctor today. I believe in better living through pharmaceuticals, in the efficacy of pills. HRT will, I imagine, flatten out the mountain range that looms in front of me every day, turning it into a gleaming white corridor down which I will stride with confidence, poise, good posture, and lovingly tended feet papoosed in chartreuse and white Pearl Izumis.

I've been to the clinic a dozen times without noticing the walls' kabeshiro thinness. This time I hear the murmur of nurses, the *whoosh* of a fetal heartbeat, the voice of my doctor speaking with another patient. I can't make out the woman's questions, only my doctor's replies. He is burly, unhandsome, and impatient, this doctor. Cursed with a Donald Duck voice. I can tell from the rising volume that he's getting fed up with the woman next door. "I'll prescribe it if you want me to," he says, "but the side effects can be miserable." He ticks them off: bloating, breast tenderness, leg cramps, migraines, indigestion, vaginal bleeding. My heart sinks. He must be talking about HRT. "Really, the thing that would help you the most right now is to stop smoking."

Phew. I am not and never have been a smoker. The body beneath this faded cotton gown is nothing to look at, really, but it's still relatively unpolluted, except by the occasional glass of wine or a margarita.

The doctor enters with his right hand already extended to shake. I take it like the well-behaved animal that I am. He meets my eyes and says "hello," just like he learned in medical school: *Look her in the eyes before you look between her legs.* He's already glanced at my chart, reminded himself I live in Hamilton and teach at the same university his daughter will be attending in the fall. We chat about this. I tell him she'll like it and that I'll keep my eye out for her.

After the exam, which he conducts in his usual brisk, no-nonsense way, he washes his hands, asks if I have any questions or concerns.

"No," I say, "Not that I can think of."

"Good," he says. "Keep up the good work. You know, you can always come to the East Syracuse location instead. It's not as long a drive for you, and I'm usually there on Tuesdays."

"Thank you," I say. "I'll do that."

"See you next year," he says, extending his paw for one last quick shake.

Narrative
"Not only do we tell stories, but stories tell us."

For the last time, my mother's foundation myth: Born at Babies Hospital in New York to a Brown- and Harvard-educated surgeon and his socialite wife. Educated at Emma Willard, Colby College, and Columbia-Presbyterian School of Nursing. On a lark, accepted a public health nurse position in Alaska. Met a guy who wasn't right for her but who happened to have an older brother he worshiped. For the older brother, it was love at first sight. They went on several dates:

curling with friends, dinner at Club 11, where they danced to "Moon River." He proposed; she demurred. He pressed his case with a Tiffany diamond and dozens of yellow roses.

The day after she said yes, Alba caught a Pan Am flight to New York. Biding his time while Carol and her mother planned a speeded-up wedding—Lent was coming—he finished the flying lessons he'd begun in Fairbanks, doing his first solo and earning his private pilot's license. On February 17, 1962, Carol Ann met him at the altar of All Saints Episcopal Church in North Adams, Massachusetts. She wore a raw silk ballgown with an Alençon lace veil. Dressed in red velvet cocktail dresses, her bridesmaids carried rabbit fur muffs rather than flowers.

On receiving, via telegram, the news of my birth, just over a year later, my surgeon grandfather pronounced me "J.P., the lumber baroness." It was a joke. At the time, my father was still working as a mechanic for Pan Am.

Decades passed. To build their company, my father and his brothers worked brutal hours in conditions so cold and dangerous, they hardly bear thinking about. There were a lot of lean years and a few profitable ones, enough to outfit us in the trappings of the middle class: Hawaiian vacations, orthodontics, college tuition, a series of Volvo station wagons.

In 2012 the company that my father founded with his father and three brothers was purchased by one of Alaska's large Native corporations. This scenario is the Alaska equivalent of winning the lottery. The Native corporation installed my brother as president of the Brice Companies. One of his first acts was to hire my father and one of my uncles—the one who'd set my parents up on their first date—as consultants. At first, this was painful for my father and his brother. Then, when the extent of their windfall sunk in, they used some of the money to buy back some of the fun they'd missed by working so hard for all those years. They bought matching airplanes, took up gold mining, built vacation cabins in remote places, then purchased the ATVs and riverboats they needed to enjoy those cabins.

My parents began spending long stretches of every winter in Key West or Hawaii. In the summer, between stays at one or the other of their cabins, they putter around the Fairbanks house. Dad builds treehouses for his grandchildren and patches the lawn. Mom grows dinner-plate-sized dahlias in the garden and throws teddy bear tea parties for the grandchildren. She is growing vague and forgetful, soft around the edges. She still bakes pies, though, with rhubarb from her garden. Before working the crust, she takes off her engagement ring and sets it on the windowsill. Sometimes in the winter, Dad puts on his Carhartt overalls to chop wood or plow the driveway.

A while back, when it became clear Mom could no longer keep track of things like reading glasses and keys, he had new locks installed, ones with a passcode they can both remember: 0-2-17. On that day, every year, Dad still brings Mom a bouquet of yellow roses.

In my professional life, I spend a lot of time thinking about the stories we tell and the ones we don't. Why do our set pieces come off in some contexts, fall flat in others? Is it an accident of timing? A trick of the light? And why do the stories that sustained us as children often lose their shine, failing to grow along with us? Every semester, I put Joan Didion's "White Album" in front of my students, pointing out the opening line: "We tell ourselves stories in order to live." I share with them Patricia Hampl's mantra, from "Memory and Imagination": "Refuse to write your life, and you have no life." If there's time, I refer them to the work of Paul Armstrong, a neuroscientist who studies the human hunger for narrative, which satisfies the brain's proclivity for pattern and consistency as well as for flexibility and openness.

Time and again, I urge my students to dig deep in the substrata of their lives, then to dig again, deeper still. *Bring up whatever shards you can find*, I tell them. Together, we'll turn those pieces into a story.

Somewhere along the way, I stopped believing my own advice. I'm not as cynical as one or two writers I can think of—one of whom recently declared, in an interview, the end of character; the other of whom asserts loudly and often, to anyone who will listen, that narrative is dead. They both make compelling intellectual arguments; sap that I am, I sometimes find myself nodding in agreement while reading or hearing them. But they're wrong, of course. The human craving for characters and stories has changed over time, with technology (the *New Yorker* profile giving way to the Instagram feed), but it hasn't disappeared altogether, and surely it won't—ever.

The danger I'm thinking of is an entirely different one. I've watched my mother use her stories sometimes as a cudgel (against my father's family and their working-class roots; against her own children, whose lives will never rise to the same level of interestingness as hers) and as cultural capital (against everyone else who washed up, for one reason or another, in one of the farthest north outposts of the continent).

Our stories ought to form a supple scaffolding, I think—a shape that can bend in the face of heavy winds. They shouldn't ossify over time but rather soften and recede. As we age, we should become more restrained in the telling and retelling of our own stories, more receptive to the stories of others. In *Darwin's Worms*, his monograph on Darwin and Freud, Adam Phillips reminds us Freud adamantly refused to write the story of his own life, nor would he allow anyone else to do it for him. His resistance to autobiography, Phillips writes, was not due to evasiveness or a desire for control (though surely that was part of it). Rather, he believed (in Phillips's telling) that a person's "life story was, in part, the ways in which a person avoided having a life story." In short, life is the thing that unfurls in resistance to—even *opposition to*—the stories we or others wish to tell about it.

Pleasure
"Literature is erotic because it is always concerned with seducing the reader."
When I was very young, two farms comprised the twin poles of my life. The first farm, in Stamford, Vermont, belonged to my maternal grandparents. I was taken there to visit only a few times as a baby or toddler, and certainly not often enough to form any images of it. The second was my paternal grandparents' farm outside Fairbanks, Alaska, where my family celebrated holidays and shared meals once or twice

a week, and where I frequently spent the weekend without any of my brothers or sisters. Both of these farms were sprawling pieces of property, made up of many acres, but neither was a farm in the Old MacDonald sense. The word *farm* as it was tossed around in my family might, in fact, have been the beginning of my love affair with language. Early on, I sensed that a single word could have more than one meaning. Also, that some of those meanings could be simultaneously true and untrue.

My father's father has not figured much in these essays. His name was Luther Liston Brice, and he loaned me the money to buy my first car. On a family vacation in the Bahamas, he offered to double my $10 gambling stake on the condition I split my winnings, if there were any. I hit the silver dollar jackpot that day, making $500, of which he claimed half. Granddad was kind and gentle, and he'd been henpecked all his life, first by his own mother, then by his wife, and then by a succession of mistresses. I loved him so much I still weep at the memory of the winter night, more than thirty years ago, when my father appeared on my doorstep, hatless and shivering from grief, not cold, to deliver the news that his own father was gone.

There was no funeral, just a priest who said a few words, none of them memorable. Dad and his brother Sam hit on the idea of spreading Granddad's ashes over the fields he'd loved and, late in life, planted with rye in an effort to make an honest farm out of the property. While forty close friends and family watched, they swooped low over the farmhouse, my uncle at the controls of the Arctic Tern, my father in the back seat holding Granddad's urn. The Tern didn't have a rear window, just a hatch door, which Dad wedged open with his foot. Those of us on the ground saw a fine spray of dust emerge from the door. The whole things seemed pretty underwhelming—until a few minutes later, when my uncle tried to land in a nearby field and hit a berm. The Tern broke a strut then toppled over in slow motion onto one wing, crumpling it. When the two men climbed out, chagrined but unhurt, they were both coated in ashes—not just their clothes but their faces and glasses. It turns out they'd failed to consider the physics of opening that door in midflight, which caused two things to happen simultaneously: (1) the Tern bucked and nearly stalled, and (2) most of the ashes blew back inside the plane, turning it black as night. It was a miracle they survived the crash.

Secrets
"Literature is about what cannot be told."

The secret at the heart of my mother's stories about her growing up—about her falling out of a tree at age ten, then having her broken arm stuffed into the sleeve of a ruffly dress, so she'd be presentable in the emergency room of the hospital where her father worked—is alcohol. Her parents were high-performing alcoholics. My father never drank, but my mother used to enjoy a glass of wine in the evening, with dinner. Then, abruptly, she stopped. When I asked her why, she said she was starting to enjoy it too much.

There's another secret, this one having to do with my other grandmother, the Alaska one. I learned about it only recently. In December of 1961, helenka was only fifty-two, at the inflection point of what would, in the end, be a long, achievement-filled life. (Her obituary was read aloud on the floor of the US Senate and entered into the Congressional Record—a story for another day.) She and Luther and three of their sons were living in a crowded cabin (not yet the farm) in the hills overlooking Fairbanks. Every penny they earned went into their collective savings for the business they eventually hoped to form.

Over dinner one night, helenka observed that her oldest son was quieter than usual. *What's wrong?* she asked. He told her about Carol Ann, how she was plucky and smart and beautiful, and there was no one else in the world he would ever want to marry. He'd already asked twice by then, but she hadn't said yes. (She hadn't said no either.) Now she was set to fly back East for the holidays. He'd been to college on the East Coast, at Columbia for a while. He knew it was full of guys who'd recognize her pluck and beauty, her *joie de vivre*, and they'd want to capture it for themselves. One of them was surely destined to sweep her off her feet, making her forget all about her whirlwind romance with the Alaska guy in grease-stained coveralls. In the story she'd eventually tell of her life, Al Brice would be lucky to be relegated to a footnote.

The next morning, helenka went down to Mount McKinley Savings Bank and emptied her account. Then she emptied her husband's account and her sons' accounts as well. (It was possible to do this, back then.) Next, she turned her formidable charm on the bank manager, cajoling him into giving her a loan. After *that*, she drove a few blocks to the AT&T office on Cushman Street, where she placed a long-distance call to New York City. *Hello? Tiffany's? This is helenka Brice, I'm calling from Fairbanks, Alaska, and I need you to help me with something right away.*

The next night, when Al straggled in from work, she met him at the door, a question in her eyes. He shrugged. Carol had let him know she'd picked up the ring, but she still hadn't decided whether to wear it.

The next morning, helenka got in her car again. This time, she went straight to the AT&T office without stopping at the bank.

Operator, she said, *get me Stamford, Vermont.*

Yes, Stamford with an "m." That's in Vermont, not Connecticut.

I'm going to need the number for the nearest florist.

ACKNOWLEDGMENTS

The phrase *Another North* is borrowed (with kind permission) from Molly McCully Brown and Susannah Nevison, who use it in their collection of epistolary poems, *In the Field Between Us*.

The writer I mention in the first paragraph of "Another North" is Scott Russell Sanders, and the essay is "Beauty."

"Playing Bridge with Robots" is forthcoming in the *Cimarron Review*. "On Keeping House" was published in *The Iron Horse Literary Review*. "In Praise of the Perfect White T-Shirt" appeared in *Under the Sun*.

The title, "I Am the Space Where I Am," comes from a line in Noël Arnaud's poem "L'état d'ébauche," as quoted in Gaston Bachelard's *The Poetics of Space*. My essay appeared in *Why We're Here: New York Essayists on Living Upstate*, edited by Robert Cowser.

The flower lexicon in "My Essay on Flowers and How Things End" comes from *Je T'Aime: The Language of Love for Lovers of Language*, by Erin McKean.

All of the headings and quotations (some lightly edited) in "Theory of Life" come from *An Introduction to Literature, Criticism, and Theory*, 2nd ed., edited by Andrew Bennett and Nicholas Royle.

My thanks to the Horned Dorset Colony and the Colgate University Research Council; to everyone at Red Hen Press, especially Rebeccah Sanhueza, Monica Fernandez, and Tobi Harper; to Peter Balakian, Brock Clarke, Lena Crown, CJ Hauser, Jane Pinchin, Lucy Schiller, Peggy Shumaker, Dana Spiotta, and Joeth Zucco; to Alan, Josie, Caroline, Kinzea, Emeline, Clara and Ruby.

For twenty-five years, Carrie Brown and I have been unspooling a conversation that has turned out to be the greatest—unsought, undeserved—gift of my life.

This book was in press when my mother died, in February 2023. She was my true north.

BIOGRAPHICAL NOTE

Jennifer Brice is the author of *The Last Settlers*, a work of documentary journalism, and *Unlearning to Fly*, a memoir. Born in Fairbanks, Alaska, she teaches contemporary literature and creative writing at Colgate University in upstate New York.